Youth Substance Abuse

Books in the **Contemporary World Issues** series address vital issues in today's society such as genetic engineering, pollution, and biodiversity. Written by professional writers, scholars, and nonacademic experts, these books are authoritative, clearly written, up-to-date, and objective. They provide a good starting point for research by high school and college students, scholars, and general readers as well as by legislators, businesspeople, activists, and others.

Each book, carefully organized and easy to use, contains an overview of the subject, a detailed chronology, biographical sketches, facts and data and/or documents and other primary source material, a forum of authoritative perspective essays, annotated lists of print and nonprint resources, and an index.

Readers of books in the Contemporary World Issues series will find the information they need in order to have a better understanding of the social, political, environmental, and economic issues facing the world today.

Youth Substance Abuse

A REFERENCE HANDBOOK

David E. Newton

ABC-CLIO ™

An Imprint of ABC-CLIO, LLC
Santa Barbara, California • Denver, Colorado

Copyright © 2016 by ABC-CLIO, LLC

Library of Congress Cataloging-in-Publication Data

Names: Newton, David E., author.
Title: Youth substance abuse : a reference handbook /
  David E. Newton.
Description: Santa Barbara, California : ABC-CLIO, [2016] |
  Series: Contemporary world issues | Includes bibliographical
  references and index.
Identifiers: LCCN 2016012284 | ISBN 9781440839825
  (alk. paper) | ISBN 9781440839832 (ebook)
Subjects: LCSH: Youth—Substance use. | Substance abuse.
Classification: LCC HV4999.Y68 N49 2016 |
  DDC 362.290835—dc23
LC record available at https://lccn.loc.gov/2016012284

ISBN: 978-1-4408-3982-5
EISBN: 978-1-4408-3983-2

20 19 18 17 16   1 2 3 4 5

This book is also available as an eBook.

ABC-CLIO
An Imprint of ABC-CLIO, LLC

ABC-CLIO, LLC
130 Cremona Drive, P.O. Box 1911
Santa Barbara, California 93116-1911
www.abc-clio.com

This book is printed on acid-free paper ∞

Manufactured in the United States of America

In January 2016, *The New York Times* printed a remarkable article about death rates among non-Hispanic white American males between 1990 and 2014. The article noted that the demographic group had experienced a pattern of mortality very different from that of other demographic groups in the country, such as non-Hispanic white women, blacks, and Hispanics. The bottom line was that the mortality rate for non-Hispanic white males was *increasing*, while that of all other groups in the United States was dropping. These results have been startling because modern scientific advances have improved the health outlook for almost everyone in both developed and developing nations. How does one explain the dramatic reversal of this pattern for white American males?

As it turns out, the answer is fairly simple: drug abuse. The number of white males between the ages of 25 and 34 who overdosed from drugs in 2014 was five times the rate of those who did so in 1999, and the number who did so in the 35 to 44 year age group tripled during that period. This one factor—drug abuse—was responsible for a change in death rates that had not been seen in the United States since the Vietnam War decade of the late 1960s and early 1970s. With data like these, can anyone any longer doubt the severity of the adolescent substance abuse problem in the United States and, as it turns out, in many other parts of the world?

The demographics of substance abuse among adolescents have traveled an irregular path over the past half century. The Monitoring the Future study, which has been tracking drug use among high school seniors since 1975, has found that the consumption of illegal substances began at a fairly high level in the earliest years of its research (about 50 percent of boys and 40 percent of girls admitted to using illegal drugs at least once during the year preceding the study), increased to its highest peak ever about five years later, dropped to its lowest levels ever in the early 1990s, and finally rose to its current levels of 40 percent use for boys and 30 percent use for girls. Experts have expressed some hope that the decreases in drug use seen in the past half decade may represent a new trend in decreasing drug use and abuse, although no one is especially confident that such is the case.

Teenagers around the world today are faced with a staggering variety of legal and illegal psychoactive substances that can bring them feelings of excitement, joy, euphoria, a sense and calm and relief, or trips into worlds far removed from reality. For a certain portion of the adolescent population in every nation of the world, such escapes from reality may be the only apparent answer to the drabness or anxieties of their everyday lives. And for an even large numbers of teenagers, the use of psychoactive materials may simply be one more "new experience" in which they want to participate.

Yet, scientific evidence and demographic reports have now shown beyond a doubt that turning to drugs for a change in mood is not a simple break from the humdrum of everyday life. Such experiences have identifiable and measurable changes on the human brain that may last long after drug use has discontinued. They often lead to dependence on and addiction to a substance which produces physical, mental, social, and psychological effects that, if they do not disable or even kill a person, can change the trajectory of his or her life.

And recovering from the pull of psychoactive substances is no simple task. Treatment programs place severe demands on a person and often have only a limited chance of success. Never starting to use addictive substances can also be difficult, but does not approach the challenges of treatment for substance abuse and/or addiction.

This book attempts to provide the basic information one needs to understand substance abuse, such as the types of psychoactive materials that are most commonly consumed, the effects they have on the body, the means by which they are obtained, the types of individuals who may be at risk for substance abuse, and the methods for prevention and treatment that are available. In addition to providing this basic information, the book attempts to provide resources that teenagers can use more to learn about substance abuse, resources such as a history of substance abuse (Chapter 1), a review of current problems, issues, and solutions (Chapter 2), some personal perspectives on substance abuse among teenagers (Chapter 3), sketches of some important individuals and organizations in the field of substance abuse (Chapter 4), important documents and data on the use and abuse of drugs (Chapter 5), an annotated bibliography of useful print and electronic sources dealing with the topic of substance abuse (Chapter 6), a chronology of substance abuse issues throughout history (Chapter 7), and a glossary of important terms in the literature of drug abuse.

Youth Substance Abuse

Alison finally seemed to have solved her drug problems. After dealing with alcohol and marijuana dependency for much too long, she appeared to have "come clean" after an extended period in a rehabilitation program. She had a new job and had moved in with her boyfriend, who was also employed. The future looked promising for this "funny, smart, gregarious, tenacious and strong-willed teenager with gusto," as her mother later described here. Then, suddenly, the roof fell in. When she failed to show up at her parents' home to do laundry, they became concerned and ran to her apartment. There they found Alison lying on the floor, dead, with a needle beside her. She had died of a heroin overdose. (Ohio Teen's Obituary Gets Parents Worldwide Attention 2015)

Jamie had no other plans than to help his friend, Hannah, celebrate her birthday at home in Aberdaron, North Wales. But he got a bit carried away and ended up drinking far more alcohol than any 16-year-old should—in fact, five times more than the legal limit for a driver in the country. When he

---

A woman wearing a diaphanous robe and holding a sickle is standing next to a coca plant offering to make cuttings for advancing Spanish explorers; a ship is in the harbor in the background. (Images from the History of Medicine (NLM))

*passed out, the hostess's mother put him to bed because she had
seen the boy drink before and didn't think his condition was
all that unusual. When partygoers later tried to revive Jamie,
they were unable to waken him and decided to rush him to
the hospital. There he died of acute alcohol poisoning brought
on by binge drinking. (Parry 2014)*

One of the most troublesome public and personal health problems facing the United States and other countries worldwide today is teenage substance abuse. The most recent report of the Monitoring the Future (MTF) study says that more than a third of twelfth graders in the United States surveyed for the study, about a quarter of tenth graders, and about 10 percent of eighth graders had used alcohol in the 30 days preceding the study. The same study found that nearly a quarter of all twelfth graders, almost 20 percent of tenth graders, and just less than 10 percent of eighth graders had used some illicit drug during that same time period. And 13.6 percent of twelfth graders, 7.2 percent of tenth graders, and 4.0 percent of eighth graders had smoked cigarettes during the 30-day period.

(The Monitoring the Future study is conducted by researchers at the Institute for Social Research at the University of Michigan. The study has been repeated annually since 1975, asking questions about substance use and about students' attitudes about the risk and availability of legal and illegal substances. The survey originally included only twelfth graders, but was expanded to include eighth and tenth graders in 1991. Data and reports for all years are available at http://www.moni toringthefuture.org/pubs.html#top [Johnston et al. 2015].)

What Is Substance Abuse?

At one time, specialists interested in the misuse of substances such as alcohol, nicotine (in cigarettes), marijuana, cocaine, heroin, and similar materials used the term *drug abuse* in much of their work. In the United States, the legal definition for the term *drug* is any article that is "intended for use in the diagnosis, cure, mitigation, treatment, or prevention of disease" or any article (other than food) "intended to affect the structure or any function of the body of man or other animals" (Is It a Cosmetic, a Drug, or Both? [Or Is It Soap?] 2015). And that definition tends to fit some of the most common ways in which people use the word *drug*. One asks a healthcare provider for a "drug" to cure one's cough, and one then goes to the "drug" store (pharmacy) to have a prescription filled for that "drug." Substances obtained in such a process are known as *prescription drugs* (or *legend drugs*) because they can be legally obtained only by getting a formal written request (the prescription) from a qualified healthcare provider. According to a recent study on prescription drugs, the U.S. Food and Drug Administration (FDA) approves only handful of new prescription drugs each year, but over its entire history, the agency has approved a total of 1,453 drugs (Kinch et al. 2014).

These prescription drugs cover a very wide range of substances depending on how useful they are in preventing and treating diseases and how risky they are to a person's health. The system used in the United States for classifying prescription drugs was first established in the Controlled Substances Act of 1970. That act established five Schedules based on the medical value and personal risk for all prescription drugs. For example, Schedule I consists of all drugs that (1) have a high potential for abuse, (2) have no currently accepted medical use in treatment in the United States, and (3) lack accepted safety for use under medical supervision. By comparison, Schedule V consists of drugs that (1) have a low potential for abuse relative to the drugs or other substances in Schedule IV, (2) have a currently accepted medical use in treatment in the United States, and (3) may, when abused or misused, lead to limited physical dependence or psychological dependence relative to the drugs or other substances in Schedule IV. Table 1.1 shows some examples of substances included in each of the five Schedules (Controlled Substances Act 1970). Complete lists of controlled substances

Table 1.1   Drug Schedules

Schedule	Description	Examples
I	No accepted medical use; High potential for abuse	Cathinone Gamma hydroxybutyric acid Heroin Marijuana Psilocybin
II	Some accepted medical use; High potential for abuse	Amphetamine Codeine Fentanyl Hydromorphone Methadone Methamphetamine Morphine Opium Oxycodone Pentobarbital
III	Some accepted medical use; Less potential for abuse than Schedules I and II	Anabolic steroids Barbituric acid derivatives Buprenorphine (Suboxone) Codeine products of low concentration Ketamine Thiopental (Pentothal)
IV	Widely accepted medical use; Low potential for abuse	Alprazolam (Xanax) Carisoprodol (Soma) Diazepam (Valium) Lorazepam (Ativan) Temazepam (Restoril) Triazolam (Halcion)
V	Widely accepted medical use; Very low potential for abuse	Codeine preparations (Robitussin) Difenoxin preparations (Motofen) Dihydrocodeine preparations Diphenoxylate preparations (Lomotil)

Source: "Controlled Substances by CSA Schedule." 2015. Drug Enforcement Administration Diversion Control Program. http://www.deadiversion.usdoj.gov/schedules/orangebook/e_cs_sched.pdf. Accessed on November 9, 2015.

by Schedule and alphabetically are available at http://www.dead iversion.usdoj.gov/schedules/orangebook/c_cs_alpha.pdf and http://www.deadiversion.usdoj.gov/schedules/orangebook/e_cs_sched.pdf, respectively.)

Many other nations and regions around the world have drug scheduling systems similar to the one used by the FDA. Canada, for example, has four categories, called Schedule I, Schedule II, Schedule III, and Unscheduled (NDS Overview 2015). The United Kingdom has six categories, one of which includes over-the-counter (OTC) drugs, and one of which (Schedule IV) has two subcategories (Schedules 2015; a list of drug classification systems in the European Union can be found at http://www.emcdda.europa.eu/html.cfm/index146601EN.html).

The term *drugs* usually applies also to another category of substances that one can buy *without* a prescription, so-called *over-the-counter* (or *OTC*) drugs. The FDC has concluded that many popular medications, such as aspirin, ibuprofen, acetaminophen, and a variety of cough and cold medicines, are safe enough to use that they can be sold and used without a prescription. Currently, there are more than 300,000 OTC products in more than 80 therapeutic classes of OTC drugs.

Another category of drugs of concern to substance abuse scholars is known as *designer drugs*, also known by a number of other technical and popular terms. Designer drugs are substances that are produced synthetically in the laboratory by modifying existing natural or synthetic drugs. Consider a very simple example, as shown in Figure 1.1. Any example from real life would be much more complicated than that shown here. But the principle involved is the same.

Suppose that the compound shown at the left in Figure 1.1 is listed by the FDA in Schedule I of drugs. That is, the drug has no medical uses and a high risk for abuse or misuse. The drug would be very difficult and illegal to obtain for recreational (or any other) purpose. But suppose a clever chemist found a way to synthesize a derivative of that drug, one that contains a methyl ($-CH_3$) group not found in the original compound. And suppose that the new compound had many chemical and biological properties similar to those of the original compound. Then, that chemist could make and, supposedly sell, the new compound to individuals who wanted to use it for recreational

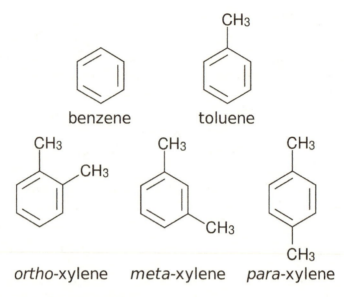

Figure 1.1   Derivatives of Benzene
(Created by Milton Beychok)

purposes. He or she could do so since the new compound was probably not restricted by the FDA drug schedule.

Of course, as soon as the FDA heard about the new compound, it could proceed to study the drug for harmful effects on animals and, if found, place the compound on Schedule I of scheduled drugs. In the meanwhile, the clever chemist might be working on another version of the original compound, one with perhaps two methyl groups attached to the ring, rather than one. The process might well be repeated again and again and again, with the FDA trying to stay ahead of clever chemists inventing new drugs, and clever chemists trying to stay ahead of FDA regulations. If you look at the two lists of scheduled drugs noted earlier, you may be able to see drug names that look very similar to each other. These drugs are examples of the process described here.

Drugs that are chemically related to each other, as in the example shown here, are known as *analogues* (or *analogs*). Many of the drugs of greatest concern to drug control agencies are designer drugs, some of which have now become illegal, and others that have not yet been acted upon by the FDA. That agency received a helping hand in dealing with the problem of designer drugs when the U.S. Congress passed the Federal Analog Act of 1986, which said essentially that "a controlled substance analogue shall, to the extent intended for human consumption, be treated, for the purposes of this title [Title I; 'Enforcement'] and title III ['Interdiction'] as a controlled substance in schedule I" (Public Law 99–570 1986; for more details, see Cooper 2015).

Yet another category of substances about which experts are concerned are those that are legal to use in the United States, but that still potentially have very serious implications for public and personal health. One could list a host of foods, drugs, and other products that are legal to buy and sell but that, used in excess, can potentially have very serious effects on a person's health, items such as sugary and fatty foods. The substances most often included in discussions of substance abuse, however, are alcohol and cigarettes. Both of these substances are entirely legal in the United States and many other parts of the world, at least for certain age groups, in spite of the fact that they are likely to have very serious health effects on an individual. Experts now know, for example, that smoking has a host of health effects including a number of cardiovascular and respiratory diseases and an increased risk for a variety of forms of cancer. The U.S. Centers for Disease Control and Prevention (CDC), for example, estimates that smoking is directly responsible for some 480,000 deaths in the United States every year, about one in every five deaths that occur in the nation. One's risk for a variety of disease increases dramatically for smokers: 2 to 4 times for coronary heart disease and stroke and 25 times for lung cancer for men and women (Smoking and Tobacco Use 2015).

Given the wide range of substances from which individuals in society today may be at risk, experts have now adopted the term *substance abuse* rather than the somewhat more limited term *drug abuse* to talk about the health issues related to the use, misuse, and abuse of prescription and non-prescription drugs, legal and illegal, of all kinds available today in the United States and other parts of the world.

Teenage Substance Abuse in History

What do scholars know about teenage substance abuse in history? The short answer is almost nothing. Indeed, that period of human life commonly referred to as *adolescence* or *the teen years* was scarcely recognized as an identifiable period worthy of study and reflection until the end of the nineteenth century. Indeed, the term *adolescent* itself probably did not appear until the middle of the fifteenth century, at which time it meant, from the Latin or Middle French, "growing towards maturity" (Adolescent 2015). The first rigorous research on the character of adolescence and the stages through which young men and women pass in the process did not appear until the historic research of pioneering American psychologist G. Stanley Hall in the first decade of the twentieth century. Since Hall's time, the study of adolescence and its characteristic "stages of development" has become a cottage industry among psychologists (Arnett 2006).

The lack of any formal academic study of adolescence does not mean, however, that such a period of human life did not exist or that some societies were not very much aware of it. One legend has it that adolescence was actually created by the Greek gods more than a million years ago, with the specific purpose of creating a situation in which immature humans (teenagers) were a constant source of annoyance to their parents and other adults, thus providing the gods with a constant source of amusement (Greydanus 2010). The characteristic features of adolescence have also been mentioned in a number of ancient texts that often sound as if they could have been written yesterday. The Greek historian Herodotus tells in the fifth century BCE, for example, of a Sumerian father who wrote a letter in which he described his son as one who "wandered about the streets . . . loitered in the public square, sought pleasure, answered his father in an insolent manner [and] seemed to have no disposition whatsoever to follow in his father's footsteps" (as quoted in Cusack 2011, 410).

In fact, the limited data that are available suggest that adolescence was, for most societies, a period in which boys and girls rather quickly passed from childhood to adulthood, taking on the roles and characteristics of adults. They were, that is, little (in size and development) adults expected to live and behave much as did their parents, neighbors, and adult friends (Kleijwegt 1991).

Some references to "substance abuse" among teenagers are available in the literature, but they are almost entirely stories of young men who had gained access to alcoholic beverages and become drunk in public. In advanced societies such as ancient Greece, such behavior was strongly condemned and subject to penalties. (See, for example, Reemtsma 2012, 29–30.)

Substance Use and Abuse in History

Whatever is or is not known about substance use and abuse among adolescents in the human history, a great deal has been learned about the topic among adults in general.

Alcoholic Beverages

It would be surprising indeed if alcoholic beverages were not known to and consumed by the earliest humans. Fermentation, the process by which various kinds of fruits and grain, are converted to ethanol (ethyl alcohol, or generally, just alcohol) is a natural process that must have become apparent to humans at an early stage in civilization. It was almost certainly a simple next step for early humans to discover and invent ways of controlling the fermentation process to make, at first, beer and wine, and later, other types of alcoholic beverages.

Alcoholic Beverages in the Ancient World

Such suppositions are confirmed by the discovery of devices used in the production of beer and wine, as well as physical and chemical traces of such products, going back nearly 10,000 years. A team of American and Chinese scientists reported in 2004, for example, that they had discovered pottery jars from the early Neolithic period in China's Henan Province that contained traces of organic material consistent with liquids made of fermented honey, rice, and fruit. They dated those finds to three periods, one between 7000 and 660 BCE, another between 6600 and 6200 BCE, and a third between 6200 and 5500 BCE. They concluded that the vessels were most likely used for religious ceremonies in which alcohol consumption was a characteristic feature (McGovern et al. 2004). Another research team from the United States, Turkey, and Georgia found what may be the earliest evidence of wine-making in Armenia, Georgia, and Turkey dating to about 6000 BCE (Vouillamoz et al. 2006).

The production of beer and wine in Egypt has been traced to about 3633–3376 BCE and in Mesopotamia, to about 3500–3100 BCE. One expert in the field has noted that archaeological evidence suggests that the people of ancient Mesopotamia "enjoyed beer so much that it was a daily dietary staple. Paintings, poems, and myths depict both human beings and their gods enjoying beer which was consumed through a straw to filter out pieces of bread or herbs in the drink" (HK24—Breweries by the Cultivation 2015; Mark 2011). The production of alcoholic beverages in the New World was, by comparison, much delayed, probably dating no earlier than 1000 BCE. At about that time, the Mayans appear to have been producing and consuming a mead-like drink made from fermented corn (Gately 2003, 10). Early Mesoamericans appear to have been one of the last cultures to discover and develop whatever benefits alcoholic beverages may have for humans because, according to one of the world's experts on the history of alcohol, "by about 1000 BC, all over the world, wherever humanity had settled in villages or towns, alcohol was consumed" (Gately 2003, 10).

The popularity of alcoholic beverages varied from region to region, however, depending on a mix of cultural, religious, and other factors. For example, the early use of such beverages by residents of the Middle East waned rapidly after the rise of Islam in the sixth century CE. At first, the Qur'an seemed to speak favorably of the use of alcoholic beverages, as being as beneficial as water, milk, and honey. But later revelations by Muhammad altered that view. Over time, he reported better understanding the evils of consuming alcohol and announced first that "in them is a great sin, and (some) benefit for men, but the sin of them is greater than their benefit," and later, more strongly, "Satan only wants to cause between you animosity and hatred through intoxicants and gambling and to avert you from the remembrance of Allah and from prayer. So will you not desist?" (Al-Ma'idah [The Table Spread] 2015, 5:91).

Other religions and cultures have varied widely in their attitudes toward the consumption of alcoholic beverages. Wine, for example, has had a long and noble role in the Jewish faith and in Hinduism. The use of alcoholic beverages is less favored or entirely discouraged in other religions, such as Buddhism and Jainism. (See, for example, A Hindu View on Drinking Alcohol 2015; Is Moderate Drinking Acceptable in Buddhism?; Taoism vs. Alcohol 2015.)

Among the many different cultures that have existed in human society, consumption of alcohol has had a variety of purposes: social, religious, medical, and recreational. For example, "having a round" (of alcoholic beverages) with friends has traditionally been a form of improving the quality of social interactions among family, friends, coworkers, and age or gender groups. The use of wine (and less often, beer) in religious ceremonies such as Holy Communion is also well known. And the therapeutic value of ethanol (ethyl alcohol) has been known for millennia (Heath 1995, Chapter 29).

Risks of Drinking Alcohol

The fundamental problem about drinking alcoholic beverages throughout history, however, has been the issue of *quantity*. In many cultures, the issue of alcohol consumption has not been one of *acceptability* ("yes" or "no," one may or may not consume alcoholic beverages), but *how much* consumption is considered appropriate (or safe or wise or mannerly or legal). This issue arises simply because the physiological effects of alcohol consumption vary dramatically with the amount of a beverage consumed. Those effects depend in a somewhat complex way on a number of factors, including one's gender, age, body weight, and manner of consumption. One way of quantifying many of these factors is a measure known as *blood alcohol content* (BAC), expressed as the percentage of alcohol present in one's body. For example, a BAC of 0.100 means that one's blood contains 0.1 percent alcohol, or one part alcohol for every 1,000 parts of blood. Tables are available for calculating BAC for a variety of conditions. (See, for example, Alcohol and Your Body 2015.)

The very wide range of effects attributable to various BACs is shown in Table 1.2. Notice that a moderate consumption of alcohol has some minimal physiological effects, while increasing amounts produce increasingly serious effects. (Although it is worth noting that experts tend to argue that there is really no entirely safe amount of alcohol consumption.)

The stark numbers in Table 1.2 explain why humans have always had a mixed feeling about alcohol consumption. At low

Table 1.2   Effects of Alcohol Consumption

Blood Alcohol Content	Physiological Effects	Emotional Effects
0.02–0.04	Very little or no impairment	Normal behavior; generally good spirits; increased sociability and talkativeness
0.05–0.07	Increased reaction time; impaired reflexes; impaired vision; impaired coordination	Mild euphoria; decreased inhibitions; decreased attention; impaired judgment; reduced sexual pleasure

Blood Alcohol Content	Physiological Effects	Emotional Effects
BAC of 0.08 is the legal limit in most states		
0.08–0.09	Some loss in balance; diminished sensory responses; impaired memory and comprehension; some loss of muscular control and coordination	Emotional instability; loss on inhibitions; reduced ability to respond appropriately to some social situations; lack of feelings
0.10–0.20	Confusion, dizziness, increased loss of motor control (inability to walk properly), impaired visual perception, decreased feelings of pain	Exaggeration of emotional responses, such as anger and fear; over-response to other's comments and actions; swings in emotional feelings
0.21–0.30	Impaired consciousness; stupor; significantly decreased response to stimulation; decreased ability to stand and walk; incontinence; reduced response to pain	Apathy; lethargy; inability to recognize and/or respond to most social situations
BAC of 0.25 is the point above which alcohol poisoning is likely to become a possibility		
0.31–0.40	Greatly reduced reflexes; impaired respiration; reduced body temperature; incontinence	Severe depression, if conscious; otherwise, largely unresponsive to personal or social stimuli
>0.40	Coma; death	None

levels, alcohol can (with some safety) produce warm, happy feelings in those who drink, conceivably a desirable outcome for at least some social and cultural purposes. But with increasing consumption come more serious physical and social effects that may create problems not only for an individual, but also for stability of a society.

Restrictions on Drinking Alcohol

It should hardly be surprising, then, that various types of prohibition or limitations on the use of alcoholic beverages have appeared since the beginning of human civilizations. Among the earliest of the laws and regulations of which we know date to the Hammurabi Code, promulgated in Babylonia in about 1754 BCE. That code had to do with the operation of taverns and the use of alcoholic beverages by priestesses (Mandelbaum 1965, 284). Similar laws were enacted in most ancient cultures of which we know. In China, for example, scholars have identified 41 different laws limiting or prohibiting the use of alcoholic beverages between 1100 BCE and 1400 CE (Hanson 1995, 3).

In most countries of the world today, consumption of alcohol is legal, although restricted by age. In the United States, for example, the legal drinking age is 21, although there are some exceptions to that regulation. Most other countries have similar laws. The most important exceptions are Muslim nations that follow Islamic shariah law, which prohibits the consumption of alcohol by any individual of any age. The penalty for violation of those laws normally involves a certain number of lashings (40, 60, or 80 is common), although it can result in a death penalty under certain circumstances (Islamic Penal Code of the Islamic Republic of Iran—Book One & Book Two 2015, section 179; Saalih al-Munajjid 2015).

One of the great experiments in modern times in banning the use of alcoholic beverages took place in the first quarter of the twentieth century. Over a period of time, proponents of a ban on alcohol won over a majority of Americans in support of their cause, and in 1919 the nation adopted the Eighteenth Amendment to the U.S. Constitution. That amendment banned the "manufacture, sale, or transportation of intoxicating liquors within, the importation thereof into, or the exportation thereof from the United States and all territory subject to the jurisdiction thereof for beverage purposes." That nation's "great experiment" with prohibition did not last very long, however. Only 14 years later, the nation adopted the Twenty-First Amendment to the Constitution, invalidating the Eighteenth Amendment (Constitution of the United States 2015; McGrew 2015).

"Hard" Liquor

During the ongoing debate over limitations on the use and abuse of beer and wine, scientists were learning about and developing other types of alcoholic beverages, often referred to collectively as *hard liquor*. Hard liquor is an alcoholic beverage produced by the distillation of the product of fermentation. Distillation removes some of the water present in the fermented liquor, thus increasing the alcoholic concentration of the substance. Hard liquors (also known as *distilled spirits*, *hard alcohol*, or simply *spirits*) may have alcoholic concentrations as great as 192 proof, which is equivalent to an alcohol concentration of 96 percent. The beverage that holds that distinction is a Polish vodka called Spirytus vodka (151 and Up: The Highest Proof Liquor 2015). (Proof is a measure of the alcohol content of a beverage and is equal to twice the percentage by volume of alcohol in the beverage.)

Today a wide array of hard liquors and other alcoholic beverages are available throughout the world, including absinthe, armagnac, aquavit, brandy, bourbon, cognac, a variety of cordials and aperitifs, gin, grappa, mezcal, rum, tequila, vodka, and whiskeys (American, Canadian, Irish, Scotch, and others). Many countries and regions also have other specialized types of hard liquors and/or specialized types of each of these general categories, such as shochu (Japan), burukutu (Nigeria), gaoliang (China), umeshu (Bulgaria), arrack (Sri Lanka), tuzemák (Czech Republic), and aila (Nepal). (Also see Types of Alcohol 2015.)

All hard liquors are inherently more risky to drink than beer or wine because their alcohol content is so much higher, causing one's BAC to rise much more quickly for the former than for the latter.

Demographics of Alcohol Consumption

Patterns and trends in alcohol consumption worldwide are reported annually in the World Health Organization (WHO) publication "Global Status Report on Alcohol and Health." Some of the major findings in the 2014 edition of that report are as follows:

• Estimated annual consumption of alcoholic beverages worldwide for individuals 15 years of age and older in 2010 (the last year for which data were available) was 6.2 liters of pure alcohol, equivalent to about half an ounce of alcohol per person per day.

• About half of that amount was consumed in the form of hard liquor.

• About a quarter of the amount was "unrecorded," that is produced and sold outside of normal governmental systems of control.

• Nearly two-thirds (61.7 percent) of the world's population had consumed no alcohol beverages in the year preceding the survey.

• Those who abstain from alcoholic beverages are more likely to live in developing nations; the rate of alcoholic consumption is positively correlated with the economic well-being of the country in which one lives.

• About 16 percent of drinkers worldwide tend to engaged in so-called *episodic* or *binge* drinking, characterized by very heavy drinking over short periods of time.

• In 2012, about 3.3 million deaths were attributed to alcohol-related factors, 5.9 percent of all deaths worldwide in that year. The death rate for males from such causes was about twice that for females, 7.6 percent to 4.0 percent. (All data are from Global Status Report on Alcohol and Health 2014, xiii–xiv.)

Data about alcohol consumption in the United States comes from a variety of sources, probably most importantly, for all adults, the National Survey on Drug Use and Health (NSDUH) and, for high school students, the Monitoring the Future (MTF) study (Center for Behavioral Health Statistics and Quality 2015; Johnston et al. 2015). According to the NSDUH study, just over half (52.7 percent) of individuals over the age of 12 reported having had an alcoholic drink at least once in the month prior to the survey. About half that number (23.0 percent) reported having engaged in binge drinking during that period and 6.2 percent said that they had done some *heavy drinking*. For the survey, binge drinking was defined as drinking five or more drinks on the same occasion on at least one day during a 30-day period, while heavy drinking was defined as drinking five or more drinks on the same occasion on five or more days in the same period of time (Center for Behavioral Health Statistics and Quality 2015, 19). These numbers have remained almost constant over the preceding decade (since 2002) (Center for Behavioral Health Statistics and Quality 2015, Table A.6B, page A-6).

The Monitoring the Future study examines the behavior and attitudes relating to a variety of substances for eighth, tenth, and twelfth graders nationwide. In the 2014 report, MTF researchers found that 0.3 percent of eighth graders, 0.8 percent of tenth graders, and 1.9 percent of twelfth graders reported that they had consumed alcoholic beverages on a daily basis in the 30 days preceding the study. These numbers had decreased for all groups compared to 1991, the first year in which this question was asked (0.5, 1.3, and 5.6 percent, respectively). The number of respondents who said they had engaged in binge drinking (as defined earlier) within a period of two weeks before the survey was 4.1 percent for eighth graders, 12.6 percent for tenth graders and 19.4 percent for twelfth graders (Johnston et al. 2015, Table 8, page 72).

Psychoactive Drugs in the Ancient World

Alcohol was by no means the only psychoactive drug known to ancient peoples. (Psychoactive drugs are substances that affect an animal's mental processes, producing unusual levels of perceptions, moods, or consciousness.) Other substances that were discovered or developed among the earliest human civilizations were the betel nut (*Areca catechu*), ephedra (ma huang; Ephedra genus); opium (*Papaver somniferum*), marijuana (also marihuana; *Cannabis sativa* and *C. indica*), cocaine (from the coca plants, varieties in the Erythroxylaceae family), and caffeine (from a variety of plants, most commonly *Coffea arabica*). The early histories of these substances have been studied in great detail, and various authors concentrate on one or another substance and/or one or another historical period and cultural setting. No brief history, such as the one given here, can provide an adequate review of this long, complex, and very interesting history. (See, for example, A Comprehensive Historical Timeline of the Relationship between Psychedelic Substances and Mammalian Brains 2012; Crocq 2007; Escohotado 1999; Gerald 2013; Timeline of Events in the History of Drugs 2015.)

Some writers claim that the earliest substance used by humans for psychoactive purposes was the betel nut, the product of the *Areca catechu* plant. The earliest date suggested for the use of the betel nut is about 9000 BCE (Erowid 2003), although better evidence suggests the earliest date may be about 7000 BCE (Ahuja and Ahuja 2011; Gorman 1970). The betel palm does not grow in the wild, but survives only with human cultivation. Historically and in the present day, nuts from the plant are mixed with other substituents (tobacco sometimes being one of them) that the user then chews to achieve a feeling of relaxation and peacefulness. The practice is not unlike that of cigarette smokers who routinely go through a pack or more of cigarettes per day (although not to achieve the same results) (Hahn 2003). According to recent estimates, some 600 million people worldwide continue to follow the practice of betel nut chewing on a regular basis (Personal Habits and Indoor Combustions 2012, 34).

Betel nuts are one of four psychoactive drugs taken in primarily by means of chewing, the others being coca, tobacco, and khat (or kat or qat). The chewing of coca leaves appears to date to nearly the same historical period as for betel nuts, although the practice seems to have originated in the New World, probably northern Peru in about 6000 BCE (Dillehay et al. 2010). Coca chewing today is largely a regionalized practice that occurs primarily in Bolivia and Peru and other parts of the Andes Mountains region. The use of coca helps residents of this region to deal with the problems of breathing the thin air in mountainous regions where many of them live.

Khat (*Cahta edulis*) is a flowering plant native to the Arabian Peninsula and the Horn of Africa. The primary psychoactive component of the plant is the alkaloid cathinone, which produces a sense of euphoria. Leaves and stems of the plant are chewed, releasing cathinone to produce a sense of ease and relaxation. Although the history of the domestication and first use of the plant is poorly known, it appears that its use was relatively widespread in the area of modern Ethiopia as early as the thirteenth century CE (Distefano 1983). Khat chewing remains a practice limited primarily to East Africa and the Arabian Peninsula, with estimates of the number of users ranging from about 30 percent in parts of Ethiopia and Somalia to 90 percent among men and more than 70 percent among women in the nation of Yemen (Khat Chewing in Yemen: Turning Over a New Leaf 2008).

The smoking, chewing, and other uses of tobacco were also known in the ancient world, but at first, only in its native regions of South America. Most experts agree that humans first began using the substance for religious, medical, and recreational uses in about the first millennium BCE, probably in the Peruvian and Ecuadorean Andes region. Authorities hypothesize that they may have tried a variety of mechanisms for ingesting the material, by inhaling it, smoking it, chewing it, and using it in enemas, for example (Gately 2003, Chapter 1). Probably the earliest visual evidence of tobacco use in the New World is a carving at the Temple of the Cross in the ruins at Palenque, dating between 684 and 702 CE. The carving shows a man apparently smoking a cigar-like item that could be a primitive cigar (Eric and Thompson 1970, 104–107, but also see other opinions, such as Borio 1993–2001 [unattributed]). The practice of tobacco use then spread throughout South America so that by the first century CE, it was being used "nearly everywhere" on the continent (Josephy and Brandon 1993, 41).

Europeans did not learn about tobacco, however, until the earliest explorers reached the continent in the late fifteenth century. Many of those explorers soon became enamored of the substance, however, and carried word of its availability and uses throughout the Western world (and probably beyond). They went so far as to carry tobacco plants and seeds with them wherever they went in their explorations, to ensure that a ready supply of tobacco would be available whenever they returned to a site (Duke and Jordan 1995, 182–183; Hanson, Venturelli, and Fleckenstein 2012, 331–332).

Tobacco Use in the Modern World

For the greatest part of the human use of tobacco, relatively little regard was given to possible health effects from its use. From time to time, physicians, researchers, or other authorities commented on possible hazards to human health from smoking, chewing, or inhaling the product. (See, for example, Tobacco Risk Awareness Timeline 2015.) But such comments were largely ignored until the middle of the twentieth century, at which point scientific research on the topic pointed so overwhelmingly to the risk posed by smoking and chewing that it could no longer be ignored, and public health authorities and government officials began imposing stronger restrictions and limitations on the advertising, sale, and consumption of the product (50 Years of Tobacco Control 2015; a summary of current laws on the use of tobacco worldwide is available at Tobacco Control Laws 2015).

Researchers estimate that the number of smokers worldwide increased from 721 million in 1980 to 967 million in 2012. The smoking rate among men was nearly five times as great as it was among women in 2012, 31.1 percent to 6.2 percent. The percentage of smokers was lowest among those in the age

15 to 19 years and over 75 years age groups and was greater in developing countries for men over the age of 35, but greater for men under 35 in developed countries. The rate of smoking among women was greater for nearly all age groups except the oldest in developed countries (Ng et al. 2014). Smoking rates vary widely from region to region and from country to country. The lowest rates (for males only) reported in 2012 were 9 percent in Ethiopia; 13 percent in Barbados and Panama; and 16 percent in Benin, Niger, and Nigeria. The highest rates were recorded in Indonesia (72 percent), Kiribati (67 percent), Jordan (64 percent), and Laos and Russia (60 percent) (Smoking Prevalence, Males [% of Adults] 2015).

Smoking rates in the United States are among the lowest in the world. According to the most recent data available, 16.8 percent of Americans currently smoke on a regular basis, nearly the same fraction of men (18.8 percent) as of women (14.8 percent). The age group with the largest fraction of smokers is those between 25 and 44 years (20 percent), followed by those in the age group 45 to 64 (18 percent), those between 18 and 24 (16.7 percent), and those over the age of 64 (8.5 percent). Smoking rates are highest among American Indians/Alaska Natives (29.2 percent) and non-Hispanic whites (18.2 percent) and lowest among non-Hispanic blacks (17.5 percent), Hispanics (11.2 percent), and non-Hispanic Asians (9.5 percent) (Current Cigarette Smoking among Adults in the United States 2015).

The prevalence of smokeless tobacco (primarily chewing tobacco and snuff) use in the United States is much lower than that for cigarette smoking, about 3.6 percent for the general population in 2012. (In statistics, the term *prevalence* refers to the number of cases of a condition that are present at some given time.) Smokeless tobacco products are nearly nine times as popular (3.6 percent to 0.4 percent) among men than among women and by far the most popular among American Indians and Native Alaskans (9.3 percent) than among other ethnic groups (non-Hispanic whites: 4.7 percent; non-Hispanic

Table 1.3 Patterns of Cigarette Smoking and Smokeless Tobacco Use among High School Students, 1991–2014 (percentage)*

Cigarette Smoking

Grade	1991	1992	1993	1994	1995	1996	1997	1998	1999	2000	2001	2002
8	14.3	15.5	16.7	18.6	19.1	21.0	19.4	19.1	17.5	14.6	12.2	10.7
10	20.8	21.5	24.7	25.4	27.9	30.4	29.8	27.6	25.7	23.9	21.3	17.7
12	28.3	27.8	29.9	31.2	33.5	34.0	36.5	35.1	34.6	31.4	29.5	26.7

Cigarette Smoking cont'd

Grade	2003	2004	2005	2006	2007	2008	2009	2010	2011	2012	2013	2014
8	10.2	9.2	9.3	8.7	7.1	6.8	6.5	7.1	6.1	4.9	4.5	4.0
10	16.7	16.0	14.9	14.5	14.0	12.3	13.1	13.6	11.8	10.8	9.1	7.2
12	24.4	25.0	23.2	21.6	21.6	20.4	20.1	19.2	18.7	17.1	16.3	13.6

Smokeless Tobacco

Grade	1991	1992	1993	1994	1995	1996	1997	1998	1999	2000	2001	2002
8	6.9	7.0	6.6	7.7	7.1	7.1	5.5	4.8	4.5	4.2	4.0	3.3
10	10.0	9.6	10.4	10.5	9.7	8.6	8.9	7.5	6.5	6.1	6.9	6.1
12	†	11.4	10.7	11.1	12.2	9.8	9.7	8.8	8.4	7.6	7.8	6.5

Smokeless Tobacco cont'd

Grade	2003	2004	2005	2006	2007	2008	2009	2010	2011	2012	2013	2014
8	4.1	4.1	3.3	3.7	3.2	3.5	3.7	4.1	3.5	2.8	2.8	3.0
10	5.3	4.9	5.6	5.7	6.1	5.0	6.5	7.5	6.6	6.4	6.4	5.3
12	6.7	6.7	7.6	6.1	6.6	6.5	8.4	8.5	8.3	7.9	8.1	8.4

*Percentage of respondents who had used substance in the 30 days preceding the study.

†Question not asked.

Source: "Trends in Lifetime Prevalence of Use of Various Drugs for Grades 8, 10, and 12 Combined." Johnston, L.D., P. M. O'Malley, R.A. Miech, J.G. Bachman, and J.E. Schulenberg. (2015). *Monitoring the Future National Survey Results on Drug Use: 1975–2014: Overview, Key Findings on Adolescent Drug Use*. Ann Arbor: Institute for Social Research, The University of Michigan. Table 7, page 71.

blacks: 1.9 percent; Hispanics: 1.2 percent; and Asian Americans: 0.4 percent) (Smokeless Tobacco Use in the United States 2015).

One of the interesting trends in the United States over the past two decades has been the significant decrease in the number of individuals who smoke cigarettes or use smokeless tobacco. Data for this trend among high school students were collected by the MTF project in 2014.

Other Psychoactive Drugs in History

In addition to the psychoactive substances discussed thus far, a number of other drugs have been known since the earliest periods of human history, all of which have had a long and complex story over the centuries. These substances produce effects in animals that are significantly different and, in some ways, more profound, than those produced by the use of alcohol, tobacco, caffeine, and other psychoactive materials. One of their most important differences is that they tend to produce dependence and addiction relatively easily and with serious long-term effects.

Some Important Terms

In the field of substance use and abuse, the term *dependence* has two distinct meanings, *physical dependence* and *psychological dependence* (Pharmacology of Drugs 2015). Physical dependence refers to a physical state in which an animal's body functions normally only when a particular chemical substance is available and provided to it. For example, people who use morphine over an extended period of time become dependent on the drug, requiring that some of it be ingested on a regular basis. Dependence occurs because physical changes take place in certain regions of a person's central nervous system (Bringing the Power of Science to Bear on Drug Abuse and Addiction 2007). When the body's cells no longer respond to the presence of some substance, they are said to have become *resistant* to that substance, a condition that results in a state known as *tolerance* to that substance. As an animal becomes more tolerant to a substance, it begins to require more and more of that substance in order to produce the same biological and physiological effects as those previously produced by smaller quantities of the substance. A common method for diagnosing physical dependence is to see what happens when a particular substance is withheld from a person. If a person has become dependent on that substance, he or she will begin to show signs of *withdrawal*. The term *withdrawal* refers to a series of symptoms such as nausea, vomiting, body aches, increase in pulse rate and blood pressure, headaches, runny nose, excessive yawning, sweating, and general feelings of malaise (Physical and Psychological Addiction 2015). The specific set of symptoms associated with the withdrawal process differs, however, upon each class of substances and, in some cases, on specific substances from which one is withdrawing (Physical Detoxification Services for Withdrawal from Specific Substances 2006).

Substance dependence and substance addiction are different from each other, although closely related. Addiction is defined as a disease of the brain in which a person has come to depend on the ingestion of some substance in order to achieve specific psychological effects, such as a sense of ease (euphoria) or heightened sensory sensations (a "high"). The need to achieve these feelings becomes so great that it takes over a person's life, and finding and ingesting the desired substance becomes the primary goal of one's existence. Substance addiction tends to brings about physical, psychological, and emotional changes that alter the character and direction of a person's life and can lead to severe chronic physical and mental disorders and, in the most extreme cases, death (Definition of Addiction 2011).

In recent years, a new term has been introduced to describe individuals who have become dependent upon or addicted to substances: substance use disorder (SUD). According the *Diagnostic and Statistical Manual of Mental Disorders*, Fifth Edition (DSM-5) of the American Psychiatric Association, a substance use disorder is "a problematic pattern of using alcohol or another substance that results in impairment in daily life or noticeable distress" (Medina 2015) It is characterized by "clinically and functionally significant impairment, such as health problems, disability, and failure to meet major responsibilities at work, school, or home" (Substance Use Disorders 2016).

Uses of Psychoactive Drugs

The reason that psychoactive substances are such a problem in modern society is that the physical, mental, and emotional changes they produce are profound, bringing peacefulness and euphoria to individuals whose lives may otherwise be beset with pain and unhappiness or a sense of excitement to other individuals whose lives may seem humdrum and depressing (more of that in the next chapter). So it would hardly be surprising that our ancestors dating back many millennia must have been aware of the same effects produced by psychoactive substances and begun using them for a variety of purposes in the earliest periods of human civilization. Those purposes generally fell (as they do today) into one of three major categories: medical, religious and cultural, and recreational.

Probably the most common medical application of psychoactive substances throughout history has been for the relief of pain (*analgesics*), although they have also been employed in the treatment of mental disorders and as anesthetics for surgical procedures. They have also been an essential part of many religious ceremonies, usually because they make possible so-called out of body experiences that allow individuals to experience a new and different way of perceiving human life and its place in the cosmos. For much the same reason on a more personal level, psychoactive substances have apparently always been used by at least some portion of the human population for recreational purposes, producing mental and emotional "highs" or "downers" (Merlin 2003; The Role of Drugs in Prehistory 2015).

Psychoactive Plants in Antiquity

Scholars who have studied ancient cultures often comment on the apparently critical role of psychoactive substances in such societies. They often point out the importance of psychoactive substances that produce altered states of consciousness (ASC) that may have contributed in a variety of ways to the development of the social fragment of early civilizations. As one team of researchers has noted, psychoactive substances and the ASC they produce "were likely involved in facilitating the social development of more symbolic forms of life and mind" (Froese, Woodward, and Ikegami 2014, 89; for an excellent review of this general question, see Guerra-Doce 2015a, 2015b).

In any case, evidence for the use of psychoactive substances, although sometimes highly speculative, dates to the earliest human societies. One reviewer of the archaeological evidence for the early use of psychoactive substances points out the abundance of such plant materials in some parts of the world (particularly South America) and the likelihood that early hunters and gatherers might reasonably be expected to have found, tested, and then used a variety of plants and minerals that have pronounced effects on the mind and body. It seems only logical, then, to expect that psychoactive substances were known to and used by early cultures. In fact, it is entirely possible, this reviewer notes, that humans and psychoactive plants may have evolved together, to the benefit of both, thus suggesting that "the search for intoxication should be better understood as a biological need common to humans and animals, a basic drive similar to the need for food, water, and sex" (Guerra-Doce 2015b, also citing Siegel 1989).

Probably the first circumstantial evidence for the use of psychoactive substances by early humans comes from archaeological research at a burial cave near Shanidar, Iraq, dating to about 60,000 BCE. The skeleton of an adult male was found there surrounded by plant material that suggested he was buried along with at least some plants with psychoactive constituents, including the stimulant ephedra (Leroi-Gourhan 1975). Other researchers have questioned this evidence, and it remains of doubtful validity (Sommer 1999).

Cocaine

In addition to the drugs mentioned earlier in this chapter, a number of other psychoactive substances were known to and used by ancient peoples, for which reliable evidence is now available. One of the best known of those drugs is cocaine, derived from the coca plant discussed earlier in this chapter. Evidence for the use of coca leaves by early Andean natives dates to at least the sixth millennium BCE (Dillehay et al. 2010), but much of what is known about the practice comes from the writings of Spanish explorers, conquerors, and adventurers from the sixteenth century. It is now clear that cocaine had a fundamental role in Inca society as related in a number of creation stories associated with the culture. Fundamentally, these stories told that the coca plant was created out of the body of an early personage known as Mama Coca, who was killed and cut into two because she was so immoral. Out of that tale grew the belief that coca was a sacred substance with profound conscious-altering properties that was available, at first, only to the elite classes of Inca societies. Over time, that view changed, and by the sixteenth century, coca use became widespread throughout the society (Karch 2006, Chapter 1; Peterson 1977, Chapter 1).

Interest in the use of coca leaves did not travel to Europe with returning Spanish and Portuguese travelers, as had been the case with tobacco however. Experts suggest that this situation resulted from the fact that coca leaves lost their potency during the long trip from South America to Europe, just the reverse of the case with tobacco leaves (Freye 2009, 13). In fact, it was more than two centuries before any European of consequence recognized and wrote about the striking effects of chewing coca leaves. Then, in 1858, Italian neurologist Paolo Mantegazza wrote of his experiences in trying out the drug in his own laboratory. He summarized those experiences in a scientific paper, "Sulle Virtù Igieniche e Medicinali Della Coca e Sugli Alimenti Nervosi in Generale" ("On the Hygienic and Medicinal Properties of Coca and on Nervine Nourishment in General"), published in the journal *Annali Universali Delle Scienze e Dell'industria* (*Annals of Universal Sciences and Industry*). In his paper, Mantegazza wrote that

> I sneered at the poor mortals condemned to live in this valley of tears while I, carried on the wings of two leaves of coca, went flying through the spaces of 77, 438 words, each more splendid than the one before. . . . (Paolo Mantegazza 2015)

Mantegazza's report appeared at about the same time that researchers were beginning a more systematic study of the coca plant and its psychoactive effects on animals. The first breakthrough occurred in 1855 when German chemist Friedrich Gaedcke isolated a compound he called erythroxyline, after the family name of the coca plant (Petersen 1977, 21, 48; Gaedcke's original paper [in German] can be found at Gaedcke 1855).

At nearly the same time that Gaedcke was conducting his research, one of the world's leading organic chemists, Friedrich Wöhler, obtained a supply of coca from South America and asked his assistant, Albert Niemann, to analyze the substance. Niemann was able to extract Gaedcke's "erythroxyline" from the material, giving it its present name of *cocaine* (Karch and Drummer 2016, 10).

The commercial potential of cocaine seemed at first to be limited, and the only company to take an interest in its production was the firm of E. Merck, in Darmstadt, Germany. By 1862, it had begun production on a modest level, producing less than 50 grams of the drug per year. But that situation soon changed as researchers began to discover the analgesic properties of cocaine. Merck's production soon increased to more than a kilogram per year (in 1883–1884) and then to more than 500 kilograms in 1889–1890 and to more than 1,500 kilograms in 1897–1898. With the entry of other producers into the market, the role of cocaine in the field of medicine was well confirmed (Friman 1999; Gootenberg 2001).

As with so many drugs, the very properties that made cocaine a useful addition to the materia medica also made it attractive for nonmedical uses, such as producing a mild and enjoyable "buzz" for users. The drug was also thought perhaps to have certain health benefits, further enhancing its popularity for non-curative purposes. By the end of the nineteenth century, a variety of coca- and cocaine-infused products were available for such purposes. These included Vin Marinani, reportedly a favorite drink of Pope Leo XIII, the new American "soft drink" called Coca-Cola, and even an injectable solution from the drug firm of Parke-Davis (Hamblin 2013; Parke, Davis & Co. Cocaine Injection Kit 2015; A Word from Our Sponsor 2015).

By 1900, evidence of the health consequences of cocaine use had become widely known, and legal prohibitions on the drug's use were being instituted. Illegal cocaine was still readily available, however, usually in the form of the salt cocaine hydrochloride, in the form of a white powder which users inhaled or dissolved in water and injected. Reports of serious damage to the nasal passages as a result of cocaine "snorting" appeared as early as 1910, although these studies appear not to have much effect on the use of the drug for recreational purposes.

Between 1900 and 1920, as the health effects of cocaine became more obvious, a campaign against the recreational use of the drug developed. Driven not only by health concerns, but also racist rhetoric against those who supposedly most abused the drug, new legislation was passed to limit or ban the use of cocaine for recreational purposes. These efforts eventually led to the listing of cocaine as a Schedule II drug, with some medical uses, but very high risk of abuse (Petersen 1977, Chapter 1).

Until the 1970s, powder cocaine was the drug of choice among many substance abusers, especially among well-to-do individuals. Its cost was usually too high for low- or moderate-income persons, accounting for its common name "the champagne of drugs" (Gahlinger 2004, 242). In the mid-1970s, a new form of cocaine became available, so-called *freebase cocaine*. The name comes from the method by which the product is made: cocaine hydrochloride is treated with a base, such as sodium bicarbonate, which neutralizes the acidic cocaine hydrochloride, leaving behind free cocaine. The cocaine is extracted from the reaction mixture with ether, which is then allowed to evaporate, leaving behind pure cocaine crystals, which can then be smoked. (A serious risk here is smoking crystals that still contain some ether, resulting in a fire when the product is lighted.) Freebase cocaine rapidly became very popular because it was generally purer than powder cocaine and, as a result of being smoked, reached the brain more rapidly.

About a decade after the discovery of freebasing, yet another form of cocaine was developed: crack cocaine. The process for making crack cocaine is essentially the same as that for making freebase cocaine. Powder cocaine is neutralized with sodium bicarbonate, sodium hydroxide, or another base, and heated. When the excess water in the mixture has evaporated, pure cocaine and additional by-products remain in the form of a rock-like crystalline substance. The substance gets its name of "crack" from the sound it makes during the chemical reaction by which it is formed. Because it is much safer and cheaper to make than freebase cocaine, crack cocaine soon became very popular among low- and middle-income individuals, resulting in an epidemic that peaked between 1984 and 1990 in the United States.

An estimated 1.5 million Americans reported using cocaine during the month preceding the most recent NSDUH study (2014), representing about 0.6 percent of the population 12 years of age and older. This number was about the same as for the preceding four years, but significantly lower than the period from 2002 to 2008 (Center for Behavioral Health Statistics and Quality 2015, 10). Data from the latest report of the MTF study (2014) indicate that an estimated 0.5 percent of eighth graders had reported using cocaine in the month prior to the survey, compared to 0.6 percent of tenth graders and 1.0 percent of twelfth graders who did so. These numbers have varied significantly over the four decades the survey has been conducted, rising in the early years of the survey (prior to 1986) and then beginning to fall until 1992, when they began to rise again. Those numbers began to fall again in about 1999, and have been dropping ever since (Johnston et al. 2015, 20; Table 7, page 69).

Opium

A second psychoactive substance of ancient origins is opium. Opium is a term used to describe the dried exudate (the liquid excreted when a plant is cut) from the unripe capsules of the *Papaver somniferum* plant. The material consists of about 25 psychoactive drugs, including as morphine, codeine, papaverine, noscapine, and thebaine. A typical analysis shows a composition of about 2.3 percent morphine, 2.6 percent codeine, 4.7 percent papaverine, and 10.2 percent noscapine (with no detectable thebaine) (Panicker, Wojno, and Ziska 2007). These values vary somewhat depending on the source of the opium being studied. The complex nature of opium was not known to the ancients and was discovered over a period of time beginning with the isolation of the first constituent, morphine, by German chemist Friedrich Sertürner in 1803.

The oldest evidence for the growth of the *P. somniferum* plant dates to Neolithic villages in Switzerland in about 5700 BCE. Additional evidence suggests that the plant was being grown in a number of locations in Central and Southern Europe for at least the next six millennia. These data suggest that a previous hypothesis that the plant originated in the Middle East may well be incorrect and that what probably happened was that the opium plant originated in Central Europe and then was transmitted over the centuries to Sumeria, Assyria, Babylon, and other Middle Eastern cultures (Merlin 2003, Table 1, 304–308; Zohary, Hopf, and Weiss 2012, 109–111). From there, transmission continued to the East, probably carried by Arab traders, to Persia, China, and Japan (Chopra 1958, 204–205).

The evolution of the role of opium in Chinese society is particularly interesting because it may well provide insight into similar patterns that have occurred in most (perhaps all) other cultures. At first, opium was used exclusively for medical purposes. In traditional Chinese medicine, the plant is thought to control the balance of bodily fluids and to preserve qi, the vital energy needed to maintain normal bodily function. Opium had long been known also as a soporific (a substance that induces sleep) and as a powerful pain reliever. Some historians have also suggested that the Chinese gave opium to their warriors to increase their strength and determination in battle (a practice that has been documented in other cultures also) (A Century of International Drug Control [2009], 19).

At first, the use of opium appears to have been restricted almost entirely to physicians and the upper classes, the former because of its health benefits, and the latter, more often, because of its psychoactive effects. Over time, however, it was the latter application that grew in popularity, and opium began to attain the role of emotional enhancement by which it is perhaps as well known today as is its medical benefits. Eventually, the psychoactive charms of opium began to expand beyond the upper classes and among commoners. One observer has noted that "[b]y the late Ming [1368–1644], opium was no longer the province of royal dabbling but a court necessity, and was working its way into the commoners' purview" (Diaz 2008). Perhaps one of the most interesting confirmations of this change in Chinese attitudes toward and use of opium came with a modification of the term used to describe the drug during the Ming dynasty, from yao ("medicine") to chun yao ("spring drug" or, more accurately, "aphrodisiac"). The new term was meant to refer to the drug's ability to "induce sexual desire, vitalise intercourse and control ejaculation or emission." It thus came to be associated less with, or at least equally valuable as, a symbol of "lust and regeneration" (Zheng 2005, 12).

While physicians and pleasure-seekers around the world were using opium in ever-increasing amounts, researchers were trying to learn more about the composition of this "marvelous" drug and to find new uses for it. One of the first breakthroughs in this area was the discovery (or invention) of a new opium-containing substance called laudanum (supposedly from the Latin verb, *laudare*, "to praise"). Although the term was used for a fairly wide variety of concoctions, it is most commonly described as a tincture of opium, opium powder dissolved in alcohol. (A tincture is, in general, any solution in which alcohol is the solvent.)

Most histories of opium ascribe the discovery of laudanum to the sixteenth-century Swiss-German alchemist and physician Paracelsus. They claimed that he discovered that opium is much more soluble in alcohol than in water, making it possible to produce a format (a tincture) that is easier to use than other forms. In fact, some recipes for laudanum recommend a high-quality wine as a solvent, to which are added a variety of herbs and spices to improve the otherwise harsh taste of the concoction. The laudanum produced as a tincture can also be reformulated in the form of pills, which can be taken as aspirin and other drugs are taken today. (The actual discovery of laudanum is probably a far more complex story than that found in most sources. For one of the best reviews of this history, see Ball 2007, 182–184.)

Whatever its precise origin, laudanum was a highly praised and eagerly sought-out medication. Paracelsus himself claimed almost endless benefits from the drug, with an ability to cure any disease whatsoever, with the one exception of leprosy. In fact, he said that laudanum could even raise the dead and, as his assistant once wrote, some patients who "seemed to be dead suddenly arose" after taking the drug (Ball 2007, 182).

Because of its efficacy in the treatment of a wide range of physical complaints, laudanum remained popular in many parts of the world until the early twentieth century. It probably reached its peak of popularity during the Victorian period in England, when it was particularly popular among women, who used the concoction for the treatment of menstrual cramps and other unspecified complaints. Among its other many uses were the treatment of pain; calming of the nerves; aid in sleeping; relief from colds and flu; and treatment of a number of more serious disorders and diseases, such as meningitis, cardiac disease, and yellow fever. The drug was also widely used by parents and nurses to reduce crying and fussiness among babies and young children (Cowell 2015).

Laudanum is still available by prescription in the United States, although it has been banned in other parts of the world. The most common use for the drug is the treatment of diarrhea and for the treatment of babies born to women who are addicted to opium. The drug is not widely used because of its serious side effects (if taken in excess it can be fatal) and because other drugs are available for most applications that are much less dangerous than is laudanum itself (Laudanum Addiction Treatment 2015).

Until the early nineteenth century, opium was used only in its natural form, as a preparation of the *P. somniferum* plant or in a concoction such as laudanum. As chemists began to research more extensively the composition of the plant, however, they begin to make an interesting discovery: natural opium leaves, seeds, sap, and other components actually consist of a complex mixture of compounds, many of which have their own characteristic psychoactive properties. The most important breakthrough in the early stages of this research was the discovery by a 19-year-old German pharmacist's assistant, Friedrich Sertürner of a compound in opium that he called *morphine*, in honor of the Greek god of dreams, Morpheus.

Chemically, morphine is classified as an alkaloid, an organic (carbon-containing) compound that contains the element nitrogen, that is present in plants, and that has physiological effects on humans. Some well-known alkaloids are caffeine, nicotine, morphine, strychnine, quinine, atropine, and curare. Morphine is perhaps the best known and most efficacious of all opiates. At one time, the term *opiate* was used to refer to any alkaloid found in the opium plant, such as morphine or codeine. Another term used to describe opium-like substances is *opioid*, which originally referred only to synthetic or semi-synthetic substances with narcotic (mood-changing) effects. The term *opioid* is sometimes reserved also for any substance that attaches to and activates cellular structures in the body known as *opioid receptors*. Some disagreement exists today as to the precise meaning of the terms *opiate* and *opioid*, with some authorities preferring to keep this original distinction, and other experts preferring to use the latter term for all opium-like substances, whether natural or synthetic. (For more on this debate, see Opiate vs. Opioid—What's the Difference? 2015.)

Morphine has a molecular structure very similar to that of other opiates and opioids, both natural and synthetic. (See, for example, Arnaud 2014, Diagram.) Its primary application is in the treatment of both acute and chronic severe pain, such as those associated with myocardial infarction, severe and multiple injuries, and post-operative distress. Its value for these uses was apparent early on. In one of the most famous statements in the history of morphine use, the famous English physician William Osler wrote about his use of morphine during the most difficult years of his life-ending medical problems. "Shunt the whole pharmacopeia," he wrote, "except for opium. It alone in some form does the job. What a comfort it has been!" (Bliss 1999, 469). Elsewhere Osler referred to morphine by a term that has ever since been associated with it: "God's own medicine" (Bliss 1999, 365).

The two most serious problems associated with the use of morphine are its effects on the respiratory system and its tendency to be addictive. When consumed in excessive amounts, morphine can cause asphyxia (a severe deficiency of oxygen in the body) and respiratory depression that can lead to death. Sertürner himself was the first person to become aware of this dangerous side effect. Soon after he discovered morphine, he decided to test its effects on animals. He fed small amounts first to mice living in his basement, and then to some unwanted dogs in the neighborhood. In all cases, the animals died from eating the drug. Not to be deterred, Sertürner then decided to try the drug on himself and some of his friends. He soon found unpleasant effects similar to those described earlier and concluded that the level of morphine used with a human was critical to its effects—beneficial or harmful—to an individual (Altman 1987, 89–90).

Sertürner's discovery of morphine was truly one of the most significant events in the history of pharmacology. As news of his research began to spread through the medical community, reports came flooding in of successful treatments for pain that had never been possible before. By the 1820s, morphine had become routinely available and without prescription in Great Britain, the United States, and other countries. These advances were made possible at least in part by the development of commercial means for manufacturing morphine from its raw ingredients, one of the first products produced by the Merck company in 1827 (Pharmaceutical Research by a Commercial House 1906). The standardization of morphine manufacture meant that physicians could prescribe very specific amounts of morphine to be taken ("take two pills twice a day") with confidence that the patient was receiving the correct dosage that would help cure his or her problem without risking serious side effects (Booth 1998, 70; see a typical Merck ad for the drug at Merck's Merits in the Manufacture of Morphine 1907).

As the availability and reliability of morphine as a medical product continued to grow through the nineteenth century, so did its appeal to individuals looking for a new recreational drug to try. But then, and even now, those medical applications of morphine have tended to outweigh their use by substance abusers. Probably the best known example of the value of morphine during the 1800s, for example, was its use in the U.S. Civil War, fought between 1861 and 1865. Two of the most challenging problems with which physicians had to deal during the war (as had been the case with nearly all preceding wars) were dysentery and surgical pain. According to the data most commonly cited, 1,525,236 Union soldiers were admitted for medical care as a result of dysentery and diarrheal disorders (caused by agents such as *Salmonella, Shigella*, and Amoeba), resulting in a total of 37,794 deaths. A total of 224,5686 men were killed by non-combat deaths, compared with 110,070 Union soldiers who died as a result of combat (Agnew 2014, 72).

Today, morphine is less commonly abused than many other types of legal and illegal substances. The Drug Awareness Warning Network (DAWN) is a survey that counts the number of admissions to emergency departments (EDs) as a result of misuse and abuse of a variety of drugs. In its most recent report DAWN noted that just less than 3 percent of all ED visits in 2011, 34,593 visits, were attributable to the misuse or abuse of a morphine product. That number had increased substantially over the preceding decade, however, up from 14,090 visits (Drug Abuse Warning Network 2013, Table 21, page 55).

The next important breakthrough in the study of opiates was the synthesis of heroin, a semi-synthetic opiate. The terms *semi-synthetic* and *synthetic* refer to compounds that are, respectively, (1) made in the laboratory beginning with a natural opiate that has been modified by chemical processes and (2) made starting "from scratch" with compounds not found in natural substances. The discovery of heroin was accomplished at St. Mary's Hospital in London in 1874. C. R. Alder Wright, a chemist working at the hospital, was trying a variety of modifications of the morphine molecule to see if he could produce a substance as effective in killing pain as morphine, but not as addictive. In one of these attempts, he added two acetyl groups to the morphine molecule, producing a new substance called diacetylmorphine or morphine diacetate. (A comparison of the molecular structure of morphine and heroin is available at Opium, Morphine, and Heroin 2015.)

Wright sent a sample of his product to a colleague, F. M. Pierce, for testing on animals. Pierce described the effect of the substance on the young dogs and rabbits that were injected with it. The most noticeable effects, Pierce said, were great prostration, fear, and sleepiness speedily following the administration, the eyes being sensitive, and pupils dilated, considerable salivation being produced in dogs, and slight tendency to vomiting in some cases, but no actual emesis. Respiration was as first quickened, but subsequently reduced, and the heart's action was diminished, and rendered irregular. Marked want of co-ordinating power over the muscular movements, and loss of power in the pelvis and hind limbs, together with a diminution of temperature in the rectum of about 4°. (Wright 1874, 1043)

These results may at least partly account for the fact that Wright went no further with his research on diacetylmorphine, a substance that attracted no further attention for more than 20 years. Then, in 1897, a researcher at the Aktiengesellschaft Farbenfabriken pharmaceutical company (later to become the giant pharmaceutical manufacturer, Bayer), Felix Hoffmann, turned his attention to the same line of research as that pursued by Wright. He rediscovered essentially the same chemical and pharmacological properties as those observed by Wright and Pierce, but also saw the marketing potential for the new drug. Heroin was about twice as efficacious as morphine, and it appeared at first to have none of the addictive properties of the natural opiate. Aktiengesellschaft Farbenfabriken began an aggressive advertising campaign for its new product (named heroin, after the German word *heroisch*, for "heroic") based on its efficacy and safety. It was recommended as a substitute for morphine and used as a constituent in cough syrups. In perhaps its most optimistic recommendation, the company even suggested that heroin could be used to wean morphine addicts off the natural opiate, a claim that very quickly turned out not to be true (Durlacher 2000).

Some other important semi-synthetic opioids are buprenorphine, etorphine, hydrocodone, hydromorphone, oxycodone, and oxymorphone. The oldest of these products is oxymorphone, first synthesized in Germany in 1914, but not made available in the United States until 1959. It is made from the opium constituent thebaine. A second semi-synthetic opioid, oxycodone was also produced in Germany two years later by chemists Martin Freund and Edmund Speyer. Oxycodone was also first made from thebaine and became available in the United States in 1939. Hydrocodone was first prepared in 1920 by German chemists Carl Mannich and Helene Löwenheim. The drug was marketed by the pharmaceutical firm of Knoll four years later under the name of Dicodid. It was approved for sale in the United States in 1943. Both hydrocodone and oxycodone are derivatives of codeine.

Hydromorphone was first synthesized in 1924, also by researchers at Knoll, which marketed the drug under the name of Dilaudid two years later. Hydromorphone is a derivative of morphine, synthesized by adding hydrogen to one of the ketone groups in morphine. Etorphine was first produced in 1960. Its synthesis is somewhat unusual in that it is made from oripavine, a constituent of opium poppy straw, rather than from the poppy seed itself.

Etorphine is up to 3,000 times as strong as morphine and is currently legal in the United States only for veterinary uses. The discovery of buprenorphine was announced in 1972 as the result of a targeted research program at the Reckitt & Coleman pharmaceutical company (now Reckitt Benckiser) to find a safer version of heroin. The most important use of buprenorphine today is for the treatment of addiction to other opioids. (For a good general introduction to semi-synthetic opioids, see Opioid 2014.)

The first synthetic opioid to have been discovered was pethidine, also known as meperidine. It was first prepared by German chemist Otto Eisleb (also given as Eislib) in 1932. Eisleb was actually looking for an anticholinergic/antispadmodic agent (a substance that interrupts nerve action), and did not realize that his new drug might have other applications. The most important of those applications, as an opium-like analgesic agent, was later discovered by German chemist Otto Schaumann in 1939 (Michaelis, Schölkens, and Rudolphi 2007). The drug was given the trade name of Dolantin, but has since become better known as Demerol. Today, nearly 150 synthetic opioids have been discovered and described, including such familiar compounds as fentanyl, methadone, propoxyphene, sufentanil, and tramadol (a naturally occurring opioid that is almost always made synthetically for commercial purposes; Overview: Opioids and Opioid Antagonists 2015).

The use of opioids for nonmedical purposes is currently regarded as one of the most serious personal and public health problems in the world today. An estimated 26 to 36 million individuals abuse opioids worldwide, and an estimated 2.1 million people in the United States have substance abuse disorders related to the misuse of opioids (Volkow 2014). In addition, 28,000 adolescents between the ages of 12 and 17 reported using heroin at least once in the year preceding the NSDUH survey, and 16,000 reported using the drug on a regular basis currently (Center for Behavioral Health Statistics and Quality 2015, 12).

Marijuana

A third psychoactive substance that has been known and widely used virtually since the origins of human civilization is marijuana. Marijuana (through much of history, the term has been spelled *marihuana*) is usually a mixture of the dried leaves and flowers of the *Cannabis sativa* plant. It is most commonly ingested by smoking, as with marijuana cigarettes, in a pipe, or in a hookah-type device. Marijuana is categorized as a psychoactive drug because it acts on molecules in the central nervous system known as cannabinoid receptors, producing a sense of relaxation and euphoria. Depending on the amount of marijuana ingested, other changes may also occur, including an altered perception of the surrounding environment, an altered perception of time and space, changes in one's mood, and, with higher doses, impaired memory, paranoia and/or anxiety, and hallucinations. (A varietal of *C. sativa* plant is used to produce a very different type of product known as *hemp*. Hemp has a number of commercial, industrial, and personal uses, but it has essentially no psychoactive effects on humans.)

As with other psychoactive plants, very little is known about the origins of cannabis use by humans. Some experts say the plant has been cultivated and used since at least 8000 BCE, and perhaps even two millennia earlier. Indeed, Carl Sagan has suggested that *C. sativa* may have been the very first plant ever cultivated by humans (10,000-Year History of Marijuana Use in the World 2015; also see video included). The original use of the plant may have been as a source of food and for the production of fibers.

Given the widespread use of cannabis as a food, it is hardly surprising that humans would rather quickly recognize the medical and psychoactive effects of the plant. One could hardly consume cannabis seeds without experiencing at least some kinds of mind-altering events from time to time. The first mention of cannabis as a medical product is usually given as about 2737 BCE, when it is described in the earliest known pharmacopeia, the Pe'n-ts'ao Ching, attributed to the legendary emperor Shen Nung. That attribution is almost certainly wrong since Shen Nung was probably not a real person, and the oldest known copy of the book actually dates to the first or second century CE. However, authorities believe that the text accurately reflects prehistoric practices, as its "earliest" mention of medical cannabis is usually taken as valid.

In any case, Chinese shamans used virtually every part of the cannabis plant to treat a variety of illnesses. A 1911 text on Chinese herbal medicine, for example, notes that "[e]very part of the hemp plant is used in medicine; the dried flowers, the ach'enia, the seeds, the oil, the leaves, the stalk, the root, and the juice" (Smith 1911). These materials were put to a plethora of applications treating a very long list of illness and disorders, including nausea, vomiting, malaria, beriberi, constipation, rheumatic pains, absent-mindedness, nervous disorders, female disorders (including postpartum depression), ulcers and other eruptions of the skin, scorpion stings, wounds, hair loss, sulfur poisoning, dryness of the throat, and worm infestations (an incomplete list at that!). Concoctions of the plant were also recommended to prevent one's hair from turning gray and from aging (Smith 1911).

In spite of a number of mentions in early Chinese documents, use of cannabis for psychoactive purposes was probably relatively limited. Observers note that Chinese society was highly ordered and activities that would disrupt that order were frowned upon and often restricted. As Martin Booth has written in his history of cannabis:

> The use of cannabis [for recreational purposes], however, never really became more than a passing phase. Chinese culture, being based on social order, family values and the reverence of ancestors and the elderly, looked down upon drugs. (Booth 2005, 23)

Evidence exists for the use of cannabis for a variety of purposes in other ancient civilizations as well. In India, for example, a drink made from cannabis buds and leaves called *bhang* was an integral part of Hindu culture as early as 1000 BCE. The drink was sometimes described as "sacred grass," and was used for both medicinal and ceremonial purposes. Because of its ability to bring about a relaxed state of mind, some practitioners of the Hindu religions still use bhang in their meditative states (Tradition of Bhang 2015). Similar acknowledgment of the spiritual benefits of cannabis preparations was expressed in a number of other religious and cultural texts from about 1000 BCE onwards. (See especially Bennett 2014.)

Over time, knowledge and use of cannabis spread from East Asia to the Middle East and then into Europe. (One of the best cannabis histories is Booth 2005.) Throughout its long history, the drug has been the source of controversy as to its potential medical benefits versus the risks posed by its use. That debate is far too extensive and complex to treat here, but the consensus appears to be that until about the second decade of the twentieth century, the general consensus appears to have been that marijuana has a number of useful medical applications and relatively few medical disadvantages if used in moderation. One of the most extensive and most recent of the major commissions appointed to study the medical and social effects of marijuana use was the National Commission on Marihuana and Drug Abuse, also known as the Schaffer Commission. The report issued by that body in 1972 offered a conclusion that was largely consistent with that of many groups that had studied the drug in the preceding two centuries. It wrote that there

> is little proven danger of physical or psychological harm from the experimental or intermittent use of the natural preparations of cannabis, including the resinous mixtures commonly used in this country. The risk of harm lies instead in the heavy, long-term use of the drug, particularly of the most potent preparations.
>
> The experimenter and the intermittent users develop little or no psychological dependence on the drug. No organ injury is demonstrable. (National Commission on Marihuana and Drug Abuse 1972, Chapter 2, Summary. For a review of other reports on marijuana, see Newton 2013, Chapter 2.)

The dawn of the twenty-first century saw a somewhat startling change of status for marijuana in the United States. Listed as a Schedule I drug since the creation of the Schedule system by the Controlled Substances Act of 1970, marijuana has recently achieved a new level of acceptance in many parts of the United States and some other regions of the world (although by no means most of them). That acceptance has come first with the recognition of certain medical benefits attributable to the ingestion of marijuana, a recognition that first took legal form in the state of California in 1996 when citizens adopted Proposition

215, allowing the use of marijuana for certain medical purposes. That action was followed rather quickly by similar actions in the states of Alaska, Oregon, and Washington (1998); Maine (1999); and Colorado, Hawaii, and Nevada (2000). As of early 2016, a total of 23 states have adopted similar legislation legalizing the use of marijuana for medical purposes. (Such actions do, however, create an awkward legal situation since, legal or not on the state level, the sale and use of marijuana is still illegal on the federal level and subject to prosecution.)

The next seemingly logical step in the ongoing evolution of attitudes toward marijuana was the legalization of the drug for recreational purposes in small quantities and under controlled conditions. Colorado and Washington were the first two states to pass such a law in 2012, followed by Alaska and Oregon in 2014, and the District of Columbia in 2015.

Today, marijuana is by far the most widely used illicit drug in the world. The United Nations Office on Drugs and Crime estimates that between 2.7 and 4.9 percent of people between the ages of 15 and 64, a total of between 128,480,000 and 232,070,000 individuals worldwide, are regular users of the drug (World Drug Report 2015, Table 1, page 6). In the United States, the numbers were even more impressive, with an estimated 22.2 million Americans reporting that they are regular users of cannabis products, about 8.4 percent of the population aged 12 and older. Of that number, about 1.8 million teenagers (7.4 percent) said they were regular users of the drug (Center for Behavioral Health Statistics and Quality 2015, 5).

Summary and Conclusion

Psychoactive substances have been an integral part of human society for more than 5,000 years, and probably much longer. They have been used for religious and ceremonial, medical, and recreational uses throughout the ages, although attitudes regarding such uses have always been mixed. That situation has not changed very much today. Opioids are still very widely used for the treatment of recalcitrant pain and other medical problems, as are cannabis products, although controversy still surrounds the validity and reliability of such applications.

A new issue has arisen in the past 75 years or so, however: the increased use, misuse, and abuse of psychoactive substances by individuals under the age of 18. Some experts have gone so far as to call youth substance abuse as the single personal and public health issue of our age.

References

"Adolescent." 2015. *Online Etymology Dictionary.* http://www .etymonline.com/index.php?term=adolescent. Accessed on December 9, 2015.

Agnew, Jeremy. 2014. *Alcohol and Opium in the Old West: Use, Abuse, and Influence.* Jefferson, NC: McFarland & Company Inc.

Ahuja, S. C. and U. Ahuja. 2011. "Betel Leaf and Betel Nut in India: History and Uses." *Asian Agri-History.* 15(1): 13–35.

"Alcohol and Your Body." 2015. Brown University Health Promotion. http://www.brown.edu/Student_Services/ Health_Services/Health_Education/alcohol,_tobacco,_&_ other_drugs/alcohol/alcohol_&_your_body.php#4. Accessed on December 11, 2015.

"Al-Ma'idah (The Table Spread)." 2015. The Noble Qur'an. http://quran.com/. Accessed on December 11, 2015.

Altman, Lawrence K. 1987. *Who Goes First?: The Story of Self-Experimentation in Medicine.* New York: Random House.

Arnaud, Celia Henry. 2014. "A Step toward Making Painkillers without Poppies Bioengineering: Modified Yeast Produce Morphine and Semisynthetic Opioids Starting from Thebaine." *C&EN.* 92(35): 11.

Arnett, Jeffrey Jensen. 2006. "G. Stanley Hall's Adolescence: Brilliance and Nonsense." *History of Psychology.* 9(3): 186–197.

Ball, Philip. 2007. *The Devil's Doctor: Paracelsus and the World of Renaissance Magic and Science*. London: Arrow.

Bennett, Chris. 2014. "The Magic and Ceremonial Use of Cannabis in the Ancient World." In Ellens, J. Harold, ed. *Seeking the Sacred with Psychoactive Substances: Chemical Paths to Spirituality and to God*. Santa Barbara, CA: Praeger.

Bliss, Michael. 1999. *William Osler: A Life in Medicine*. Oxford; New York: Oxford University Press.

Booth, Martin. 1998. *Opium: A History*. New York: St. Martin's Press.

Booth, Martin. 2005. *Cannabis: A History*. New York: Picador Press.

Borio, Gene. 1993–2001. "Tobacco Timeline." http://archive .tobacco.org/History/Tobacco_History.html. Accessed on December 15, 2015.

"Bringing the Power of Science to Bear on Drug Abuse and Addiction." 2007. National Institute on Drug Abuse. http://www.drugabuse.gov/publications/teaching-packets/ power-science/section-I. Accessed on December 16, 2015.

Center for Behavioral Health Statistics and Quality. 2015. "Behavioral Health Trends in the United States: Results from the 2014 National Survey on Drug Use and Health. http://www.samhsa.gov/data/. Accessed on December 12, 2015.

"A Century of International Drug Control." 2009. United Nations Office on Drugs and Crime. http://www.unodc .org/documents/data-and-analysis/Studies/100_Years_of_ Drug_Control.pdf. Accessed on December 21, 2015.

Chopra, R. N. 1958. *Indigenous Drugs of India*. Calcutta: Dhur.

"A Comprehensive Historical Timeline of the Relationship between Psychedelic Substances and Mammalian Brains." 2012. The Cosmic LOL. https://cl.nfshost.com/ psychedelics-chronology.html. Accessed on December 13, 2015.

"Constitution of the United States." 2015. The Charters of Freedom. http://www.archives.gov/exhibits/charters/constitution_amendments_11-27.html. Accessed on December 12, 2015.

"Controlled Substances Act." 1970. U.S. Food and Drug Administration. http://www.fda.gov/regulatoryinformation/legislation/ucm148726.htm. Accessed on December 9, 2015.

Cooper, Donald A. 2015. "Future Synthetic Drugs of Abuse." Vaults of Erowid. https://www.erowid.org/library/books_online/future_synthetic/future_synthetic.shtml#Introduction. Accessed on December 9, 2015.

Cowell, Stephanie. 2015. "Poetry, Pain, and Opium in Victorian England." Wonders & Marvels. http://www.wondersandmarvels.com/2013/02/poetry-pain-and-opium-in-victorian-england-elizabeth-barrett-brownings-use-of-laudanum.html. Accessed on December 21, 2015.

Crocq, Marc-Antoine. 2007. "Historical and Cultural Aspects of Man's Relationship with Addictive Drugs." *Dialogues of Clinical Neuroscience*. 9(4): 355–361.

"Current Cigarette Smoking among Adults in the United States." 2015. Centers for Disease Control and Prevention. http://www.cdc.gov/tobacco/data_statistics/fact_sheets/adult_data/cig_smoking/. Accessed on December 15, 2015.

Cusack, Carole M. 2011. "Some Recent Trends in the Study of Religion and Youth." *Journal of Religious History*. 35(3): 409–418.

"Definition of Addiction." 2011. American Society of Addiction Medicine. http://www.asam.org/for-the-public/definition-of-addiction. Accessed on December 16, 2015.

Diaz, Ernie. 2008. "China's Unofficial Opium Story." China Expat. http://www.chinaexpat.com/2008/12/11/chinas-unofficial-opium-story.html/. Accessed on December 21, 2015.

Dillehay, Tom C., et al. 2010. "Early Holocene Coca Chewing in Northern Peru." *Antiquity.* 84(326): 939–953.

Distefano, John A. 1983. "An Enquiry into the History of Qat." Proceedings of the 2nd International Conference on Somalia. http://www.everythingharar.com/publication/An%20Enquiry%20Into%20The%20History%20of%20Qat%20-%20Distefano.pdf. Accessed on December 14, 2015.

"Drug Abuse Warning Network, 2013: National Estimates of Drug-Related Emergency Department Visits." 2013. Washington, DC: Center for Behavioral Health Statistics and Quality. Substance Abuse and Mental Health Services Administration.

Duke, Maurince, and Daniel P. Jordan. 1995. *Tobacco Merchant: The Story of Universal Leaf Tobacco Company.* Lexington: University Press of Kentucky.

Durlacher, Julian. 2000. *Heroin: Its History and Lore.* London: Carlton Books.

Eric, John, and Sidney Thompson. 1970. *Maya History and Religion.* Norman: University of Oklahoma Press.

Erowid, Fire. 2003. "Psychoactives in History." The Vaults of Erowide. https://www.erowid.org/psychoactives/history/history_article1.shtml. Accessed on December 14, 2015.

Escohotado, Antonio. 1999. *A Brief History of Drugs: From the Stone Age to the Stoned Age.* Rochester, VT: Park Street Press.

"50 Years of Tobacco Control." 2015. Robert Wood Johnson Foundation. http://www.rwjf.org/maketobaccohistory. Accessed on December 15, 2015.

Freye, Enno. 2009. *Pharmacology and Abuse of Cocaine, Amphetamines, Ecstasy and Related Designer Drugs: A Comprehensive Review on Their Mode of Action, Treatment of Abuse and Intoxication.* Dordrecht; New York: Springer.

Friman, H. Richard. 1999. "Germany and the Transformations of Cocaine, 1860–1920." In Gootenberg, Paul, ed. *Cocaine: Global Histories.* London; New York: Rutledge, 83–104.

Froese, Tom, Alexander Woodward, and Takashi Ikegami. 2014. "Are Altered States of Consciousness Detrimental, Neutral or Helpful for the Origins of Symbolic Cognition? A Response to Hodgson and Lewis-Williams." *Adaptive Behavior.* 22(1): 89–95.

Gaedcke, F. 1855. "Ueber Das Erythroxylin, Dargestellt Aus Den Blättern Des in Südamerika Cultivirten Strauches Erythroxylon Coca Lam." *Archiv der Pharmazie.* 132(2): 141–150. Available online at http://onlinelibrary.wiley.com/doi/10.1002/ardp.18551320208/abstract;jsessionid=DACA8A93DA1AE75BDE2E96A45A84EA0C.f01t01. Accessed on December 18, 2015.

Gahlinger, Paul. 2004. *Illegal Drugs: A Complete Guide to Their History, Chemistry, Use and Abuse.* New York: Plume.

Gately, Iain. 2003. *Tobacco: A Cultural History of How an Exotic Plant Seduced Civilization.* New York: Grove Press.

Gately, Iain. 2008. *Drink: A Cultural History of Alcohol.* New York: Gotham Books.

Gerald, Michael C. 2013. *The Drug Book: From Arsenic to Xanax, 250 Milestones in the History of Drugs.* New York: Sterling.

"Global Status Report on Alcohol and Health 2014." 2014. World Health Organization. http://apps.who.int/iris/bitstream/10665/112736/1/9789240692763_eng.pdf?ua=1. Accessed on December 12, 2015.

Gootenberg, Paul. 2001. "The Rise and Demise of Coca and Cocaine: As Licit Global 'Commodity Chains,' 1860–1950." Latin America and Global Trade. http://www.mamacoca.org/docs_de_base/Consumo/gootenberg_rise_and_demise_coca_cocaine.pdf. Accessed on December 21, 2015.

Gorman, Chester F. 1970. "Excavations at Spirit Cave, North Thailand: Some Interim Interpretations." *Asian Perspectives*. 13: 79–107.

Greydanus, D. E. 2010. "Adolescence across the Ages: From Homer to Hesiod to Hall to Hoffmann." http://www.iatrikion line.gr/Deltio_57d_2010/1.pdf. Accessed on December 9, 2015.

Guerra-Doce, Elisa. 2015a. "The Origins of Inebriation: Archaeological Evidence of the Consumption of Fermented Beverages and Drugs in Prehistoric Eurasia." *Journal of Archaeological Method and Theory*. 22(3): 751–782.

Guerra-Doce, Elisa. 2015b. "Psychoactive Substances in Prehistoric Times: Examining the Archaeological Evidence." *Time and Mind*. 8(1): 91–112.

Hahn, Robert "Rio." 2003. "Swami's Sacred Plant." *Vernal Equinox*. 12(1): 1–6, 40. Also available online at http://www.riohahn.com/expedition_docs/EnthrogenReview DaturaArticle.pdf. Accessed on December 14, 2015.

Hamblin, James. 2013. "Why We Took the Cocaine Out of Soda." *The Atlantic*. http://www.theatlantic.com/health/archive/2013/01/why-we-took-cocaine-out-of-soda/272694/. Accessed on December 21, 2015.

Hanson, David J. 1995. *Preventing Alcohol Abuse: Alcohol, Culture, and Control*. Westport, CT: Praeger.

Hanson, Glen, Peter J. Venturelli, and Annette E. Fleckenstein. 2012. *Drugs and Society*, 11th ed. Sudbury, MA: Jones & Bartlett Learning.

Heath, Dwight B. 1995. "An Anthropological View of Alcohol and Culture in Historic Perspective." In Heath, Dwight B., ed. *International Handbook on Alcohol and Culture*. Westport, CT: Greenwood Press.

"A Hindu View on Drinking Alcohol." 2015. Hindu Human Rights. http://www.hinduhumanrights.info/a-hindu-view-on-drinking-alcohol/. Accessed on December 11, 2015.

"HK24—Breweries by the Cultivation." 2015. Hierakonpolis: City of the Hawk. http://www.hierakonpolis-online.org/ index.php/explore-the-predynastic-settlement/hk24-brewe ries-by-the-cultivation. Accessed on December 10, 2015.

"Is It a Cosmetic, a Drug, or Both? (Or Is It Soap?)" 2015. U.S. Food and Drug Administration. http://www.fda.gov/ Cosmetics/GuidanceRegulation/LawsRegulations/ucm 074201.htm#Definedrug. Accessed on December 9, 2015.

"Is Moderate Drinking Acceptable in Buddhism?" 2015. Buddhism Beta. http://buddhism.stackexchange.com/ questions/2512/is-moderate-drinking-acceptable-in-buddhism. Accessed on December 11, 2015.

"Islamic Penal Code of the Islamic Republic of Iran—Book One & Book Two." 2015. Iran Human Rights Documentation Center. http://www.iranhrdc.org/english/ human-rights-documents/iranian-codes/3200-islamic-penal-code-of-the-islamic-republic-of-iran-book-one-and-book-two.html. Accessed on December 11, 2015.

Johnston, Lloyd D., et al. 2015. "Monitoring the Future: National Survey Results on Drug Use." Ann Arbor: Institute for Social Research. University of Michigan. Available online at http://www.monitoringthefuture .org/pubs/monographs/mtf-overview2014.pdf. Accessed on December 9, 2015.

Josephy, Alvin M., and William Brandon. 1993. *American Heritage Book of Indians*. New York: American Heritage/ Wings Books.

Karch, Steven B. 2006. *A Brief History of Cocaine: From Inca Monarchs to Cali Cartels: 500 Years of Cocaine Dealing*, 2nd ed. Boca Raton, FL: CRC/Taylor & Francis.

Karch, Steven B., and Olaf H. Drummer. 2016. *Karch's Pathology of Drug Abuse*, 5th ed. Boca Raton, FL: CRC Press/Taylor & Francis Group.

"Khat Chewing in Yemen: Turning Over a New Leaf." 2008. *Bulletin of the World Health Organization.* 86(10): 741–742. Also available online at http://www.who.int/bulletin/volumes/86/10/08-011008/en/. Accessed on December 14, 2015.

Kinch, Michael S., et al. 2014. "An Overview of FDA-approved New Molecular Entities: 1827–2013." *Drug Discovery Today.* 19(8): 1033–1039.

Kleijwegt, Marc. 1991. *Ancient Youth: The Ambiguity of Youth and the Absence of Adolescence in Greco-Roman Society.* Amsterdam: J. C. Gieben.

"Laudanum Addiction Treatment." 2015. Project Know. http://www.projectknow.com/research/laudanum/. Accessed on December 21, 2015.

Leroi-Gourhan, Arlette. 1975. "The Flowers Found with Shanidar IV, a Neanderthal Burial in Iraq." *Science.* 190(4214): 562–564.

Mandelbaum, David Goodman. 1965. "Alcohol and Culture." *Current Anthropology.* 6(3): 281–293.

Mark, Joshua J. 2011. "Beer in the Ancient World." Ancient History Encyclopedia. http://www.ancient.eu/article/223/. Accessed on December 10, 2015.

McGovern, Patrick E., et al. 2004. "Fermented Beverages of Pre- and Proto-Historic China." *Proceedings of the National Academy of Science U.S.A.* 101(51): 17593–17598.

McGrew, Jane Lang. 2015. "History of Alcohol Prohibition." Schaffer Library of Drug Policy. http://www.druglibrary.org/schaffer/library/studies/nc/nc2a.htm. Accessed on December 13, 2015.

Medina, Johnna. 2015. "Symptoms of Substance Use Disorders (Revised for DSM-5)." PsychCentral. http://psychcentral.com/disorders/revised-alcohol substance-use-disorder/. Accessed on January 1, 2016.

"Merck's Merits in the Manufacture of Morphine." 1907. The Merck Report, January 1907. https://books.google.com/bo oks?id=bTlHAQAAMAAJ&pg=PA28&lpg=PA28&dq=me rck+morphine+1827&source=bl&ots=hZez5WhuaV&sig= ABMfEDqZhTzVSNkUccnr7a0xJu0&hl=en&sa=X&ei= SugrVamYFMipogSWhIBQ&ved=0CD8Q6AEwBQ# v=onepage&q=merck%20morphine%201827&f=false. Accessed on December 21, 2015.

Merlin, M. D. 2003. "Archaeological Evidence for the Tradition of Psychoactive Plant Use in the Old World." *Economic Botany.* 57(3): 295–323.

Michaelis, Martin, Bernward Schölkens, and Karl Rudolphi. 2007. "An Anthology from Naunyn-Schmiedeberg's Archives of Pharmacology." *Naunyn-Schmiedeberg's Archives of Pharmacology.* 375(2): 81–84. Available online at http:// link.springer.com/article/10.1007%2Fs00210-007-0136-z. Accessed on April 11, 2016.

National Commission on Marihuana and Drug Abuse. 1972. *Marihuana: A Signal of Misunderstanding.* New York: New American Library. Full report available online at http:// www.druglibrary.org/schaffer/library/studies/nc/ncmenu .htm. Accessed on December 22, 2015.

"NDS Overview." 2015. National Association of Pharmacy Regulatory Authorities. http://napra.ca/pages/Schedules/ Overview.aspx?id=1925. Accessed on December 9, 2015.

Newton, David E. 2013. *Marijuana: A Reference Handbook.* Santa Barbara, CA: ABC-CLIO.

Ng, Marie, et al. 2014. "Smoking Prevalence and Cigarette Consumption in 187 Countries, 1980–2012." *JAMA.* 311(2): 183–192.

Ohio Teen's Obituary Gets Parents Worldwide Attention. 2015. http://www.cbsnews.com/news/ohio-teen-alison-shuemake-obituary-heroin/. Accessed on April 11, 2016.

"151 and Up: The Highest Proof Liquor." 2015. *The Daily Meal.* http://www.thedailymeal.com/151-and-highest-proof-liquor. Accessed on December 12, 2015.

"Opiate vs. Opioid—What's the Difference?" 2015. *Opium.* http://opium.com/derivatives/opiate-vs-opioid-whats-difference/. Accessed on December 21, 2015.

"Opioid." 2014. Mahalo. http://www.mahalo.com/opioid#ref_38. Accessed on December 21, 2015.

"Opium, Morphine, and Heroin." 2015. http://www.ch.ic.ac.uk/rzepa/mim/drugs/html/morphine_text.htm. Accessed on December 21, 2015.

"Overview: Opioids, Opioid Antagonists." 2015. National Library of Medicine. http://livertox.nih.gov/Opioids.htm. Accessed on December 21, 2015.

Panicker, Sini, Heidi Wojno, and Lewis H. Ziska. 2007. "Quantitation of the Major Alkaloids in Opium from *Papaver Setigerum* DC." *Microgram Journal.* 5(1–4): 13–19.

"Paolo Mantegazza." 2015. http://cocaine.org/mantegazza/. Accessed on December 18, 2015.

"Parke, Davis & Co. Cocaine Injection Kit." 2015. Herb Museum. http://herbmuseum.ca/content/parke-davis-co-cocaine-injection-kit. Accessed on December 21, 2015.

Parry, Lizzie. 2014. "Schoolboy, 16, Was Five Times the Drink-drive Limit When He Died of Alcohol Poisoning after Marquee Garden Party at Friend's Home." *Daily Mail.* http://www.dailymail.co.uk/news/article-2580318/Schoolboy-16-five-times-drink-drive-limit-died-alcohol-poisoning-marquee-garden-party-friends-home.html. Accessed on April 10, 2016.

"Personal Habits and Indoor Combustions." 2012. IARC Monographs on the Evaluation of Carcinogenic Risks to Humans. Lyon, France: International Agency for Research on Cancer.

Petersen, Robert D. 1977. "History of Cocaine." In Petersen, Robert D., and Robert C. Stilllman, eds. *Cocaine: 1977*. Washington, DC: U.S. Government Printing Office. Available online at https://archives.drugabuse.gov/pdf/monographs/13.pdf. Accessed on December 18, 2015.

"Pharmaceutical Research by a Commercial House." 1906. American Druggist and Pharmaceutical Record. February 26, 1906. https://books.google.com/books?id=U343AQAAMAAJ&pg=PA122-IA4&lpg=PA122-IA4&dq=history+of+merck+corporation+morphine+1827&source=bl&ots=5REjJlN0W3&sig=DtvTlQeD2XRlHWfXlFlEZ3wXcMk&hl=en&sa=X&ei=EvMrVYz6HpCQoQSf3YHgCg&ved=0CEgQ6AEwBw#v=onepage&q=history%20of%20merck%20corporation%20morphine%201827&f=false. Accessed on December 21, 2015.

"Pharmacology of Drugs." 2015. ForCon. Forensic Counseling. http://www.forcon.ca/learning/pharmacology.html. Accessed on December 16, 2015.

"Physical and Psychological Addiction." 2015. AlcoholRehab.com. http://alcoholrehab.com/addiction-articles/physical-and-psychological-addiction/. Accessed on December 16, 2015.

"Physical Detoxification Services for Withdrawal from Specific Substances." 2006. Treatment Improvement Protocol (TIP) Series, No. 45. Washington, DC: Substance Abuse and Mental Health Services Administration. Available online at http://www.ncbi.nlm.nih.gov/books/NBK64116/. Accessed on December 16, 2015.

"Public Law 99–570." 1986. U.S. Statutes. https://www.gpo.gov/fdsys/pkg/STATUTE-100/pdf/STATUTE-100-Pg3207.pdf. Accessed on December 9, 2015.

Reemtsma, Jan Phillipp. 2012. *Trust and Violence: An Essay on a Modern Relationship*. Princeton, NJ: Princeton University Press.

"The Role of Drugs in Prehistory." 2015. Ancient Wisdom. http://www.ancient-wisdom.com/prehistoricdrugs.htm. Accessed on December 16, 2015.

Saalih al-Munajjid, Shaykh Muhammad. 2015. "Islam Question and Answer." https://islamqa.info/en/20037. Accessed on December 11, 2015.

"Schedules." 2015. Release. http://www.release.org.uk/law/schedules. Accessed on December 9, 2015.

Siegel, Ronald K. 1989. *Intoxication: Life in Pursuit of Artificial Paradise.* New York: Dutton.

Smith, F. Porter. *Chinese Materia Medica: Vegetable Kingdom.* Shanghai: American Presbyterian Mission Press, 1911. Available online at http://www.biodiversitylibrary.org/bibliography/25114#/summary. Accessed on December 22, 2015.

"Smokeless Tobacco Use in the United States." 2015. Centers for Disease Control and Prevention. http://www.cdc.gov/tobacco/data_statistics/fact_sheets/smokeless/use_us/index.htm. Accessed on December 15, 2015.

"Smoking and Tobacco Use." 2015. Centers for Disease Control and Prevention. http://www.cdc.gov/tobacco/data_statistics/fact_sheets/health_effects/effects_cig_smoking/#definition. Accessed on December 9, 2015.

"Smoking Prevalence, Males (% of Adults). 2015. World Bank. http://data.worldbank.org/indicator/SH.PRV.SMOK.MA. Accessed on December 15, 2015.

Sommer, Jeffrey D. 1999. "The Shanidar IV 'Flower Burial': A Re-evaluation of Neanderthal Burial Ritual." *Cambridge Archaeological Journal.* 9(1) : 127–129.

"Substance Use Disorders." 2015. Substance Abuse and Mental Health Services Administration. http://www.samhsa.gov/disorders/substance-use. Accessed on January 1, 2016.

"Taoism vs. Alcohol." 2015. http://www.taoistmasterblog.com/taoism-vs-alcohol/. Accessed on December 11, 2015.

"10,000-Year History of Marijuana Use in the World." 2015. Advanced Holistic Health. http://www.advancedholistichealth.org/history.html. Accessed on December 22, 2015.

"Timeline of Events in the History of Drugs." 2015. INPUD's International Diaries. https://inpud.wordpress .com/timeline-of-events-in-the-history-of-drugs/. Accessed on December 13, 2015.

"Tobacco Control Laws." 2015. Campaign for Tobacco-Free Kids. http://tobaccocontrollaws.org/. Accessed on December 15, 2015.

"Tobacco Risk Awareness Timeline." 2015. Brown & Williamson Tobacco. http://www.cigarette.com/images/ timeline.pdf. Accessed on December 15, 2015.

"Tradition of Bhang." 2015. Holi. http://www.holifestival .org/tradition-of-bhang.html. Accessed on December 22, 2015.

"Types of Alcohol." 2015. icohol. http://icohol.com/ types-of-alcohol/. Accessed on December 12, 2015.

Volkow, Nora. 2014. "America's Addiction to Opioids: Heroin and Prescription Drug Abuse." National Institute on Drug Abuse. http://www.drugabuse.gov/about-nida/ legislative-activities/testimony-to-congress/2015/ americas-addiction-to-opioids-heroin-prescription-drug-abuse. Accessed on December 22, 2015.

Vouillamoz, José F., et al. 2006. "Genetic Characterization and Relationships of Traditional Grape Cultivars from Transcaucasia and Anatolia." *Plant Genetic Resources: Characterization and Utilization.* 4(2): 144–158.

"A Word from Our Sponsor . . ." 2015. Cocaine.org. http:// cocaine.org/popecoke.htm. Accessed on December 21, 2015.

"World Drug Report 2015." 2015. Vienna: United Nations Office on Drugs and Crime. Available online at https:// www.unodc.org/documents/mexicoandcentralamerica/ eventos/2015/WDD2015/World_Drug_Report_2015 .pdf. Accessed on December 23, 2015.

Wright, C. R. A. 1874. "On the Action of Organic Acids and Their Anhydrides on the Natural Alkaloids. Part I." *Journal of the Chemical Society.* 27: 1031–1043. Available online at https://www.thevespiary.org/rhodium/Rhodium/Vespiary/talk/files/4132-On-the-action-of-organic-acids-and-their-anhydrides-on-the-natural-alkalo%C3%AFds.-Part-I6d99.pdf?topic=1698.0. Accessed on December 21, 2015.

Zheng, Yangwen. 2005. *The Social Life of Opium in China.* Cambridge, UK; New York: Cambridge University Press.

Zohary, Daniel, Maria Hopf, and Ehud Weiss. 2012. *Domestication of Plants in the Old World: The Origin and Spread of Domesticated Plants in Southwest Asia, Europe, and the Mediterranean Basin.* Oxford, OK: Oxford University Press.

2 Problems, Issues, and Solutions

What do we know about the abuse and misuse of psychoactive substances among adolescents in the world today? In contrast to our previous answer to this question historically ("not much"), the current answer is "a great deal indeed!" For example, we know that

- The use of illegal drugs is largely a phenomenon of youth throughout the world. In most countries, illicit drug use tends to begin during adolescence, increase to the age of 18 to 25, and then begin to drop off. By the time individuals reach maturity, their use of illicit drugs tends to be quite low (World Drug Report 2012 2012, 59).
- By contrast, the use of legal psychoactive substances (e.g., alcohol and tobacco) tends in the other direction, with first use occurring during one's teen years and then tending to remain into old age (World Drug Report 2012 2012, 59).
- A number of nations have conducted studies on the use and abuse of specific psychoactive substances among their youth. These data are available in publications such as the United Nations Office on Drug and Crime annual reports. (See, for example, World Drug Report 2015, Annex 1, x–xvii.)
- Marijuana is by far the most popular of all illegal substances used by adolescents worldwide with a prevalence of at least

Alcohol consumption is sometimes ignored, but remains one of the most serious types of substance abuse among young adults. (iStockPhoto.com)

10 times that for heroin and cocaine and about 5 times that for amphetamines in most countries of the world. (Data for individual countries are available at http://www.unodc .org/documents/data-and-analysis/WDR2011/Youth_ta bles_complete_WDR2011.pdf; accessed on December 23, 2015.)

- The most widely used psychoactive drug by high school students in the United States in 2014 was alcohol. More than a third (37.4 percent) of twelfth graders surveyed by MTF researchers said that they had used alcohol at least once in the 30 days preceding the survey. Comparable numbers for eighth and tenth graders were 9.0 percent and 23.5 percent, respectively (Johnston et al. 2014, Table 7, page 70).

- So-called *binge* drinking continues to be relatively widespread among U.S. high school students. In the 2014 MTF survey, 19.4 percent of twelfth graders reported that they had taken five or more drinks in a row during the two-week period preceding the survey, the survey's definition of binge drinking. The comparable numbers of eighth and tenth graders were 4.1 percent and 12.6 percent, respectively. A not insignificant number of high school seniors have reported even more extreme drinking patterns for a number of years. In the 2012 MTF survey, for example, about 10 percent of seniors said that they had consumed 10 to 14 drinks in one drinking episode, and slightly more than 5 percent said they consumed 15 or more drinks at a time (Johnston et al. 2014, Table 7, page 72; Hingson and White 2013, 996).

- Marijuana was the most widely used psychoactive drug by high school students other than alcohol in the United States in 2014. It had held that position for all 40 years during which the Institute for Social Research at the University of Michigan had been conducting its Monitoring the Future (MTF) survey of high school student substance use and abuse. The 2014 MTF study found that 21.2 percent of all twelfth grade students had used marijuana at least once in the 30 days preceding the survey compared to 37.4 percent who had used alcohol, 6.4 percent who had used a prescription drug for nonmedical purposes (the next most popular substance), and 3.8 percent who had used amphetamines (Johnston et al. 2015, Table 7, pages 67–71).

- Patterns of substance abuse among eighth, tenth, and twelfth graders in 2014 were very similar for nearly all psychoactive substances, with usage rates ranging from nearly zero to as high as nearly 3 percent. (As noted in Chapter 1, data with respect to use of and attitudes toward psychoactive substances have been collected for twelfth graders since 1975 and for eighth and tenth graders since 1991. Annual MTF reports are a treasure trove of detailed information on the practices and attitudes relating to drug use and abuse in the United States. For complete annual reports, see http:// www.monitoringthefuture.org/pubs.html; accessed on December 23, 2015.)

- Long-term trends for nearly all psychoactive substances among all three grades have been remarkably similar. The percentage of twelfth graders saying that they had used any illegal drug sometime during the year preceding the survey in 1975 was 45 percent. That number grew to a peak of 54.2 percent in 1979, after which it dropped regularly and gradually to a low of 29.4 percent in 1991. It then began to increase once more, reaching a new high of 42.4 percent in 1997. It has since remained relatively constant, varying between a low of 35.9 percent in 2009 and its current high of 40.3 percent (Johnston et al. 2014, Table 3, pages 346–347).

- Trends for nearly all illicit substances are similar for eighth and tenth graders since they were first included in the MTF survey in 1991 (Johnston et al. 2015, graphs, page 11).

- MTF measures trends not only in usage of psychoactive substances, but also student attitudes toward such materials. In 2015, for example, MTF researchers found that eighth graders viewed the most harmful drugs presented for their consideration to be heroin, with 73.2 percent saying they thought that practice posed "great risk" to users. The next most harmful drug they mentioned was cocaine, whether in "crack" or powder form (65.5 percent and 61.8 percent saying a "great risk," respectively). Tenth and twelfth graders agreed that heroin and cocaine were the most dangerous of all drugs listed in the survey (Johnston et al. 2015, Tables 9–11, pages 76–82).

- In general, all three age groups tended to view nearly all sub-stances as *less harmful* over the period between 1991 and 2014. For example, 83.8 percent of eighth graders in 1991 thought that smoking marijuana regularly posed a "great risk" to users, while that number dropped to 58.9 percent in the 2014 survey. The only two substances for which all three grade levels expressed greater concerns about potential harm between 1991 and 2014 were alcohol and tobacco products. Just over half (51.6 percent) of eighth graders said in 1991 that smoking a pack or more of cigarettes a day was harm-ful, but that number had increased to 62.1 percent by 2014 (Johnston et al. 2015, Tables 9–11, pages 76–82).

- All three age groups also expressed significant levels of disap-proval for the use of nearly all psychoactive drugs. Among eighth graders, that level of disapproval was very near the 90 percent mark for nearly all drugs at virtually all times between 1991 and 2014. The three exceptions to that rule were LSD, ecstasy, and marijuana, whose disapproval lev-els were at about 50 percent, 60 percent, and 70 percent, respectively. Responses from tenth graders were similar, ex-cept all disapproval levels were roughly 10 percent higher for nearly all substances. And among twelfth graders, those levels were at or above 90 percent for essentially all drugs (Johnston et al. 2015, Tables 12–14, pages 83–86).

- A final variable measured by MTF researchers was students' views of the availability of substances studied in the survey. As might be expected, eighth graders tended to view most illegal drugs as being very hard to obtain, with "easy to get responses" at about 10 percent except for marijuana (36.9 percent "easy to get" in 2014) and the two legal drugs, alcohol and cigarettes (54.4 percent and 47.2 percent, respectively in 2014). These numbers all represented decreases of at least half compared to results from the 1991 survey. Both tenth and twelfth graders followed similar patterns in their views on availability, although the percentage reporting that substances were "easy to get" increased regularly with respondents' ages (Johnston et al. 2015, Tables 15–17, pages 87–90).

• One of the intriguing findings in the 2014 MTF survey with regard to drug availability is that all three age groups showed for almost all substances surveyed a significant decrease in the availability of substances from 1991 to 2014, usually by a factor of about half. Some examples of this trend are shown in Table 2.1. (Johnston et al. 2015, Tables 15–17, pages 87–90).

Table 2.1   Students' Perception of the Availability of Certain Substances*

	1992	1996	2001	2005	2010	2014	% Change**
Eighth Graders							
Crack cocaine	25.6	27.9	24.4	20.8	17.9	12.0	−53.1
LSD	21.5	23.6	17.6	11.5	10.0	6.9	−67.9
Heroin	19.7	20.6	16.9	13.2	11.6	8.6	−56.3
Amphetamines	32.2	32.6	26.2	21.0	19.6	12.1‡	−62.4
Marijuana	42.3	54.8	48.1	41.1	41.4	36.9	−12.8
Alcohol	76.2	75.3	70.6	64.2	61.1	54.4	−28.6
Cigarettes	77.8	76.9	67.7	59.1	55.5	47.2	−39.3
Tenth Graders							
Crack cocaine	33.7	36.4	30.6	31.0	22.5	15.1	−55.2
Ecstasy	–	–	41.4	30.2	25.7	20.1	–
Heroin	24.3	24.8	22.3	19.3	14.5	10.9	−55.1
Amphetamines	43.4	47.2	40.6	35.6	32.6‡	25.2	−41.9

(Continued)

Table 2.1   Continued

	1992	1996	2001	2005	2010	2014	% Change**
Marijuana	65.2	81.1	77.4	72.6	69.4	66.9	+2.6
Alcohol	88.6	90.4	87.7	83.7	80.0	75.3	−15.0
Cigarettes	89.1	91.3	86.3	81.5	75.6	69.0	−22.6
Twelfth Graders							
Crack cocaine	43.5	40.7	40.2	39.3	26.1	20.1	−53.8
Ecstasy	24.2	36.9	61.5	40.3	36.4	35.1	+45.0
Heroin	34.9	32.2	32.3	27.3	24.1	20.2	−42.0
Amphetamines	58.8	59.4	57.1	51.2	44.1‡	44.5	−24.3
Marijuana	82.7	88.7	88.5	85.6	82.1	81.3	−1.7
Alcohol	–	–	94.3	93.0	90.4	87.6	–
Cigarettes	(not asked)						

*Percentage saying substance is "fairly easy" or "very easy" to obtain.

**1992 to 2014.

‡ Some change in question.

Source: Johnston, Lloyd D., et al. 2015. "Monitoring the Future: National Survey Results on Drug Use." Ann Arbor: Institute for Social Research. University of Michigan, Tables 15–17, pages 87–90. Available online at http://www .monitoringthefuture.org/pubs/monographs/mtf-overview2014.pdf. Accessed on December 23, 2015.

- Teenagers make up a significant portion of those individuals in the United States who use prescription medications for nonmedical purposes, one of the most troubling of all substance abuse issues in the nation today. According to one study on the topic, approximately 1.5 million boys and girls and men and women between the ages of 15 and 24 reported abusing prescription drugs in the month preceding the study in 2011. This number was the largest of all age groups, exceeding that in the age group 25 to 34 (about 1.2 million individuals), age group 35 to 44 (about 650,000), age group 45 to 54 (about 600,000), age group 55 to 64 (about 250,000), and age group age 65 and over (about 100,000; Kolodny et al. 2015, Figure 4, page 564).

- Some recent studies suggest that the use of electronic cigarettes may be highest in the United States among high
school–age boys and girls, with usage rates reaching as high
as 10 percent. This rate significantly exceeds that of the next
highest group, young adults aged 20 to 28 years, where the
prevalence in 2011 ranged from 4.9 percent to 7 percent in
various studies (Chapman and Wu 2014, 43).

A better understanding of some of these basic statistics can be
gained by examining the patterns of substance use, misuse, and
abuse among adolescents today.

Alcohol

To the average non-scientist, the term *alcohol* refers to one specific member of the chemical family, ethanol, also known as
ethyl alcohol, grain alcohol, or, sometimes, "drinking alcohol."
Alcohol is produced naturally by the process known as *fermentation*, in which a sugar such as glucose, fructose, or sucrose
is converted by the action of yeasts into ethanol and carbon
dioxide. This chemical reaction is the mechanism by which
essentially all alcoholic beverages are produced.

What Are the Effects of Ethanol on the Human Body?

Alcohol ingested into the human body is absorbed primarily
in the stomach and small intestine, after which it is distributed
throughout the human body by the bloodstream. It is metabolized primarily in the liver, where it is converted to water and
carbon dioxide in a three-step process. In the first of those
steps, ethanol is converted to ethanal (acetaldehyde), which, in
the second step, is converted to ethanoic acid (acetic acid). In
the final step, acetic acid (or, in its ionic form, *acetate*) is converted to carbon dioxide and water, which are eliminated from
the body in urine and the respiratory system.

Ethanol has both stimulant and depressant effects on the
body, a phenomenon known as a *biphasic response*. The balance of

stimulation and depression depends on a complex mix of factors, including the amount of ethanol ingested, the rate of ingestion, the presence of food in the body, a person's genetic constitution, and perhaps other factors (Holdstock and de Wit 1998).

Scientists now know that acetaldehyde is responsible for many of the effects traditionally attributed to ethanol. It may cause damage to the liver, pancreas, brain, and gastrointestinal system, although the extent, mechanism, and characteristics of these effects are not yet well understood (Alcohol Metabolism: An Update 2007). In any case, acetaldehyde does not remain in the body very long, but is metabolized relatively quickly to produce acetic acid. A person who ingests alcohol at a moderate rate, then, is likely to avoid the most serious damage done to his or her body because the acetaldehyde produced during alcohol metabolism is itself metabolized before it can produce significant harm to the body (Biochemistry of Alcohol 2015; Pierini 2015; for a more advanced explanation of this process, see King 2015).

The consumption of alcohol, especially at too rapid a rate and in too large quantities, can effect a number of organs and systems in the human body, such as:

- the heart: arrhythmias (irregular heartbeat), high blood pressure, stroke, and cardiomyopathy;
- the liver: alcoholic hepatitis, steatosis ("fatty liver"), cirrhosis, and fibrosis;
- the pancreas: pancreatitis and related digestive disorders;
- the brain: disruption of the neural transmission system, resulting in confusion, disorientation, changes in mood and emotions, and other variations in normal brain function;
- the immune system: disruption of normal immune functions can result in a variety of diseases, such as pneumonia and tuberculosis; and
- cancer of a number of organs and tissue, such as those of the mouth, esophagus, throat, liver, and breast (Beyond Hangovers 2015).

Among pregnant women, consumption of alcohol poses another risk to the body: the possibility of fetal alcohol syndrome (FAS). FAS is a condition that occurs in newborn children as a result of the mother's consumption of alcohol during pregnancy. It is characterized by symptoms such as wide-set eyes and an unusually thin upper lip; deformities of the joints and limbs; slow physical growth; problems with vision and hearing; an unusually small head; poor coordination and balance, as well as other diminished mental processes; and a variety of social and behavioral problems, including inability to get along with peers and difficulty in staying with a task to its completion (Facts about FASDs 2015).

Having recognized the large number of serious health problems associated with excessive consumption of alcohol, it is worthwhile to mention that certain health benefits have been attributed to the moderate drinking of alcohol. One problem with such a discussion is what one means by "moderate" drinking, with no generally agreed-upon definition yet having been developed. In most cases, it may mean "one drink per day," although some researchers use more generous amounts for the definition. In any case, a considerable body of research now suggests that the consumption of modest amounts of alcohol may provide health benefits such as reduced risk of cardiovascular disease (the most common benefit mentioned by researchers), as well as reduced risk of type 2 diabetes, and gallstones, as well as improved digestion and some relief from emotional stress (Alcohol: Balancing Risks and Benefits 2015).

Causes of Alcohol Abuse, Dependence, and Addiction

Despite decades of research, scientists are still uncertain as to the precise factors that cause a person to overuse alcoholic beverages and become dependent upon or addicted to them. The evidence collected thus far appears to suggest that one's genetic background and environment both have an influence on a person's tendency to drink more than is safe. Psychological and social factors, such as a low self-esteem and/or ability to get along well with others, may also contribute to alcohol dependence and addiction.

Although the causes of alcohol problems are not well known, a number of factors appear to be associated with the development of such issues. For example, individuals who begin to drink heavily at an early age are more likely to become alcoholic than those who do not. Also, coming from a family in which alcohol is regularly over-used may be a risk factor also. The presence of various stress factors may also be a factor. The ease with which alcoholic beverages are available may also influence one's tendency to drink excessively. (For more details on this issue, see Youth Risk Behavior Surveillance 2014.)

Individuals who consume quantities of alcohol that begin to disrupt their physical, social, mental, or social health may be diagnosed as having *alcohol use disorder* (AUD). This condition is a formal diagnosis defined and described in the *Diagnostic and Statistical Manual of Mental Disorders*, fifth edition (DSM-5), which is the "bible" of the psychiatric profession that formally describes all mental disorders with which the profession deals. According to DSM-5, AUD is diagnosed on the basis of a number of signs and symptoms, such as the tendency to drink more than one intends, a craving for drinking that may dominate a person's thoughts, choosing to drink in preference to some other activity in which one is interested, and finding that drinking and the desire to drink begin to interfere with one's other normal family, personal, and social responsibilities (Alcohol Use Disorder 2015). A diagnosis of AUD suggests that one is in need of professional help to deal with this problem.

Treatment

Treatment of alcohol-related disorders generally fall into one of three categories: medications, behavior modification, and group therapy, also known as mutual-help groups (MHGs). Three medications have been approved by the U.S. Food and Drug Administration for use with alcoholism: naltrexone (trade names: Revia and Depade), disulfiram (Antabuse), and acamprosate (Campral). Each of these drugs produces an unpleasant physical effect upon ingesting alcohol or shortly thereafter.

For example, disulfiram interferes with the action of the enzyme acetaldehyde dehydrogenase, which brings about the breakdown of acetaldehyde in the liver. As a result of taking disulfiram, acetaldehyde begins to build up in the body very soon after one begins to drink, producing the most unpleasant consequences of alcohol overdose almost immediately. One is induced to stop drinking, then, after the first drink, not the tenth. Researchers are constantly looking for new drugs that can also be used for the treatment of alcohol-related problems.

Behavior modification is a psychological procedure in which a person is taught to exhibit certain desirable behaviors (such as not drinking) and to *not* exhibit less desirable behaviors (such as drinking). A simplistic explanation of the procedure might involve imagining that a person has icy cold water dumped on his or her head every time he or she looks at a bottle of beer. That treatment might be expected to decrease the likelihood that the person would then look at a bottle of beer again in the future. Therapists use far more sophisticated techniques in behavior modification, of course, but the principle is the same: "correct" behavior is rewarded, while "incorrect" behavior is punished.

By far the most popular form of treatment for alcohol use disorder today in the United States is MHG therapy. In this form of treatment, a group of individuals with a common problem (such as AUD) get together and talk about that problem. Probably the best known of such groups is Alcoholics Anonymous (AA), a group first formed in 1935 and now boasting more than two million members worldwide in more than 100,000 local groups (A. A. Fact File 2013, 4). According to a number of research studies, MHGs such as AA are powerful methods for helping people deal with alcoholic problems, often more successful than either medication or behavioral therapy (Exploring Treatment Options for Alcohol Use Disorder 2010).

Prevention

As with many medical problems, preventing an adverse condition is usually a better option than trying to treat that condition after it develops. A number of approaches have been suggested for reducing the likelihood that children and adolescents will begin drinking. Most of these approaches are based on one of four levels of contact: individual, family, school, and community. For example, a number of programs have been devised to identify girls and boys, young men and women, who may be at risk for developing an alcohol use disorder and then provide individual counseling. The most recent version of this approach is called Electronic Screening and Brief Intervention (e-SBI), in which some type of electronic device, such as a computer or smart phone, is used to monitor a person's alcohol consumption and then to provide brief messages about the consequences of such actions ("Preventing Excessive Alcohol Consumption: Electronic Screening and Brief Intervention (e-SBI)" 2015; see also Alcohol Screening and Brief Intervention for Youth: A Practitioner's Guide n.d.).

The principle behind most family-oriented programs is that families have been found to have the strongest influence on a young person's behaviors, including the decision to start drinking alcohol. Family prevention programs, then, are designed to educate families about the risks of excessive alcohol consumption and the mechanisms by which abstinence or moderate drinking can be encouraged. An example of a family-oriented substance abuse prevention program is the Creating Lasting Family Connections program of the Council on Prevention and Education: Substances Inc. That program attempts to identify individuals or groups of individuals at risk for substance abuse, such as AUD, and then provide intensive training programs for parents and families of those individuals. The program makes use of trained counselors who identify families in high-risk environments and then provide a series of training sessions that explain the nature of substance abuse and methods that can be used to help young adults avoid becoming dependent on substances (Council on Prevention and Education: Substances Inc. 2015).

School programs are especially attractive venues for offering alcohol prevention programs. Large numbers of adolescents are brought together in a common place on a regular basis, so that integrating education about alcohol into the normal school program (or added as an extracurricular activity) is relatively easy to do. As a result, alcohol prevention programs of one kind or another have become widely popular for students at a wide range of grades in American schools. A popular example of such programs is the Botvin Life Skills Training program, a privately operated system with curricula designed for elementary, middle, and high school students, as well as for young adults transitioning from high school to college or the workplace, as well as for parents (Botvin Life Skills®Training 2015). The program claims to reduce alcohol use by 60 percent, a claim that is repeated in the peer-reviewed literature. (See, for example, Griffin and Botvin 2010.)

Community programs to reduce adolescent alcohol abuse tend to be more ambitious and broad-ranging, including some or all of the elements mentioned earlier for dealing on an individual, family, and school level with such problems. In addition, community programs deal with issues such as sale of alcohol to adolescents, institutions where alcohol may be obtained, and the use of alcohol at social functions and by drivers in the community. Educating both teenagers and their parents about the risks of excessive consumption of alcohol is almost always an important element of such community programs (Fagan, Hawkins, and Catalano 2011; for an excellent overview of this topic, see Scheier 2015).

Tobacco

Tobacco is a product made from the leaves of the tobacco plant in the genus Nicotiana. Sixty-six species of Nicotiana are currently recognized, and the status of more than 150 other varieties remains unresolved (Nicotiana 2015). The species most commonly used to make commercial tobacco is *N. tabacum.* The leaves of the plant are normally harvested and then *cured* for a period of time. Curing is a process that allows tobacco leaves to age, bringing about changes in the chemical constitution of the leaves to bring about desirable odors and tastes preferred by smokers.

Scientists have been interested for many years in the chemical composition of tobacco leaves, both smoked and raw. (See, for example, Leffingwell 1999.) Today, they know that nearly 9,600 different compounds occur in the leaf and its ashes (Rodgman and Perfetti 2013). Many of these constituents occur in vanishingly small amounts and/or are totally harmless to human health. Some occur in larger quantities and/or are known to be toxic, carcinogenic, teratogenic, or mutagenic. Possibly the best known and most hazardous of the chemicals in tobacco is nicotine, the substance responsible for the addictive properties of tobacco. In addition to the natural ingredients found in tobacco, tobacco companies add other substances to cigarette tobacco to augment flavor, odor, color, and other properties. (See, for example, 599 Ingredients Added to Cigarettes 2015.)

What Are the Effects of Tobacco on the Human Body?

Summarizing the effects of tobacco on the human body is a challenging task partly because there are so many different chemicals involved, partly because these effects are only partially known, partially because the effects that are known can be complex, and partially because the effects may be known at either the molecular or systemic level, or both. One of the best available summaries of these effects is a factsheet prepared by the Campaign for Tobacco-Free Kids (Smoking's Immediate Effects on the Body 2009). Some of the effects listed in that report are as follows:

• Smoking appears to produce changes in brain chemistry, altering the ability of certain nerve cells to respond to messages passing through the brain. These changes may be responsible for mood changes and may increase one's risk for dependence upon and addiction to chemicals found in tobacco.

- Some chemicals in tobacco smoke appear to inactivate cilia that line the respiratory system and provide a means for keeping that system clean. As a result, mucus may accumulate in the respiratory system, resulting in the familiar "smoker's cough" and respiratory problems with which it is associated.

- Nicotine and other components of tobacco smoke pass from the respiratory system into the bloodstream, where they may attack the walls of arteries and veins, increasing their tendency to collect plaque that is the first step in the development of atherosclerosis.

- Chemicals in tobacco smoke may have a tendency to alter the pH (acidity) of the stomach, reducing its ability to neutralize acidic foods, thereby contributing to the risk for gastrointestinal disorders.

- Tobacco chemicals appear to alter the blood supply and natural healing mechanisms in the mouth that protect against infections, resulting in an increased risk for periodontal disease.

- Smoking appears to compromise the immune system, resulting in greater risk for a wide variety of localized infectious diseases, such as otitis media (infection of the middle ear), sinusitis, rhinitis, and pneumonia.

- Tobacco chemicals have been implicated in decreased ability of the body's digestive system to absorb necessary vitamins and minerals, leading to the possibility of vitamin-deficiency disorders such as scurvy and anemia. (All citations are from Smoking's Immediate Effects on the Body 2009. Also see Ambrose and Barua 2004; Das 2003; Hecht 1999; Smoking: A Danger to Healthy Gums 2015.)

Causes of Tobacco Abuse, Dependence, and Addiction

Smoking is a habit that typically begins relatively early in a person's life. According to the Campaign for Tobacco-Free Kids (based on data from SAMHSA), 90 percent of adults smokers began to use tobacco in their teen years and two-thirds were regular smokers before the age of 19 (Smoking and Kids 2015). A number of reasons are traditionally given for the appeal of smoking to children and adolescents. For example, children who grow up on homes where adults smoke are twice as likely to take up smoking than are those who live in smoke-free homes (Hill et al. 2005). Children who come from lower socioeconomic conditions are also at greater risk for taking up smoking, as are those who tend to have poorer social skills or lower self-esteem (Conrad, Flay, and Hill 1992). Peer pressure and the impact of cigarette advertising have also been found to be strong factors in determining whether or not one chooses to smoke (Smoking and Kids 2015).

Treatment

Most people who smoke want to quit. A recent survey by the CDC found that 68.8 percent of smokers interviewed expressed that desire, and 52.4 percent had made at least one attempt to quit in the year preceding the survey. The number who successfully gave up smoking, however, was much lower, about 6.2 percent of all smokers (Quitting Smoking among Adults 2011). Interestingly enough, the majority of those who attempted to quit did not take advantage of the scientifically proven methods available for that objective, but did so as an act of will (Quitting Smoking among Adults 2011).

The U.S. government's online help program, called Smoke-Free.gov, lists more than a dozen ways to quit smoking, most of them being some form of medication. These medications deliver nicotine in the form of a patch, gum, inhaler, lozenge, or nasal spray to satisfy the smoker's addiction to nicotine without ingesting the other numerous harmful chemicals associated with tobacco. SmokeFree.gov also recommends self-help programs, in which a person can obtain information and advice from print or electronic materials, as well as a variety of counseling programs that help him or her through the stages of withdrawal and cessation. Other cessation techniques that have been used successfully by some individuals include acupuncture, laser treatments, and hypnosis (Find a Quit Method That Works for You 2015).

Prevention

Because most smokers begin using tobacco at an early age, prevention programs tend to focus on children and adolescents. Those programs often have two major elements: actions by government to reduce access to tobacco products by young people and educational programs to inform the general public and adolescents in particular about the health risks of smoking. For example, prevention programs often push for an increase in the cost of cigarettes by raising taxes on them, the hope being that higher costs make cigarettes and other tobacco products less available to young people. State and local laws may also punish retailers who sell tobacco products to underage individuals or otherwise ignore laws designed to restrict tobacco access to children and teenagers. Advertising programs are generally designed to provide information about health risks associated with smoking through schools and community outlets with the hope that those who are better informed will be less likely to start smoking (Youth Tobacco Prevention 2015).

Electronic Cigarettes

Possibly the most revolutionary development in the history of smoking has taken place within the last half century: the invention of the electronic cigarette, or e-cigarette. In spite of its name, the device is also made in the shape of a cigar or a pipe. Credit for the invention of the first e-cigarette is usually given to American inventor Herbert A. Gilbert who received a patent for a "smokeless non-tobacco cigarette" in 1963 (Dunworth 2013). A somewhat different and more advanced version of that device was later invented by Chinese inventor Hon Lik in the early 2000s. Both men saw the e-cigarette as an alternative means of delivering the flavor and aroma of tobacco smoking, along with the nicotine found in tobacco in Hon's case.

An e-cigarette consists of a small number of essential parts: an inhaler, which contains a replaceable cartridge that holds a liquid consisting of nicotine, water, and other liquids; an atomizing chamber, in which the liquid is converted to a vapor; a battery, used to bring about the vaporization process; and an LED light to replicate the burning tip of a traditional cigarette. (For a diagram of an e-cigarette, see http://www.e-cig-bargains .com/HowItWorks.jsp.) Because of the method by which the e-cigarette operates, the process of using it is sometimes referred to as *vaping* (from "vaporization" of the constituents).

In today's world, e-cigarettes are sometimes touted also as being safer than traditional cigarettes because they do not produce the large maze of harmful chemicals associated with tobacco smoke. At the very least, some researchers say, allowing their use would reduce the number of individuals who smoke tobacco and, thus, be an important part of solving the world's smoking problems. (See, for example, Hajek et al. 2014.) U.S. regulators have been hesitant to impose restrictions on the use of e-cigarettes because, they say, insufficient data are available to determine their overall safety and possible effectiveness in combating conventional cigarette smoking. In late 2015, however, the FDA announced plans to establish a new rule under which electronic devices would be regulated in essentially the same way as other tobacco products are regulated (E-cig Firms Steel for Legal Battle 2015). As of April 2016 the FDA had not yet announced this rule.

Illicit Drugs

In addition to the two legal substances discussed so far, alcohol and tobacco, a vast array of illicit (illegal) drugs are the subject of concern among those who study substance abuse, drugs such as heroin, cocaine, marijuana, LSD, amphetamines, ecstasy, and PCP. The vast majority of these drugs can be classified into one of three major categories: stimulants, depressants, and hallucinogens.

Stimulants

Stimulants are defined as substances that temporarily increase the nervous or physiological activity of the body or some part of the body. They increase heart rate, blood pressure, and rate of respiration and increase one's energy, attention, and alertness. Because of these actions, stimulants are sometimes referred to as "uppers," since they increase one's physical and mental activity. Some of the most common stimulants are cocaine, methamphetamine, MDMA (ecstasy), and the prescription drugs methylphenidate (Ritalin) and dextroamphetamine (Adderall).

What Are the Effects of Stimulants on the Human Body?

The thoughts and emotions that humans experience as a consequence of electrical and chemical changes occur in the central nervous system (CNS), primarily the brain. That system consists mainly of two parts: neurons (nerve cells) and neurotransmitters (substances that carry a nerve message between neurons). (A number of good diagrams are available online with which to follow this discussion. See, for example, http://hyperphysics.phy-astr.gsu.edu/hbase/biology/neurtran.html.)

Most "messages" to the brain begin as electrical pulses transmitted from sensory neurons in the eyes, ears, skin, nose, and other organs. These messages travel along sensory neurons in much the same way that an electrical current travels through a wire. The messages eventually reach the brain where they begin the process of recognition and action.

An electrical message originates in a sensory neuron when the portion of the neuron in contact with the external environment, the *dendrites*, is stimulated to produce an electrical impulse. That impulse travels from the dendrites through the central core of the neuron, the nucleus, and out into long arms of the neurons, called *axons*. Axons carry the electrical impulse to the very end of the neuron, located in the CNS. When the electrical impulse reaches the end of the neuron, it stimulates the release of chemicals known as *neurotransmitters*.

As their name suggests, neurotransmitters pass an electrical current from one neuron to a second, adjacent neuron. Some of the most common neurotransmitters are acetylcholine, epinephrine, norepinephrine, dopamine, seratonin, glycine, and gamma-aminobutyric acid (GABA).

Neurotransmitters travel from the end of a sensory neuron to dendrites in nearby CNS neurons. The space between the two neurons across which a neurotransmitter passes is known as a *synapse*. (The neurons on either side of the synapse are known, therefore, as the *presynaptic* ["before the synapse"] and *postsynaptic* ["after the synapse"] neurons.) When a neurotransmitter reaches the postsynaptic neuron, it searches for and attaches to a pocket in the dendrites known as a *receptor*. Receptors are regions in a cell whose shape perfectly matches the three-dimensional shape of one specific neurotransmitter. When that neurotransmitter recognizes and approaches the receptor site, it is able to slide into that pocket, where it fits tightly in place. Once it is placed, the neurotransmitter may stimulate the receptor site to emit an electrical signal identical to the one by which the neurotransmitter was originally produced. That signal then continues through the second neuron in the same way it did in the first: from dendrite to nucleus to axon.

Two types of neurotransmitters occur in the nervous system: excitatory and inhibitory. As their names suggest, excitatory neurotransmitters stimulate a cell to produce an electrical impulse; it gets the cell "excited." Inhibitory neurotransmitters prevent an electrical impulse from developing; they "close a cell down" and "put it to sleep," in a manner of speaking. Of the neurotransmitters listed earlier, GABA is the most common inhibitory neurotransmitter, with glycine and dopamine also having this function all, most, or some of the time. The other neurotransmitters listed are all excitatory substances.

After a neurotransmitter has been docked at a receptor site for a period of time, it is released and returns to the synapse. There it is acted upon by enzymes that break it down into its component parts, which return to the neuron from which the neurotransmitter originally came. There, the component parts are reassembled into the neurotransmitter once more, and the process of nerve transmission is repeated again and again and again.

This process of nerve transmission occurs continually untold numbers of time, day and night, every day of a person's life. It is responsible for the ideas we generate, the things we learn, the fears we feel, the movements we make, and every other brain activity that occurs. Normal nerve transmission is also affected, however, by a number of natural and non-natural factors. For example, for reasons that are still unknown, some people begin to produce less dopamine as they grow older. The functions that depend on dopamine transmission, then, tend to diminish in quality and quantity. When this change occurs, a person may develop a brain disease such as Parkinson's disease, senility, or depression.

But synthetic chemicals can also affect the transmission of nerve messages in the brain, resulting in changes in one's motor, mental, and/or emotional states. Such is the case with the class of illicit drugs known as stimulants. These substances act on the nervous system in a variety of ways, all of which tend to result in an increased utilization of excitatory neurotransmitters. When cocaine reaches the nervous system, for example, it tends to increase the amount of dopamine released from one cell, thus increasing the excitatory effects on a receptor cell (the whole system becomes more "excited"). At the same time, cocaine has a second effect on the nervous system by blocking the reuptake of dopamine molecules trying to return to the original neuron. This inhibitory effect further increases the number of dopamine molecules available within the synapse and, hence, their overall effect on the CNS (How Drugs Affect Neurotransmitters 2015; for videos illustrating this effect, see https://www.youtube.com/watch?v=Ju_qha2OBL4 or https://www.youtube.com/watch?v=4OS2C4NemJI).

Substance Addiction as a Brain Disease

Most societies in modern times have considered substance abuse to be a criminal issue. In the United States, possession of any controlled substance is punishable for a fine of not less than $1,000 and a prison sentence of up to one year. For a second offense, the penalty is a fine of not less than $2,500 and a prison sentence of 15 days to two years, or, for a third offense, a fine of not less than $5,000 and a prison term of 90 days to three years (Yeh 2015, 8; state laws may impose additional penalties and different widely from state to state; see Possession of a Controlled Substance: Drug Possession Laws 2015). Many researchers, however, have changed their perception of substance abuse, dependence, and addiction, taking the view that such conditions are actually brain diseases, brought about by casual use of a substance that results in changes in brain structure and function that can be identified and measured.

This change in outlook reflects an even more fundamental change in views about the brain itself. At one time, researchers thought that the brain was essentially formed in its final condition relatively early in life, and that changes in its structure and function were rare after that point. A more recent view is that the brain is capable of adapting to external stimuli, with neurons developing new shapes and functions and neural networks developing new connections and pathways, a possibility known as *neuronal plasticity* or *neuroplasticity*. Some of the changes made by a brain are brought about by the introduction of outside substances and forces, such as illicit drugs.

For example, an intake of cocaine dramatically increases the amount of dopamine available in a user's brain (as described earlier). The brain's natural system for moving dopamine back and forth across synapses is overwhelmed, and it makes adjustments to deal with the new situation. It activates more dopamine receptors and creates new neural pathways to carry signals away from a receiving neuron. Eventually, the normal structure of the neural system is inactivated and is unable to carry out its normal functions, replaced by a new network of neurons and connections. What this means is that the addicted person is no longer to respond to normal stimuli that would previously have been recognized and responded to by the original neural system.

The changes described here can be visualized by a variety of imaging technologies, such as positron-emission tomography (PET), that allow researchers to see where neural activity is at its highest and lowest levels, and to follow those changes over time. One interesting observation is that substance-induced neural changes have a tendency to remain in place for extended periods of time, as long as a person remains addicted to a substance. If a person is able to overcome the addiction, however, his or her brain chemistry gradually returns to something approaching its pre-addiction, "normal" structure and function. (For some typical PET scans of addicted and non-addicted brains, see Addiction Brain Scans, Unscrambled 2015; for more on this general topic, see Drug Use Changes the Brain Over Time 2015; Horvath et al. 2015; Neuroaddiction: The Reward Pathway 2010.)

Signs and Symptoms of Stimulant Abuse

Stimulants promote an increase in energy and activity in the body, resulting in a number of characteristic signs and symptoms that may suggest overuse or abuse of the substances. These signs and symptoms include:

- Increased energy and restlessness
- Increased alertness
- Rapid and/or rambling speech
- Dilated pupils
- Changes in mood
- Increases in heart rate and blood pressure
- Impaired judgment
- Nausea and/or vomiting
- Unusual weight loss
- Nasal congestion and/or runny nose
- An expanded sense of confidence and self-esteem

- Insomnia
- Excessive sweating
- Loss of appetite
- Fatigue

Depressants

Depressants are substances that reduce neural (nerve) activity in the body, thus reducing those motor and mental activities that are controlled by the nervous system, such as vision, sense of balance, gait, sense of judgment, rational thought, memory, and sensitivity to pain. Because their effects on the body are just the opposite of stimulants ("uppers"), depressants are sometimes referred to in common parlance as "downers." They are also called more specifically *central nervous system* (*CNS*) *depressants* because that is the part of the body on which they exert their influence.

In the broadest possible sense, the category of CNS depressants can be associated with, and sometimes equated with, a number of other classes of drugs such as sedatives, tranquilizers, hypnotics, dissociatives, anti-convulsants, and analgesics. (It should be noted that many authorities in the field of substance use and abuse prefer to use a more restricted definition of the term *depressant*, as noted later.) Each of these terms has a more restricted meaning than the general term, CNS depressant:

A *sedative* (or *soporific*) a substance that tends to put a person to sleep.

A *tranquilizer* is a substance that calms a person down without necessarily putting him or her to sleep.

A *hypnotic* is a substance that puts a person into a trance-like state that is not equivalent to sleep.

A *dissociative* is a substance that tends to make a person feel removed from (dissociated from) his or her environment and, indeed, from his or her own body.

An *anti-convulsant* (also known as an *anti-epileptic* or *anti-seizure*) substance is one that acts very specifically on muscular action to prevent or bring under control violent muscular spasms, such as those associated with an epileptic event.

An *analgesic* is a substance that relieves pain. This very large class of compounds includes drugs used to treat mild pain, such as soreness resulting from physical activity (e.g., aspirin, acetaminophen, and ibuprofen) to severe, chronic pain associated with cancer, post-surgical pain, and other discomfort not treatable by milder agents.

Some substances most commonly categorized as CNS depressants are alcohol, barbiturates, benzodiazepines, and opioids. Barbiturates are among the oldest synthetic substances produced for medical purposes. They are derivatives of barbituric acid, from which they get their name. Barbituric acid was first synthesized by German chemist Adolph von Baeyer in 1864, but it had no medical use at the time. In fact, it was not until 1903 that German chemists Emil Fischer and Joseph von Mering synthesized the first derivative of barbituric acid, a compound they called *barbitone*. Barbitone was later made available commercially under the trade name of Veronal, a drug that was later to become one of the most popular CNS depressants ever discovered. Today more than 2,500 barbiturates are known although no more than about a dozen have medical applications. They include such familiar names as amobarbital (listed as a Schedule II drug), barbital (Schedule IV), butabarbital (Schedule III), pentobarbital (Schedule II), phenobarbital (Schedule IV), and secobarbital (Schedule II) (What Are Barbiturates? 2015).

Today, barbiturates have been largely replaced by another category of CNS depressants, benzodiazepines, because they are safer and more effective. Benzodiazepines are derivatives of a parent compound consisting of a benzene ring attached to a diazepine ring to which one or more substituents have been added. The first member of the family was discovered accidentally by Polish American chemist Leo Sternbach in 1955. It was first made commercially available five years later by the pharmaceutical firm of Hoffman-La Roche, and by 1977, benzodiazepines were the most widely prescribed drugs in the world. Probably the best known members of the family are Ativan (lorazepam), Halcion (triazolam), Librium (chlordiazepoxide), and Valium (diazepam).

Opioids were discussed in Chapter 1 of this book. They are a family of compounds of immense importance both because of their invaluable role in the treatment of chronic, intractable pain, and because of their very high risk of abuse by individuals of all ages.

What Are the Effects of Depressants on the Human Body?

As dopamine is the key to the way in which stimulants affect the human brain, so it is that a second neurotransmitter, GABA, is the key to explaining changes that result from the use of depressants. GABA is the common abbreviation for the compound gamma-aminobutyric acid (or γ-aminobutyric acid). Recall that GABA is an inhibitory neurotransmitter. When it docks at a receptor site on a post-synaptic neuron (the neuron that *receives* neurotransmitters passing across the synaptic gap), it allows chloride ions to flow into that neuron, causing changes that reduce the neuron's ability to accept excitatory neurotransmitters. (See, for example, diagrams at Ashton 2002, Figure 1; Drugs and Behavior 65.2 2016, slide 16.) The neuron is, therefore, less likely to "fire," that is, transmit a neural message, reducing the general activity of the system. GABA is the most important of all inhibitory neurotransmitters in the human CNS and is involved in a variety of actions that tend to slow neural and muscular actions in the body. (Technically the cells being discussed here are $GABA_A$ in contrast to a second type of cell known as the $GABA_B$ neuron.)

The neurons described here have a second receptor site in addition to the one keyed for GABA molecules. This second receptor site is designed to accept depressant molecules, such as those of barbiturates and benzodiazepines. These "depressant" receptor sites increase the likelihood that the neuron will accept GABA molecules. So a person who has ingested some type of depressant has simply increased the number of GABA molecules passing through the system, decreasing the tendency of the system to transmit nerve messages and slowing down the nervous system in general (Olsen and DeLorey 1998, 2016).

As is the case with stimulants, long-term use of depressants can actually make permanent changes in the structure and function of GABA-accepting neurons. Some receptor sites actually change shape as a result of the action of depressant molecules acting on the cell, and the normal sequence of actions that occurs in the cell is disrupted. If and when depressant use is decreased or ended, the cell is "thrown into confusion." The GABA receptor sites that formally accepted GABA neurotransmitters with their accompanying inhibitory effect no longer function in that way. Instead, the cell may appear to be unable to recognize GABA neurotransmitters and will begin to accept excitatory neurotransmitters (such as glutamate) only. The nervous system is then thrown into "overdrive" in which physical, mental, and emotional reactions increase rapidly to much higher than normal levels. These changes account for the characteristic and often dangerous effects that occur when a person withdraws from depressant abuse without some external control (Vinkers and Olivier 2012).

Signs and Symptoms of Depressant Abuse
The signs and symptoms of excessive depressant abuse are those that might be expected of someone whose body functions have slowed down, such as:

- Drowsiness or excessive sleepiness
- Slowed or slurred speech
- Lack of coordination and/or concentration

- A sense of dizziness or vertigo
- Slowed vital signs, that is, reduced heartbeat, blood pressure, and respiration rate
- Reduced or limited control of one's actions
- Confusion
- Increased fatigue
- Dilated pupils
- Difficulty in urinating or inability to urinate

Hallucinogens

A hallucinogen is a substance that produces hallucinations, profound distortions of a person's perceptions of reality. Hallucinogens are also known as *psychedelics*. That term is also sometimes used to describe a subcategory of hallucinogens, although the different between the two terms is largely one of semantics. Some experts divide hallucinogens into three major categories: classical hallucinogens, such as lysergic acid diethylamide (LSD), psilocibin, and mescaline; dissociatives, such as amantadine, phencyclidine, dextromethorphan, and nitrous oxide; and deliriants, such as atropine, scopolamine, dicyclomine, and diphenhydramine (Baumeister et al. 2014; Rastegar and Fingerhood 2015, Chapter 9; The Subjective Components of a Delirious Trip 2016).

The hallucinogens are a fascinating family of compounds, consisting of some of the oldest psychoactive drugs known, which are also among those producing the most extreme and most terrifying of experiences for the drug user. The deadly nightshade (*Atropa belladonna*), for example, has been used for at least 2,000 years for both beneficial and harmful purposes. In ancient times, it was used as an anesthetic for surgery, but it was probably better known as a poison for the killing of prey by humans (in poison-tipped arrows) and political rivals (such as competitors for a throne) (Lee 2007).

Hallucinogens have long been, and continue to be, one of the most popular drugs of abuse among teenagers. When the

Monitoring the Future first began its student of substance abuse by high school seniors in 1975, 7.2 percent of twelfth graders reported using LSD at least once in the year preceding the survey. An even larger fraction of that population (9.4 percent) reported using some hallucinogen other than LSD. The number of LSD users rose to its maximum level of 8.8 percent of twelfth graders in 1996, before beginning to drop off to its current (2014) level of 2.5 percent. Meanwhile the use of non-LSD hallucinogens followed a different trend, dropping to its lowest number of 1.7 percent in 1992 before beginning to rise to its current (2014) level of 3.0 percent (Johnston, et al. 2014, 2015).

Among the most popular non-LSD drugs are psilocybin, peyote, dimethyltryptamine, and ayahuasca. All of these substances can be found in naturally occurring plants. Psilocybin (a naturally occurring type of tryptamine) occurs in more than 200 mushrooms belonging to the genus Psilocybe. When produced for recreational use, the substance may be known as "magic mushrooms," "shrooms," "boomers," or "little smoke." Peyote is a small, spineless species of cactus whose systematic name is *Lophophora williamsii*. It contains a powerful psychedelic compound known as mescaline, which is responsible for its psychoactive effects. In the United States and Canada, the use of peyote is specifically excluded from federal regulations about drug use because it has traditionally been a part of the ceremonies of Native Indian tribes (in the United States, the Native American Church). Ayahuasca is a tea made out of the *Banisteriopsis caapi* vine, native to the Amazon region of South America. It has been used for centuries by residents of the area for ceremonial and religious purposes and has recently been adopted by recreational drug users in other parts of the world because of its hallucinogenic effects. One component of the plant source of the tea is dimethyltryptamine, which is also made synthetically for use by recreational drug users (D'Orazio 2015; Entheogens Including Salvia, LSD, Peyote, and Mushrooms 2014; Halpern 2004).

What Are the Effects of Hallucinogens on the Human Body?

The psychoactive effects of hallucinogens make use of yet another type of neurotransmitter, serotonin. The vast majority of serotonin is found in the human body in the gastrointestinal system, where it regulates bowel function and other GI activities. A smaller amount of serotonin is found in the CNS, especially the brain, where it is thought to be responsible for a variety of emotional responses. The traditional view has been that serotonin is a "happy" neurotransmitter, which produces feelings of ease and comfort and the lack of which may produce anxiety, depression, and suicidal feelings. Current evidence suggests that this view may be true to a large extent, but the action of serotonin on the brain is actually far more complex than is suggested by this simplistic model. (See, for example, Teissier et al. 2015.)

In any case, the normal pathway for the serotonin neurotransmitter begins in the presynaptic neuron, where serotonin is synthesized and stored in small packets known as *vesicles*. Serotonin molecules are then released from the presynaptic neuron, travel across the synaptic gap, and dock at receptor sites, one type of which is known as the 5-HT_{2A} receptor. (For a diagram of this process, see Chatterjee 2015.) At its receptor site, serotonin then stimulates the postsynaptic neuron to produce the physiological effects with which it is associated.

Over the past two decades, researchers have learned that LSD and other hallucinogens "highjack" the serotonin system to produce their own distinctive psychoactive effects. One of the two key points uncovered is that 5-HT_{2A} receptors have a greater affinity for hallucinogen molecules than they do for serotonin itself, so that whenever those molecules are available, 5-HT_{2A} receptor sites "gobble them up" and begin to produce greatly enhanced responses in the brain. In other words, once a person consumes a hallucinogen, the brain not only becomes "happy," but may become "deliriously happy," producing the bizarre psychoactive effects associated with this class of drugs. The second key point, uncovered only in 2007, is that the 5-HT_{2A} receptor is actually the key to the whole hallucinogenic process, distinguishing between molecules of hallucinogens and non-hallucinogens (Chatterjee 2015; the 2007 research is reported at González-Maeso et al. 2007; for an excellent general review of this topic, see Fantegrossi, Murnane, and Reissig 2008).

Signs and Symptoms of Hallucinogen Abuse

The signs and symptoms associated with hallucinogen abuse are usually quite obvious and often quite frightening, both to the person who has taken a hallucinogen and to friends, families, and others who observe the abusers. Some of those signs and symptoms are as follows:

- Increase in body vital signs, such as elevated body temperature, increased heart rate, increased respiration rate, and increased blood pressure
- Profuse sweating
- Changes in patterns of salivation, including "dry mouth"
- Nausea and vomiting
- Loss of ability to perform certain common motor tasks, such as operating devices and driving
- Dilated or "floating" pupils
- Tingling in fingers and toes
- Numbness of extremities
- Loss of coordination
- Sleeplessness
- Dizziness
- Visual and/or auditory hallucinations, which may include distortions of time, space, and shape; altered perceptions of speed; a sense of being "out of one's own body"; intensified sense of sound, color, and touch; and confusion of sensory experience that may involve "hearing" colors and "visualizing" sounds
- Anxiety

- Confusion
- Agitation
- Violent behavior

(For a general overview of the topic of hallucinogens, see Hallucinogens and Dissociative Drugs 2015.)

Licit Drugs

Concerns about drug abuse date back well over a century in the United States. The first laws prohibiting possession and/or use of certain drugs were adopted in the 1870s. In another sense, public concerns about drug abuse have only a more recent origin, dating to the early 1970s when President Richard M. Nixon announced a "war on drugs." On June 17, 1971, Nixon announced that drug abuse in the United States had become a "national emergency" that had "swept America in the last decade." He described a plan not only to continue and expand enforcement of the newly adopted Controlled Substances Act of 1970, but also to begin programs for the rehabilitation of drug users themselves (Nixon 1971). And for the next half century, the federal, state, and local governments have worked to bring under control the abuse of illegal drugs by Americans of all ages.

In the early twenty-first century, however a quite different problem had arisen to challenge those who are fighting drug abuse in the United States (and most other parts of the world): the abuse of legal drugs. The problem has arisen for two reasons. First, individuals looking for substances to use for recreational purposes are always on the lookout for new products with which to experiment. And, second, chemists are always looking for new products that will be of value to the medical profession in dealing with a host of health problems (as well as those who are looking specifically for new legal psychoactive drugs to use for recreational purposes). As a consequence, the first two decades have seen an upsurge in the number of people who are using legal, prescription drugs for non-medical purposes, resulting in a whole new population of individuals who abuse those drugs, and/or have become dependent upon and/or addicted to them (Drug Facts: Prescription Drugs 2015).

An important element in the current prescription drug abuse crisis is that most individuals, both adults and teenagers, believe that prescription drugs are safer to use than are illicit drugs. After all, those drugs were developed for beneficial purposes—to cure or prevent disease—so they probably should be relatively safe for a person to take. In a 2013 study of parent and adolescent views on this issue, one in six parents (16 percent) and one in four teenagers (27 percent) agreed with this line of thinking. In fact, an even larger percentage of teenagers (33 percent) agreed with the statement that "it's okay to use prescription drugs that were not prescribed to them to deal with an injury, illness or physical pain" (2012 Partnership Attitude Tracking Study 2013, 10). One of the many flaws with this argument, of course, is that substance abusers may take drugs for purposes for which they were not intended in the medical field. Also, many substance abusers use more—often far more—of a drug than is intended for human consumption or is safe to take.

Prescription Drugs of Abuse

The prescription drugs most susceptible to abuse fall into three general categories, two of which have been discussed earlier: stimulants and depressants (which include tranquilizers). The third category consists of opioids, the vast majority of which are narcotic opioids that have been developed for the treatment of chronic and intractable pain. According to the most recent MTF study (2015), 18.3 percent of twelfth graders interviewed for the research had used a prescription drug for nonmedical purposes at least once in their lifetime. (Eighth and tenth graders were not asked questions about prescription drug abuse.) About 1 out of 10 twelfth graders (12.9 percent) said they have used a prescription drug for non-medical purposes in the last year, and 5.9 percent reporting doing so in the month preceding the survey (Monitoring the Future Study: Trends in Prevalence of Various Drugs 2015).

Of the drugs that were thus misused, the most popular was Adderall (a stimulant), listed as having been misused by 7.5 percent of twelfth graders in 2015, followed by Vicodin (an opioid narcotic), named by 4.4 percent of twelfth graders, OxyContin (an opioid narcotic), by 3.7 percent of twelfth graders, and Ritalin (a stimulant), by 2.0 percent of twelfth graders (Monitoring the Future Study: Trends in Prevalence of Various Drugs. 2015). The comparable data for eighth and tenth graders, as well as trends in these data, are given in Table 2.2.

Table 2.2   Trends in Non-Medical Use of Prescription Drugs among Adolescents (past year; percentage of respondents)

Eight Graders				
Substance	2012	2013	2014	2015
Adderall	1.70	1.80	1.30	1.00
Vicodin	1.30	1.40	1.00	0.90
OxyContin	1.60	2.00	1.00*	0.80
Ritalin	0.70	1.10	0.90	0.60
Cough Medicine	3.00	2.90	2.00*	1.60
Bath Salts	0.80	1.00	0.50*	0.40
Tenth Graders				
Substance	2012	2013	2014	2015
Adderall	4.50	4.40	4.60	5.20
Vicodin	4.40	4.60	3.40	2.50
OxyContin	3.00	3.40	3.00	2.60
Ritalin	1.90	1.80	1.80	1.60
Cough Medicine	4.70	4.30	3.70	3.30
Bath Salts	0.60	0.90	0.90	0.70
Twelfth Graders				
Substance	2012	2013	2014	2015
Adderall	7.60	7.40	6.80	7.50
Vicodin	7.50	5.30*	4.80	4.40

Twelfth Graders				
OxyContin	4.30	3.60	3.30	3.70
Ritalin	2.60	2.30	1.80	2.00
Cough Medicine	5.60	5.00	4.10	4.60
Bath Salts	1.30	0.90	0.90	1.00

* Statistically significant difference from previous year.

Source: "Monitoring the Future Study: Trends in Prevalence of Various Drugs." 2015. National Institute on Drug Abuse. http://www.drugabuse.gov/trends-statistics/ monitoring-future/monitoring-future-study-trends-in-prevalence-various-drugs. Accessed on January 4, 2016.

The last two rows of Table 2.2 show data for over-the-counter (OTC) substances that are sometimes misused also. OTC drugs do not require a prescription; one can just walk into a drug store and buy them "over the counter." The OTC products that are most widely misused are cold and cough medicines because most of them contain one or more psychoactive substances. The most common of these substances is dextromethorphan (DXM), a sedative that has some dissociative properties and is used in OTC products because it is a cough suppressant (Cough and Cold Medicine [DXM and Codeine Syrup] 2015). Another category of OTC products that are sometimes misused are called "bath salts," although they have nothing at all to do with the substances that are added to bath water to make it softer and foamy. In the context used here, *bath salts* are products that contain members of the cathinone family, a group of chemicals that have psychoactive properties similar to those of amphetamine. These products are said to produce a sense of euphoria and an increased sociability and, some say, enhanced sex drive (DrugFacts: Synthetic Cathinones ["Bath Salts"] 2012).

How Do Users Get Access to Prescription Drugs?

One of the questions of special interest to those who work on the problem of prescription drug abuse is how young adults are able to get access to drugs such as Adderall, Vicodin, and OxyContin. After all, it would be relatively rare that someone under the age of 18 would receive a prescription for one of these drugs for his or her own medical problem.

A fair amount of research has now been conducted to answer this question, and it appears that a number of avenues exist by which teenagers can gain access to prescription drugs rather easily. In some cases, teenagers actually do receive prescriptions for medications intended for their own use. In such cases, however, it appears that parents seldom pay much attention to the use of those prescription drugs, and their sons and daughters can use more than the quantities prescribed as they wish. In one study, for example, only one parent out of 31 interviewed said that any effort was made to prevent children from gaining easy access to their medications. (One other parent said she threw out excess medications [Friese et al. 2013; see also Ross-Durow, McCabe, and Boyd 2013].)

Other studies have highlighted the importance of friends as sources of prescription drugs. A very limited study of the misuse of prescription drugs in Rice County, Minnesota, for example, found that 73 percent of respondents had obtained their drugs from friends, compared to 41 percent who bought them from drug dealers and 38 percent who got them at home. (Respondents were allowed to select more than one source; Prunty and Hotho 2015.)

In most larger studies, however, it appears that the most common source for prescription drugs for teenagers is their own home. The 2013 Partnership Attitude Tracking Study conducted by the Partnership for Drug-Free Kids and the MetLife Foundation, for example, found that more than half of parents surveyed said that "anyone can access their medicine cabinet," and 73 percent of prescription-drug-using teenagers themselves reported that gaining access to their parents' drugs was not a problem (The Partnership Attitude Tracking Study 2014, 18). In fact, according to some authorities, a number of locations in the home can provide easy access to prescription drugs for teenagers, including the bathroom counter and trash can, the parents' bedroom, mom's purse, the refrigerator, and the kitchen counter. (Where Are Teens Getting Prescription Drugs? 2015)

Causes of Teenage Substance Abuse

Stimulants, depressants, and hallucinogens are very different types of substances with very different effects on the human body. People begin to take—and continue taking—these substances for a wide variety of reasons with varying effects on their present lives and varying outlooks for their future lives. The factors that lead to a person's choice of abusing one or more kinds of illicit substances vary to some extent, depending on the type of drug one chooses. One might, for example, decide to start using a stimulant because his or her life is disappointing, depressing, and unfulfilling. Or he or she might choose to start using a hallucinogen just because of the thrill of a new experience.

In spite of these differences in one's motivation for beginning substance abuse, certain common themes occur in (1) the factors that tend to drive one to use excessive quantities of a drug and become dependent on and/or addicted to that drug, (2) the methods of treatment that are available for a person who has developed a substance use disorder (SUD), and (3) the methods that have been developed to reduce the likelihood of (to prevent) one's becoming dependent upon or addicted to an illicit substance. The next sections of this chapter review these three issues relating to adolescent substance abuse.

Causes of Substance Abuse

Factors that place an individual teenager at risk for substance abuse have now been studied in considerable detail, and some conclusions can be drawn with relative confidence. Among the factors that appear to be predictive of SUD later in life for all forms of illegal substances are the following.

Being an Adolescent

Ironically, one of the risk factors for developing a substance use disorder may simply result from being a teenager. During this period in one's life, the brain is still growing and undergoing some critical changes. Any alterations made in the brain, such as those that occur during the use of psychoactive substances, may have a greater chance of producing changes in brain structure and function that may last for very long periods of time, certainly into adulthood (Winters and Arria 2011).

Family Influences

Risk factors for substance abuse appear from the very moment of conception. A number of studies have demonstrated that tendency toward the misuse of drugs has genetic roots that are passed down from parent to children (Meyers and Dick 2010). But a host of family characteristics have also been implicated in an increased risk for substance abuse, factors such as physical or emotion abuse or neglect of a child by its parents, a history of substance abuse by parents themselves, disregard or actual approval of substance use by one's parents, poorly developed family relationships, marital status of parents, and level of parents' educational attainments and their socioeconomic status also pose potential problems for parents' ability to understand and/or deal with a child's interest in experimenting with psychoactive substances (Buu et al. 2009; Vakalahi 2001; Whitesell et al. 2013).

Physical, Emotional, and Sexual Abuse

One of the strongest risk factors for future substance abuse appears to be some form of other abuse within the family, by other family members, or by acquaintances. In one of the pioneering studies on this topic, researchers found that a sample of tenth through twelfth graders in six Oregon schools were at significantly increased risk for tobacco, alcohol, and illicit drug abuse when they had a history of emotional, physical, and/or sexual abuse (Moran, Vuchinich, and Hall 2004; also see Tonmyr et al. 2010). Some evidence suggests that physical or sexual abuse can increase the risk of later substance abuse by a factor of as much as four times (Wall and Kohl 2007; also see White-sell et al. 2013).

Neglect

Some children grow up in homes where they are not provided with the minimal food, clothing, shelter, and other basic needs. A number of studies have shown that such an environment tends to increase the risk of such children's developing sub-stance use disorder problems later in life (Chen et al. 2011). At least one recent study suggests that such early experiences may actually result in physical changes in the brain that may lead to greater risk for adult substance abuse (Oswald et al. 2014).

Peer Pressure

Just as the influence of one's family on one's future substance use should be obvious, so should the influence of one's friends and social network. If all or most of the individuals that one spends time with as a child and adolescent approve of and per-haps themselves use psychoactive substances, such behaviors may seem acceptable and even desirable in order to "fit in" with one's peers. This intuitive conclusion has now been con-firmed by a number of research studies. In one recent study, for example, a population of sixth through eighth graders con-firmed that peers who smoked, drank alcohol, and used mari-juana were generally thought to be the most popular members of their peer group (Tucker et al. 2011). Interestingly enough, there is some evidence that the effects of peer pressure on the development of substance abuse is related to family influences, with the greater the strength of familial attitudes on the topic, the less significant the influence of peer attitudes and practices (Bahr, Hoffmann, and Yang 2005).

Individual Traits

An individual's personality and emotional state are also factors in determining whether or not one will begin experimenting with psychoactive substances. An individual who is depressed, lonely, anxious, afraid, or otherwise upset may choose to try taking a drug to escape from such unhappy moods. Certainly research has now confirmed that such is the case with many individuals who begin taking drugs during childhood and adolescence and then continue that practice into adulthood (Taylor 2011; Volkow 2004). The question of risk factors during adolescence for future substance abuse has been studied extensively. Useful overviews are Cleveland et al. 2008 and Kilpatrick et al. 2000.

Treatment

In the vast majority of human societies throughout recorded history, the excessive and/or intemperate use of psychoactive substances has been regarded as a problem for and by at least some individuals, and a host of actions have been proposed and put into practice to deal with this problem. In the United States, for example, treatments for alcoholism were being offered in the very earliest days of the nation's history. In 1784, for example, the eminent physician Benjamin Rush suggested that alcoholism was a medical problem that should be treated in much the same way as other medical problems (an idea that was far ahead of its time for most experts in the area; Katcher 1993).

For much of American history, the use of psychoactive substances (primarily alcohol for most of that time) was considered an act of weak character by individuals who could not control their behavior. The proper "treatment" for such individuals often fell into one of two categories: (1) groups organized by and/or for other "deviants" where common problems could be addressed and, hopefully, resolved, or (2) mandatory incarceration, where "deviants" could be removed from contact with "normal" people. Alcoholics Anonymous is perhaps the best known example of the first approach today (although it is by no means the only group of its kind in history), and the drug laws instituted in the United States beginning in the 1910s are examples of the second approach. (For one of the best available treatments of the history of substance treatment in the United States, see White 1998.)

The notion of substance as a disease did not gain much traction in the United States until the mid-twentieth century, largely as a result of the involvement of a handful of influential researchers and through the adoption of the concept by major professional groups, such as the American Medical Association which, in 1963, officially defined alcoholism as a "treatable illness." Among the leading researchers in the field was Stanford University physiologist E. Morton Jellinek, who devoted most of his professional career to studying and promoting the concept of alcoholism as a disease. (See, especially, Jellinek 1960; but note that the disease concept of substance abuse is by no means universally accepted by researchers in the field. See, for example, Satel and Lilienfeld 2013, Chapter 3, 2014.)

Today, a well-developed protocol of treatment for substance abuse is available through a number of sources. Some of the basic principles that underlie this protocol, as outlined by the National Institute on Drug Abuse, are the following:

- "Addiction is a complex but treatable disease that affects brain function and behavior."
- "No single treatment is appropriate for everyone."
- "Effective treatment attends to multiple needs of the individual, not just his or her drug abuse."
- "Remaining in treatment for an adequate period of time is critical."
- "Counseling—individual and/or group—and other behavioral therapies are the most commonly used forms of drug abuse treatment."

- "Medications are an important element of treatment for many patients, especially when combined with counseling and other behavioral therapies."
- "Medically assisted detoxification is only the first stage of addiction treatment and by itself does little to change long-term drug abuse."
- "Treatment does not need to be voluntary to be effective" (Drug Facts: Treatment Approaches for Drug Addiction 2009).

This approach to treatment is based on the presumption that excessive substance use has brought about specific changes in the physical structure and function of the brain, and treatment involves at least some measure of restructuring the brain to its original form and function. One of the elements of treatment, then, can be the use of various medications that tend to phase out the inappropriate structures and functions and prompt the brain to restore its original characteristics. For example, the U.S. Food and Drug Administration (FDA) has approved three drugs for the treatment of alcohol dependence and abuse, disulfiram (Antabuse), naltrexone (ReVia), and acamprosate (Campral), as well as two medications for tobacco withdrawal, bupropion and varenicline, along with a variety of nicotine replacements therapies (Addiction Medications 2016; Smith 2007). Drugs are also available for treatment of opioid dependence and addictions, including buprenophrine, methadone, and injectable naltrexone (Rinaldo and Rinaldo 2013).

One of the exciting frontiers of research on addiction medications is the attempt to develop a vaccine that would protect against dependence and addiction. Studies in this field have been going on now for a number of years, and progress is encouraging. Some experts predict that vaccines will soon be available against one or more of the most commonly abused substances, including alcohol, amphetamines, cocaine, heroin, and nicotine (Rainey 2013; Schlosburg et al. 2013).

Medications are usually employed during a period of *detoxification*. Detoxification is a procedure during which substances that have been ingested by an individual with harmful effects on his or her body are gradually removed from the person's use. Detoxification is generally a period of profound discomfort while an individual's central nervous system "re-learns" how to function without access to substances on which it has become dependent. An important adjunct to the use of medications during detoxification is the use of individual (one-on-one) or group counseling, which often includes behavior modification procedures. The dependent or addicted individual requires not only changes in his or her brain function, but also the guidance and support of family, friends, and professional counselors to learn how to live once more without the crutch of a psychoactive substance. Such treatment programs may take place in an out-patient setting or in a residential setting, that may include a place of incarceration. (For an excellent overview of treatment options, see Rastegar and Fingerhood 2015.)

Treatment programs can sometimes be especially complicated and risky when they involve withdrawal with certain types of addictive substances. For example, a condition known as *benzodiazepine withdrawal syndrome* (or sometimes just *benzo withdrawal*) occurs when a person who is dependent upon or addicted to benzodiazepines stops using the drug too quickly. It appears that brain systems that have become adapted to the presence of benzodiazepines are unable to adjust to their absence quickly enough, resulting in a set of troubling and dangerous systems, including headache, sweating, tremors, palpitations, confusion, panic attacks, hallucinations, seizures, and suicidal thoughts, some of which may lead to self-injury and/or death. The treatment of benzo withdrawal, therefore, requires gradual and carefully monitored reduction in the quantity of drug being ingested (Why Benzo Withdrawal Syndrome Is Deadly 2014).

A second example of treatment issues is called *hallucinogen persisting perception disorder* (HPPD), in which perceptual misinterpretations persist for extended periods of time among individuals who had abused hallucinogens for months or years. Such individuals, even with otherwise successful treatment for their dependence on a hallucinogen, continue to experience frightening visions similar to those that occurred during their period of addiction. Again, it appears that brain systems remain fixed on structures adapted during the period of dependence and/or addiction and are unable to return to a normal status even after the aggravating substance is discontinued (Litjens 2014).

Prevention

The search for effective methods of preventing substance abuse among children and young adults has occupied the attention of researchers for well over half a century in the United States. At this point, experts in the field have developed a number of general principles, as well as a variety of specific programs, for achieving this result.   Among those general principles are the following:

- Prevention programs should take cognizance of risk factors that tend to lead to substance abuse later in life (see above) as well as protective factors. *Protective factors* are individual, family, and community factors that tend to reduce the risk that individuals will develop a dependence on or addiction to psychoactive substances.

- Prevention programs should be directed at both individual substances, such as opioids or hallucinogens, and the general topic of psychoactive substances that includes alcohol, tobacco, and other potentially problematic substances.

- Prevention programs should, on occasion, be targeted at particular populations at special risk for substance abuse, such as lesbian, gay, bisexual, and transgender (LGBT) individuals; Native Americans; and veterans and military families.

- Prevention programs should have a long-term focus (since substance abuse problems are not easily resolved), and should include repeated interventions to strengthen earlier learning.

- Prevention programs appear to be most successful when they involve extensive interactions between educators, counselors, and trainers and their clients.
- Prevention programs tend to be more effective and less costly than treatment programs that attempt to deal with substance abuse problems after they have developed (Preventing Drug Use among Children and Adolescents 2003).

Much of the research on risk factors for substance abuse discussed earlier has a secondary component, the search for factors that tend to reduce a person's becoming dependent upon or addicted to a psychoactive substances. Table 2.3 summarizes the results of this research, with protective factors divided by age group and individual, family, or group setting.

Table 2.3   Risk and Protective Factors for Substance Abuse

Age	Target Audience	Protective Factors
Early childhood	Individual	Self-regulation Secure attachment Mastery of communication and language skills Ability to make friends and get along with others
	Family	Reliable support and discipline from caregivers Responsiveness Protection from harm and fear Opportunities to resolve conflict Adequate socioeconomic resources for the family
	Peer, School, Community	Support for early learning Access to supplemental services such as feeding, and screening for vision and hearing Stable, secure attachment to childcare provider Low ratio of caregivers to children Regulatory systems that support high quality of care

(Continued)

Table 2.3   Continued

Age	Target Audience	Protective Factors
Middle School	Individual	Mastery of academic skills (math, reading, writing) Following rules for behavior at home, at school, and in public places Ability to make friends Good peer relationships
	Family	Consistent discipline Language-based, rather than physical, discipline Extended family support
	Peer, School, Community	Healthy peer groups School engagement Positive teacher expectations Effective classroom management Positive partnering between school and family School policies and practices to reduce bullying High academic standards
Adolescence	Individual	Positive physical development Emotional self-regulation High self-esteem Good coping skills and problem-solving skills Engagement and connections in two or more of the following contexts: at school, with peers, in athletics, employment, religion, culture
	Family	Family provides structure, limits, rules, monitoring, and predictability Supportive relationships with family members Clear expectations for behavior and values
	Peer, School, Community	Presence of mentors and support for development of skills and interests Opportunities for engagement within school and community Positive norms Clear expectations for behavior Physical and psychological safety
Young adulthood	Individual	Identity exploration in love, work, and worldview Subjective sense of adult status

Age	Target Audience	Protective Factors
		Subjective sense of self-sufficiency, making independent decisions, becoming financially independent
		Future orientation
		Achievement motivation
	Family	Balance of autonomy and relatedness to family
		Behavioral and emotional autonomy
	Peer, School, Community	Opportunities for exploration in work and school
		Connectedness to adults outside of family

Source: Adapted from "Risk and Protective Factors." 2016. Youth.gov. http://youth.gov/youth-topics/substance-abuse/risk-and-protective-factors-substance-use-abuse-and-dependence. Accessed on January 6, 2016.

The evidence that researchers have collected on risk and protective factors provides a key element in the design of any prevention program. Such programs obviously need to reduce risk factors and emphasize protective factors whenever, wherever, and in whatever way they can (Brook et al. 2015; Prevention of Substance Abuse and Mental Illness 2015).

Some examples of substance abuse prevention programs are the following:

ParentUp Vermont is a campaign designed to provide parents in Vermont with the tools they need to help their children deal with substance abuse issues. It provides background information about substance abuse among adolescents and lists a variety of resources that parents can use in dealing with problems in their own home, such as telephone and Internet contacts with state, local, and non-governmental organizations; district state health department offices; specialized groups, such as LGBT organizations and poison control centers; community coalitions; and substance abuse and mental health groups (Contact: http://parentupvt.org/).

School-based prevention programs are especially appealing because the target audience is already gathered together on a regular basis in a convenient location for the presentation of information about and training in needed skills related to substance abuse. One of the best-known examples of school-based programs is Project ALERT, developed by the Rand Corporation. The program is designed for seventh and eighth graders and consists of 11 core lessons taught once a week in the seventh grade, followed by three booster lessons taught once per week in eighth grade. As of early 2016, Rand reported that more than 60,000 teachers had used the program, resulting in a 40 percent decrease in regular smoking behavior, 24 percent decrease in the use of alcohol, and a 60 percent decrease in marijuana use. The program makes use of online lesson plans and teacher training modules, interactive student videos, projectable classroom posters, an electronic newsletter, and a toll-free telephone line for support and technical assistance (Contact: http://www.projectalert.com/).

Experts in substance abuse prevention have long recommended that greater attention be paid to the needs of special groups of children and adolescents in developing programs with this focus. (See, for example, A Provider's Introduction to Substance Abuse Treatment for Lesbian, Gay, Bisexual, and Transgender Individuals 2012.) A survey of current programs in the field suggests that, thus far, these recommendations have largely been ignored, with relatively few prevention programs having been designed and sustained on a long-term basis. (See, for example, Substance Abuse Prevention at http://youth .gov/youth-topics/substance-abuse and SAMHSA's Prevention Efforts for Specific Populations at http://www.samhsa.gov/pre vention/specific-populations, accessed on January 7, 2016.) The type of opportunity that can and should be provided for specialized groups, however, can be found in efforts by Native American Indian tribal councils to provide substance abuse prevention programs for their children and adolescents, largely supported by the federal Indian Alcohol and Substance Abuse Prevention and Treatment Act of 1986 (Alcohol and Substance Abuse 2016).

In 1993, for example, the Boys and Girls Club of the Northern Cheyenne Nation adopted the parent organization's SMART MOVES (Skills Mastery and Resistance Training) program as a way of educating tribal youth about the risks posed by substance abuse. The program is designed for youth of three age groups (SMART Kids, age 6 through 9; Start SMART, age 10 through 12; and Stay SMART, age 13 through 15) and makes use of formal instruction, discussion, interactive activities, and play experiences to provide youngsters with the factual knowledge and coping skills needed to understand the risks posed by substance abuse and methods for becoming trapped in a cycle of dependence and addiction (Promising Practices and Strategies to Reduce Alcohol and Substance Abuse among American Indians and Alaska Natives 2000; SMARTmoves: A Skills Mastery and Resistance Training Program: A Facilitator's Guide 2011).

One of the critical questions one might ask about prevention programs is how successful they are. Do such programs actually achieve the objectives for which they were designed and carried out? That question is very difficult to answer, however, as there are so many different prevention programs in operation with so many different objectives. One of the best indicators of the success of substance abuse prevention programs, however, is the annual report produced for the Drug-Free Communities Support Program of the Office of National Drug Control Policy. That program has been in existence since 1997 and in 2011 covered federal support for a total of 726 drug prevention programs in all 50 states, the District of Columbia, Puerto Rico and the U.S. Virgin Islands, American Samoa, and Palau. The success (or failure) of these 726 programs was studied in great detail, attempting to determine changes in substance use practices by adolescents along with attitudes about substance use and abuse and the availability of drugs in their communities. In carrying out their local drug prevention programs, the 726 respondents reported using a staggering variety of techniques for achieving their basic objectives, including the production and distribution of flyers, posters, press releases, and brochures; the release of news stories to local media about their efforts; fairs and other types of celebrations; face-to-face information systems with adolescents, their parents, and community members; educational articles on local radio and television and in local newspapers; and the distribution of information on social media and the Internet.

By comparing the 2012 results with those from the preceding 10 years, researchers were able to draw a number of conclusions about the success, or lack of it, of such programs. They were able to make two major conclusions:

• Respondents reported a significant decrease in long-term (annual) use of tobacco, alcohol, and marijuana, and a significant decrease in short-term (30-day) use for the first two substances, but a significant increase in short-term marijuana use.

• Respondents reported a significant increase in their own disapproval and that of their parents about the use of tobacco and alcohol, but not for marijuana, for which no change was reported.

Authors of the report concluded finally that

> While it cannot be determined for certain that the work of DFC community coalitions caused any of the significant changes, the data are consistent with what would be expected if the program were having an impact with only two exceptions (i.e., increases in prevalence of past 30-day marijuana use by high school students and a lack of significant findings in perception of risk of marijuana use at the middle and high school levels). (Drug-Free Communities Support Program 2012; note that some individual states carry out similar evaluation programs for their own states. See, for example, White, Guard, and Arndt 2011.)

Another useful consequence of evaluation programs is their ability to identify features of programs that are likely to be effective and features that are likely to be less effective. In one such study conducted by researchers from EMT Associates Inc., ORC/Macro Inc., and the Center for Substance Abuse Prevention, previous studies identified four variables that contributed to the success of substance abuse prevention programs:

- Content: The most effective types of content in prevention programs confirmed what earlier studies had shown, namely that the most effective type of content focused on individual behavioral and life skills rather than on knowledge about substance use and abuse.

- Delivery: Programs that depended primarily on interaction between students and instructors were generally more effective than those that followed a more traditional classroom-style lecture approach.

- Coherence: Programs that involved logical, well-connected steps between a variety of elements were more effective than those that presented lessons on a more random basis.

- Contact time: The density of contact between facilitators and students appears to be an important factor in bringing about change. Researchers recommended four or more hours of contact per week as the most effective allocation of time (Springer, Hermann, and Sambrano 2002; also see Griffin and Botvin 2010; Nation et al. 2003).

Conclusion

The use of psychoactive substances throughout human history has consistently been marked by the risks of misusing and abusing such substances to the detriment of human health and life and social coherence. Over the past half century, some children and adolescents in the United States and other parts of the world have been drawn into this vortex of dependence and addiction. Over the past few years, some evidence suggests that substance abuse has gradually become less of a crisis than it had once been not so many years ago. But no one can tell if the recent downturn in misuse and abuse statistics is a trend or a temporary blip in the direction of the battle against substance abuse. History suggests that efforts continue to be made to educate the general public, and adolescents in particular, about the inherent risks in using psychoactive substances for recreational purposes, with the hope that education will bring wise choices in the use of alcohol, tobacco, marijuana, cocaine, and other hazardous substances.

References

"A. A. Fact File." 2013. http://www.aa.org/assets/en_US/ m-24_aafactfile.pdf. Accessed on December 26, 2015. Available online at http://www.aa.org/assets/en_US/m-24_ aafactfile.pdf. Accessed on December 26, 2015.

"Addiction Brain Scans, Unscrambled." 2015. The Fix. https://www.thefix.com/content/brain-scans-addiction 90916. Accessed on December 31, 2015.

"Addiction Medications." 2016. New York State Office of Alcoholism and Substance Abuse Services. https:// www.oasas.ny.gov/AdMed/meds/meds.cfm. Accessed on January 6, 2016.

"Alcohol and Substance Abuse." 2016. Tribal Court Clearinghouse. http://www.tribal-institute.org/lists/alcohol .htm. Accessed on January 7, 2016.

"Alcohol: Balancing Risks and Benefits." 2015. The Nutrition Source. Harvard T. H. Chan School of Public Health. http://www.hsph.harvard.edu/nutritionsource/ alcohol-full-story/. Accessed on December 26, 2015.

"Alcohol Metabolism: An Update." 2007. Alcohol Alert. http://pubs.niaaa.nih.gov/publications/AA72/AA72.htm. Accessed on December 26, 2015.

"Alcohol Screening and Brief Intervention for Youth: A Practitioner's Guide." n.d. Washington, DC: National Institute on Alcohol Abuse and Alcoholism. Available online at http://www.integration.samhsa.gov/clinical-practice/sbirt/Guide_for_Youth_Screening_and_Brief_Intervention.pdf. Accessed on December 29, 2015.

"Alcohol Use Disorder." 2015. National Institute on Alcohol Abuse and Alcoholism. http://www.niaaa.nih.gov/alcohol-health/overview-alcohol-consumption/alcohol-use-disorders. Accessed on December 26, 2015.

Ambrose, John A., and Rajat S. Barua. 2004. "The Pathophysiology of Cigarette Smoking and Cardiovascular Disease: An Update." *Journal of the American College of Cardiology*. 43(10): 1731–1737.

Ashton, C. Heather. 2002. "Benzodiazepines: How They Work and How to Withdraw." http://www.benzo.org.uk/manual/bzcha01.htm. Accessed on January 1, 2016.

Bahr, Stephen J., John P. Hoffmann, and Xiaoyan Yang. 2005. "Parental and Peer Influences on the Risk of Adolescent Drug Use." *Journal of Primary Prevention*. 26(6): 529–551.

Baumeister, David, et al. 2014. "Classical Hallucinogens as Antidepressants? A Review of Pharmacodynamics and Putative Clinical Roles." *Therapeutic Advances in Psychopharmacology*. 4(4): 156–169.

"Beyond Hangovers: Understanding Alcohol's Impact on Your Health." 2015. National Institute on Alcohol Abuse and Alcoholism. http://pubs.niaaa.nih.gov/publications/Hangovers/beyondHangovers.pdf. Accessed on December 26, 2015.

"Biochemistry of Alcohol." 2015. Substance Abuse: CNS Depressants—Alcohol. https://www.nurseslearning.com/courses/corexcel/cxnrp-1600/Chap3/course/chap1/P2.html. Accessed on December 26, 2015.

"Botvin Life Skills®Training." 2015. http://www.lifeskills training.com/index.php. Accessed on December 29, 2015.

Brook, Judith S., et al. 2015. "Risk and Protective Factors for Substance Use and Abuse." In el-Guebaly, Nady, Giuseppe Carra, and Marc Galanter, eds. *Textbook of Addiction Treatment International Perspectives*. Milan: Springer Reference, 2279–2305.

Buu, Anne, et al. 2009. "Parent, Family, and Neighborhood Effects on the Development of Child Substance Use and Other Psychopathology from Preschool to the Start of Adulthood." *Journal of Studies on Alcohol and Drugs*. 70(4): 489–498.

Chapman, Shawna L. Carroll, and Li-Tzy Wu. 2014. "E-Cigarette Prevalence and Correlates of Use among Adolescents versus Adults: A Review and Comparison." *Journal of Psychiatric Research*. 54: 43–54.

Chatterjee, Anirban. 2015. "What Is LSD's Mechanism of Action in the Brain?" Quora. https://www.quora.com/ What-is-LSDs-mechanism-of-action-in-the-brain. Accessed on January 3, 2016.

Chen, Wan-Yi, et al. 2011. "Child Neglect and Its Association with Subsequent Juvenile Drug and Alcohol Offense." *Child and Adolescent Social Work Journal*. 28(4): 273–290.

Cleveland, Michael J., et al. 2008. "The Role of Risk and Protective Factors in Substance Use across Adolescence." *Journal of Adolescent Health*. 43(2): 157–164.

Conrad, Karen M., Brian R. Flay, and David Hill. 1992. "Why Children Start Smoking Cigarettes: Predictors of Onset." *Addiction*. 87(12): 1711–1724.

"Cough and Cold Medicine (DXM and Codeine Syrup). 2015. NIDA for Teens. http://teens.drugabuse.gov/ drug-facts/cough-and-cold-medicine-dxm- and-codeine-syrup. Accessed on January 4, 2016.

Council on Prevention and Education: Substances, Inc. 2015. http://copes.org/index.php. Accessed on December 29, 2015.

Das, Salil K. 2003. "Harmful Health Effects of Cigarette Smoking." *Molecular and Cellular Biochemistry.* 253(1–2): 159–165.

D'Orazio, Joseph L. 2015. "Hallucinogen Toxicity." http://emedicine.medscape.com/article/814848-overview#a4. Accessed on January 2, 2016.

"Drug Facts: Prescription Drugs." 2015. NIDA for Teens. https://teens.drugabuse.gov/drug-facts/prescription-drugs. Accessed on January 4, 2016.

"DrugFacts: Synthetic Cathinones ('Bath Salts')." 2012. National Institute on Drug Abuse. http://www.drugabuse .gov/publications/drugfacts/synthetic-cathinones-bath-salts. Accessed on January 4, 2016.

"Drug Facts: Treatment Approaches for Drug Addiction." 2009. National Institute on Drug Abuse. http://www .drugabuse.gov/publications/drugfacts/treatment-approaches-drug-addiction. Accessed on January 6, 2016/

"Drug-Free Communities Support Program." 2012. Office of National Drug Control Policy. https://www.whitehouse .gov/sites/default/files/dfc_2012_interim_report_annual_ report_-_final.pdf. Accessed on January 7, 2015.

"Drug Use Changes the Brain Over Time." 2015. Learn. Genetics. http://learn.genetics.utah.edu/content/addiction/ brainchange/. Accessed on December 31, 2015.

"Drugs and Behavior 65.2." 2016. SlideShare. http://www .slideshare.net/SairaNawaz2/sedative-hypnotics-anxiolytics1. Accessed on January 1, 2016.

Dunworth, James. 2013. "An Interview with the Inventor of the Electronic Cigarette, Herbert A. Gilbert." Ashtray Blog. http://www.ecigarettedirect.co.uk/ashtray-blog/2013/10/ interview-inventor-e-cigarette-herbert-a-gilbert.html. Accessed on December 30, 2015.

"E-Cig Firms Steel for Legal Battle." 2015. The Hill. http://thehill.com/regulation/258465-e-cig-firms-steel-for-legal-battle. Accessed on December 30, 2015.

"Entheogens Including Salvia, LSD, Peyote, and Mushrooms." 2014. Get the Facts. DrugWarFacts.org. http://www.drugwarfacts.org/cms/Entheogens# sthash.925H4qgT.UHZlZK39.dpbs. Accessed on January 2, 2016.

"Exploring Treatment Options for Alcohol Use Disorder." 2010. National Institute for Alcohol Abuse and Alcoholism. http://pubs.niaaa.nih.gov/publications/AA81/ AA81.htm. Accessed on December 26, 2015.

"Facts about FASDs." 2015. Centers for Disease Control and Prevention. http://www.cdc.gov/ncbddd/fasd/facts.html. Accessed on December 26, 2015.

Fagan, Abigail A., J. David Hawkins, and Richard F. Catalano. 2011. "Engaging Communities to Prevent Underage Drinking." *Alcohol Research & Health*. 34(2): 167–174.

Fantegrossi, William E., Kevin S. Murnane, and Chad J. Reissig. 2008. "The Behavioral Pharmacology of Hallucinogens." *Biochemical Pharmacology*. 75(1): 17–33.

"Find a Quit Method That Works for You." 2015. SmokeFree. gov. http://smokefree.gov/explore-quit-methods. Accessed on December 30, 2015.

"599 Ingredients Added to Cigarettes." 2015. Tobacco.org. http://archive.tobacco.org/Resources/599ingredients.html. Accessed on December 29, 2015.

Friese, Bettina, et al. 2013. "How Parents of Teens Store and Monitor Prescription Drugs in the Home." *Journal of Drug Education*. 43(3): 223–233.

González-Maeso, Javier, et al. 2007. "Hallucinogens Recruit Specific Cortical 5-HT2A Receptor-Mediated Signaling Pathways to Affect Behavior." *Neuron*. 53(3): 439–452.

Griffin, Kenneth W., and Gilbert J. Botvin. 2010. "Evidence-Based Interventions for Preventing Substance Use Disorders in Adolescents Child." *Adolescent Psychiatric Clinics of North America*. 19(3): 505–526.

Hajek, Peter, et al. 2014. "Electronic Cigarettes: Review of Use, Content, Safety, Effects on Smokers and Potential for Harm and Benefit." *Addiction*. 109(11): 1801–1810.

"Hallucinogens and Dissociative Drugs." 2015. National Institute on Drug Abuse. http://www.drugabuse. gov/publications/research-reports/hallucinogens-dissociative-drugs/director. Accessed on January 4, 2015.

Halpern, John H. 2004. "Hallucinogens and Dissociative Agents Naturally Growing in the United States." *Pharmacology & Therapeutics*. 102(2): 131–138.

Hecht, Stephen S. 1999. "Tobacco Smoke Carcinogens and Lung Cancer." *JNCI*. 91(14): 1194–1210.

Hill, Karl G., et al. 2005. "Family Influences on the Risk of Daily Smoking Initiation." *Journal of Adolescent Health*. 37(3): 202–210.

Hingson, Ralph W., and Aaron White. 2013. "Trends in Extreme Binge Drinking among US High School Seniors." *JAMA Pediatrics*. 167(11): 996–998.

Holdstock, Louis, and Harriet de Wit. 1998. "Individual Differences in the Biphasic Effects of Ethanol." *Alcoholism: Clinical and Experimental Research*. 22(9): 1903–1911.

Horvath, A. Tom, et al. 2015. "How Does Addiction Affect the Brain?" AMHC. http://www.amhc.org/ 1408-addictions/article/48370-how-does-addiction-affect-the-brain. Accessed on December 31, 2015.

"How Drugs Affect Neurotransmitters." 2015. The Brain from Top to Bottom. http://thebrain.mcgill.ca/flash/i/ i_03/i_03_m/i_03_m_par/i_03_m_par.html. Accessed on December 31, 2015.

Jellinek, E. M. 1960. *The Disease Concept of Alcoholism*. New Haven, CT: Hillhouse Press.

Johnston, Lloyd D., et al. 2014. "Monitoring the Future: Demographic Subgroup Trends among Adolescents in the Use of Various Licit and Illicit Drugs, 1975–2013." Ann Arbor: Institute for Social Research. University of Michigan. Available online at http://www.monitoringthefuture.org/pubs/occpapers/mtf-occ81.pdf. Accessed on December 23, 2015.

Johnston, Lloyd D., et al. 2015. "Monitoring the Future: National Survey Results on Drug Use." Ann Arbor: Institute for Social Research. University of Michigan. Available online at http://www.monitoringthefuture.org/pubs/monographs/mtf-overview2014.pdf. Accessed on December 9, 2015.

Katcher, B. S. 1993. "Benjamin Rush's Educational Campaign against Hard Drinking." *American Journal of Public Health*. 83(2): 273–281.

Kilpatrick, Dean G., et al. 2000. "Risk Factors for Adolescent Substance Abuse and Dependence: Data From a National Sample." *Journal of Consulting and Clinical Psychology*. 68(1): 19–30.

King, Michael W. 2015. "Ethanol Metabolism." Medical Biochemistry. http://themedicalbiochemistrypage.org/ethanol-metabolism.php. Accessed on December 26, 2015.

Kolodny, Andrew, et al. 2015. "The Prescription Opioid and Heroin Crisis: A Public Health Approach to an Epidemic of Addiction." *Annual Review of Public Health*. 36: 559–574. Also available online at http://www.annualreviews.org/doi/pdf/10.1146/annurev-publhealth-031914-122957. Accessed on December 24, 2015.

Lee, M. R. 2007. "Solanaceae IV: Atropa belladonna, Deadly Nightshade." *The Journal of the Royal College of Physicians of Edinburgh*. 37(1): 77–84.

Leffingwell, J. C. 1999. "Basic Chemical Constituents of Tobacco Leaf and Differences among Tobacco Types." In Davis, D. Layten, and Mark T. Nielson, eds. *Tobacco: Production, Chemistry, and Technology.* Boston: Blackwell Science. Available online at http://www.leffingwell.com/ download/Leffingwell%20-%20Tobacco%20production% 20chemistry%20and%20technology.pdf. Accessed on December 29, 2015.

Litjens, Ruud P. W., et al. 2014. "Hallucinogen Persisting Perception Disorder and the Serotonergic System: A Comprehensive Review Including New MDMA-Related Clinical Cases." *European Neuropsychopharmacology.* 24(8): 1309–1323.

Meyers, Jacquelyn L., and Danielle M. Dick. 2010. "Genetic and Environmental Risk Factors for Adolescent-Onset Substance Use Disorders." *Child and Adolescent Psychiatric Clinics of North America.* 19(3): 465–477.

"Monitoring the Future Study: Trends in Prevalence of Various Drugs." 2015. National Institute on Drug Abuse. http://www.drugabuse.gov/trends-statistics/ monitoring-future/monitoring-future-study-trends- in-prevalence-various-drugs. Accessed on January 4, 2016.

Moran, Patricia B., Sam Vuchinich, and Nancy K. Hall. 2004. "Associations between Types of Maltreatment and Substance Use during Adolescence." *Child Abuse & Neglect.* 28(5): 565–574.

Nation, Maury, et al. 2003. "What Works in Prevention. Principles of Effective Prevention Programs." *The American Psychologist.* 58(6–7): 449–456.

"Neuroaddiction: The Reward Pathway." 2010. The Chemical Carousel. http://www.dirkhanson.org/neuroaddiction.html. Accessed on December 31, 2015.

"Nicotiana." 2015. The Plant List. http://www.theplantlist .org/tpl1.1/search?q=nicotiana. Accessed on December 29, 2015.

Nixon, Richard M. 1971. "Special Message to the Congress on Drug Abuse Prevention and Control." The American Presidency Project. http://www.presidency.ucsb.edu/ws/?pid=3048. Accessed on January 4, 2016.

Olsen, Richard W., and Timothy M. DeLorey. 1998. "GABA Receptor Physiology and Pharmacology." In Siegel, George J., et al., eds. *Basic Neurochemistry: Molecular, Cellular, and Medical Aspects*, 6th ed. Philadelphia: Lippincott Williams & Wilkins. Available online at http://www.ncbi.nlm.nih.gov/books/NBK28090/. Accessed on January 1, 2016.

Oswald, Lynn M., et al. 2014. "History of Childhood Adversity Is Positively Associated with Ventral Striatal Dopamine Responses to Amphetamine." *Psychopharmacology*. 231(12): 2417–2433.

"The Partnership Attitude Tracking Study." 2014. Partnership for Drug-Free Kids and MetLife Foundation. http://drugfree.scdn1.secure.raxcdn.com/wp-content/uploads/2014/07/PATS-2013-FULL-REPORT.pdf. Accessed on January 4, 2015.

Pierini, Carolyn. 2015. "A Health-Destroying Toxin We Can't Avoid And Must Detoxify." Vitamin Research Products. http://www.vrp.com/digestive-health/a-health-destroying-toxin-we-cant-avoid-and-must-detoxify. Accessed on December 26, 2015.

"Possession of a Controlled Substance: Drug Possession Laws." 2015. Criminal Defense Lawyer. http://www.criminaldefenselawyer.com/crime-penalties/federal/Possession-Controlled-Substance.htm#states. Accessed on December 31, 2015.

"Preventing Drug Use among Children and Adolescents: A Research-Based Guide for Parents, Educators, and Community Leaders," 2nd ed. 2003. National Institute on Drug Abuse. https://www.drugabuse.gov/sites/default/files/preventingdruguse_2.pdf. Accessed on January 6, 2015.

"Preventing Excessive Alcohol Consumption: Electronic Screening and Brief Intervention (e-SBI)." 2015. Community Preventive Services Task Force. http://www .thecommunityguide.org/alcohol/eSBI.html. Accessed on December 29, 2015.

"Prevention of Substance Abuse and Mental Illness." 2015. Substance Abuse and Mental Health Services Administration. http://www.samhsa.gov/prevention. Accessed on January 6, 2016.

"Promising Practices and Strategies to Reduce Alcohol and Substance Abuse among American Indians and Alaska Natives." 2000. American Indian Development Associates. http://www.aidainc.net/Publications/Alcohol%20promise .pdf. Accessed on January 7, 2016.

"A Provider's Introduction to Substance Abuse Treatment for Lesbian, Gay, Bisexual, and Transgender Individuals." 2012. U.S. Department of Health and Human Services. Substance Abuse and Mental Health Services Administration. Center for Substance Abuse Treatment. https://store.samhsa.gov/shin/content/SMA12-4104/ SMA12-4104.pdf. Accessed on January 7, 2016.

Prunty, Maggie M., and Devyn M. Hotho. 2015. "Adolescents' Access to Prescription Drugs for Non-medical Use." http://www.ncurproceedings.org/ojs/index .php/NCUR2015/article/view/1367/687. Accessed on January 4, 2016.

"Quitting Smoking among Adults—United States, 2001– 2010." 2011. *Morbidity and Mortality Weekly Report.* 60(44): 1513–1519.

Rainey, Clint. 2013. "Measles, Mumps, Rubella, Cocaine." *New York Magazine.* http://nymag.com/news/intelligencer/ cocaine-vaccine-2013-9/. Accessed on January 6, 2016.

Rastegar, Darius, and Michael Fingerhood, eds. 2015. *The American Society of Addiction Medicine Handbook of Addiction Medicine.* New York: Oxford University Press.

Rinaldo, Suzanne Gelber Rinaldo, and David W. Rinaldo. 2013. "Advancing Access to Addiction Medications: Implications for Opioid Addiction Treatment." American Society of Addictive Medicine. http://www.asam.org/docs/default-source/advocacy/aaam_implications-for-opioid-addiction-treatment_final. Accessed on January 6, 2016.

Rodgman, Alan, and Thomas Albert Perfetti. 2013. *The Chemical Components of Tobacco and Tobacco Smoke*, 2nd ed. Boca Raton, FL: CRC Press.

Ross-Durow, Paula Lynn, Sean Esteban McCabe, and Carol J. Boyd. 2013. "Adolescents' Access to Their Own Prescription Medications in the Home." *Journal of Adolescent Health.* 53(2): 260–264.

Satel, Sally, and Scott O. Lilienfeld. 2013. *Brainwashed: The Seductive Appeal of Mindless Neuroscience.* New York: Basic Books.

Satel, Sally, and Scott O. Lilienfeld. 2014. "Addiction and the Brain-Disease Fallacy." *Frontiers in Psychiatry.* 4: 141. doi: 10.3389/fpsyt.2013.00141. PMCID: PMC3939769. http://www.ncbi.nlm.nih.gov/pmc/articles/PMC3939769/. Accessed on January 6, 2016.

Scheier, Lawrence M., ed. 2015. *Handbook of Adolescent Drug Use Prevention: Research, Intervention Strategies, and Practice.* Washington, DC: American Psychological Association.

Schlosburg, Joel E., et al. 2013. "Dynamic Vaccine Blocks Relapse to Compulsive Intake of Heroin." *Proceedings of the National Academy of Sciences of the United States of America.* 110(22): 9036–9041.

"SMARTmoves: A Skills Mastery and Resistance Training Program: A Facilitator's Guide." 2011. Boys & Girls Clubs of America. http://bgcutah.org/wp-content/uploads/2014/08/SMART-Facilitators_single.pdf. Accessed on January 7, 2016.

Smith, John K. 2007. "Drugs for Drugs—Medications to Treat Addiction." *Social Work Today.* 7(6): 40–43. Available

online at http://www.socialworktoday.com/archive/
novdec2007p40.shtml. Accessed on January 6, 2016.

"Smoking: A Danger to Healthy Gums." 2015. Colgate Oral
Care Center. http://www.colgate.com/en/us/oc/oral-health/
basics/threats-to-dental-health/article/smoking-a-danger-
to-healthy-gums. Accessed on December 30, 2015.

"Smoking and Kids." 2015. Campaign for Tobacco-Free
Kids." https://www.tobaccofreekids.org/research/factsheets/
pdf/0001.pdf. Accessed on December 30, 2015.

"Smoking's Immediate Effects on the Body." 2009. Campaign for
Tobacco-Free Kids. https://www.tobaccofreekids.org/research/
factsheets/pdf/0264.pdf. Accessed on December 30, 2015.

Springer, J. Fred, Jack Hermann, and Soledad Sambrano.
2002. "Characteristics of Effective Substance Abuse
Prevention Programs for High-Risk Youth." Prevention
Tactics. http://www.cars-rp.org/publications/Prevention%
20Tactics/PT6.3.02.pdf. Accessed on January 7, 2016.

"The Subjective Components of a Delirious Trip." 2011.
Disregard Everything I Say. http://disregardeverything
isay.com/post/13543540109/the-subjective-components-
of-a-delirious-trip. Accessed on January 2, 2015.

Taylor, Ozietta D. 2011. "Adolescent Depression as a
Contributing Factor to the Development of Substance
Use Disorders." *Journal of Human Behavior in the Social
Environment.* 21(6): 696–710.

Teissier, Anne, et al. 2015. "Activity of Raphé Serotonergic
Neurons Controls Emotional Behaviors." Cell Reports.
http://www.cell.com/cell-reports/pdf/S2211-1247(15)
01250-4.pdf. Accessed on January 3, 2016.

Tonmyr, Lil, et al. 2010. "A Review of Childhood
Maltreatment and Adolescent Substance Use Relationship."
Current Psychiatry Reviews. 6(3): 223–234.

Tucker, Joan S., et al. 2011. "Substance Use among Middle School
Students: Associations with Self-Rated and Peer-Nominated
Popularity." *Journal of Adolescence.* 34(3): 513–519.

"2012 Partnership Attitude Tracking Study." 2013. MetLife Foundation and The Partnership at DrugFree.org. http://www.drugfree.org/wp-content/uploads/2013/04/PATS-2012-FULL-REPORT2.pdf. Accessed on January 4, 2016.

Vakalahi, Halaevalu F. 2001. "Adolescent Substance Use and Family-Based Risk and Protective Factors: A Literature Review." *Journal of Drug Education.* 31(1): 29–46.

Vinkers, Christiaan H., and Berend Olivier. 2012. "Mechanisms Underlying Tolerance after Long-Term Benzodiazepine Use: A Future for Subtype-Selective Receptor Modulators?" *Advances in Pharmacological Sciences.* 2012: 1–19.

Volkow, Nora D. 2004. "The Reality of Comorbidity: Depression and Drug Abuse." *Biological Psychiatry.* 56(10): 714–717.

Wall, Ariana E., and Patricia L. Kohl. 2007. "Substance Use in Maltreated Youth: Findings from the National Survey of Child and Adolescent Well-Being." *Child Maltreatment.* 12(1): 20–30.

"What Are Barbiturates?" 2015. Drug Laws. http://drugs.laws.com/barbiturates. Accessed on January 1, 2016.

"Where Are Teens Getting Prescription Drugs? The Search Starts at Home." 2015. Casco Bay CAN. http://www.cascobaycan.org/prescriptions.htm. Accessed on January 4, 2016.

White, Kristin, Molly Guard, and Stephen Arndt. 2011. "Comprehensive Substance Abuse Prevention Program Evaluation Report." Iowa City: Iowa Consortium for Substance Abuse Research and Evaluation. http://iconsortium.subst-abuse.uiowa.edu/downloads/IDPH/Comprehensive%20Prevention%20Project%20Evaluation%20Annual%20Report%202011.pdf. Accessed on January 7, 2016/

White, William L. 1998. *Slaying the Dragon: The History of Addiction Treatment and Recovery in America.* Bloomington, IL: Chestnut Health Systems/Lighthouse Institute.

Whitesell, Mackenzie, et al. 2013. "Familial, Social, and Individual Factors Contributing to Risk for Adolescent Substance Use." *Journal of Addiction*. 2013: 1–9.

"Why Benzo Withdrawal Syndrome Is Deadly." 2014. The Recovery Way. http://www.therecoveryway.com/ drug-abuse-facts/benzos-withdrawal-symptoms-can-deadly. Accessed on January 6, 2016.

Winters, Ken C., and Amelia Arria. 2011. "Adolescent Brain Development and Drugs." *Prevention Researcher*. 18(2): 21–24. Available online at http://www.ncbi.nlm.nih.gov/ pmc/articles/PMC3399589/. Accessed on January 4, 2016.

"World Drug Report 2012." 2012. Vienna: United Nations Office on Drugs and Crime. Available online at https:// www.unodc.org/documents/data-and-analysis/WDR2012/ WDR_2012_web_small.pdf. Accessed on December 23, 2015.

"World Drug Report 2015." 2015. Vienna: United Nations Office on Drugs and Crime. Available online at https:// www.unodc.org/documents/mexicoandcentralamerica/ eventos/2015/WDD2015/World_Drug_Report_2015.pdf. Accessed on December 23, 2015.

Yeh, Brian T. 2015. "Drug Offenses: Maximum Fines and Terms of Imprisonment for Violation of the Federal Controlled Substances Act and Related Laws." Congressional Research Service. https://www.fas.org/sgp/ crs/misc/RL30722.pdf. Accessed on December 31, 2015.

"Youth Risk Behavior Surveillance—United States, 2013." 2014. *Morbidity and Mortality Weekly*. 63(4): whole.

"Youth Tobacco Prevention." 2015. Centers for Disease Control and Prevention. http://www.cdc.gov/tobacco/basic_infor mation/youth/. Accessed on December 30, 2015.

Introduction

The topic of youth substance abuse has both an intellectual and academic aspect to it, as well as a very personal and emotional aspect. One can talk about demographics of substance abuse, the effects of psychoactive substances on the brain, procedures for prevention and treatment, and other important topics. But the fact is that substance abuse often has profound effects on the personal lives of friends, family, the community as a whole, and abusers themselves. This chapter provides individuals with an opportunity to write about both aspects of the youth substance abuse issue.

All Are Welcome to Change
Billy Beaton

Dying Ourselves

We were all doing homework on the floor when Ian got a call from work. We had to finish a group paper on the Steller sea lion but spent most of the night laughing over our attempts to remember its scientific name. Cats climbed over laptops and snow boots. Nintendo 64 was waiting when we were finished. I had only been close with this group of friends for a while, but already they had taught me much about being a compassionate member of our college community.

Teenage boys using a hookah pipe to ingest drugs. Hookahs are used in many cultures to injest tobacco, or shisha, but they are sometimes used for ingesting illicit drugs. (ktaylorg/iStockphoto.com)

Ian came back from the bedroom, phone in hand. Some-one had to cover our friend Alex's shift at the hotel tonight, he said. But he had to repeat himself before we understood—Alex wasn't going to be there because he was dead.

The feeling fell over us slowly. Shock blinded sadness, but horror was immediate. He was alone. He overdosed. He's gone. We each tried to remember the last time we heard Alex laugh, then realized we never would again.

I think we got the email from the university before Ian left for work. The president and his wife sent their thoughts and prayers with the curt news of Alex's death. It was the same tem-plate email they sent out a few weeks before, when another student died after an accidental house fire. Counselors would be available. Class would continue as scheduled.

At the University of North Dakota in Grand Forks (UND), there are few young people who don't know someone whose life has been impacted—or ended—by drug use. I went through high school in town and joined the ranks of those afflicted just a month after graduation, when Christian, the friendly football player I sat next to in English class, was found dead in the grass outside his parents' home.

The same week, 17-year-old Elijah overdosed in a similar way. He and his brother Justin ate chocolate they were told was cooked with psilocybin—the ingredient in psychedelic mush-rooms. But Justin later told police that when the effects began to kick in, he knew it was something else. By the time the ambulance arrived, he knew, too, that his brother was gone.

Autopsies later found that substances called NBOMe and powdered fentanyl were to blame for many of the recent over-dose deaths in town. These substances are cheaper to produce than hallucinogens like LSD, but since their effects are some-what similar, dealers often sell these extremely potent drugs as something safer and more marketable than what they really are. Often, dealers themselves don't even know what they're pushing.

When I returned home from my friends' house, our sea lion paper was nowhere near finished. Somewhere far away, Alex's family grieved. On campus, police scrambled to figure out how to keep us safe.

That night in bed, I didn't know what to dream, and I didn't dream at all. But in the morning I found a new email from university police, this time encouraging students to turn in their roommates for "unusual behavior" and to "keep (their) eyes open for such things as small pieces of tin foil (and) baggies." "(Due) to the nature of the way (designer drugs) are being obtained," campus police explained, "users cannot be certain of what substance(s) they are actually ingesting."

On this, the university is right. Many of the substances that have killed my classmates were bought online, by other young people who are now in prison for it. They didn't know what they had or how to use it safely—this is why overdose happens. But the university's emphasis on promoting fear and its recent investment in a police drug dog send conflicting messages. Are all welcome in Grand Forks? Or are a few personal decisions assumed to invalidate a student's right to sincere protection?

Three months after Alex died, so did my friend Evan. He, too, was alone. He, too, overdosed. He, too, is gone forever. Wondering after the fact if he should have been arrested does nothing to bring him back.

Testing Ourselves

It was dark inside the tent. Music and voices swirled outside, rolling down the hill toward the stage. Three of us huddled over a clean zip-seal bag in the lamplight. That's when a young man I'll call Roger showed me something I'd never known about. "I think I have some high quality MDMA," he said. "But we're going to test it to see if it's MDMA at all."

Zip. Click. Snap. He tapped the side of the bag with his thumb, gently holding a plastic test tube in his other hand. A tiny amount of white powder trickled to the bottom of the clear container. Closing the bag, he produced a small vial of yellow liquid.

Pop. Drip. Drip. Two drops slid along the inside of the tube. When it made contact with the powder, it bubbled, fizzed, and began to change color. He snapped the lid closed and flicked the side of the tube. When the reaction ended, I held the light closer.

Black.

"What does that mean?" I asked.

Roger grabbed the Bunk Police substance testing kit someone brought to the music festival I found myself at. Flipping it over, he studied the colorful diagram inside. "It's MDMA," he exclaimed. "I almost don't believe it."

Months later, I learned why he was so surprised. Far from the muffled excitement of that dim tent, at the University of Colorado Boulder, I met James. At the age of 19, James had gone to war as an army combat medic. Returning home with post-traumatic stress disorder, he sought every kind of treatment imaginable. Nothing helped. When it seemed all hope was gone, he found a military-sponsored treatment utilizing the psychoactive properties of the illegal party drug MDMA (or "Molly", "Ecstasy") to treat PTSD. "MDMA therapy helped give me my life back," James told me. "And now I want to give my life to spreading perspective on drugs."

That perspective is changing worldwide, and the new name of the drug use safety game is "harm reduction." But the concept goes far beyond making medicines available to those in need. It's about reducing the amount of dangerous situations that substance users, community members, and police officers are exposed to on a daily basis. It includes enforcement and detection but emphasizes education—not just of the health risks of using mind-altering substances, but of practical, empowering actions that directly reduce overdose and arrest rates.

Enter, the Psychedelic Club—a student organization James founded with a handful of friends at CU Boulder. At first, the group consisted of five like-minded classmates chatting beneath a tree in the campus garden. Today, more than 45 students attend their meetings every week—and that's just in Boulder. Chapters have been founded at four other universities, and with official support from MAPS—the world's largest scientific organization dedicated to researching psychedelic substances—the club is just beginning to have a serious impact on reducing harm at schools across the country.

Just one of the services they provide is easy access to free substance testing. Bring a $20 bill to a Psychedelic Club meeting, and leave with a Bunk Police test kit. Bring it back the next day, and your $20 is returned. Of those who used the Club's kits to test what they thought was MDMA last year, over 88 percent actually had meth.

That statistic is so horrifying, I must write it again—nearly 9 out of 10 students at CU Boulder bought methamphetamine from dealers who said they were selling them Molly. Others found bath salts in their Ecstasy. Another 40 percent of LSD tested with the Club's kits were actually research chemicals like NBOMe—the same stuff that's killing my classmates in North Dakota.

None can say if the testing prevented the university from having to send more death notice emails. But if someone you knew decided to try a powder, would you want them to know what's in it?

Empowering Ourselves

When I returned to North Dakota, my good friend Larry and I wrote an article in our student newspaper. We talked about substance testing. We explained the fatal weaknesses of our university's "abstinence-only" attitude. We expressed our love for those who are gone. Like many articles we've written in the student paper, it seemed to have no impact. Those who didn't know the kids who died still saw no problem. Those who did still saw no solution.

Then I met Cara. She's the one at UND responsible for calling the parents of students who die on campus, and she's done it way more than she wishes she's had to. As we agree, one call is too many.

I was in her office with a fellow student for an unrelated reason, when she caught me on the way out her door. "Do you have an extra minute?" I remember she asked me. "I'd like to know more about these substance testing kits you wrote about in the paper."

In my whole life growing up in Grand Forks, I would never have imagined that an adult like Cara in a position of influence would ever want to start a conversation with a student about substance use that didn't start and end with "just say no." To say the least I was surprised. As we continued talking, I realized the depth of her sincerity. "All are welcome," she told me. "That's the message we need to get across."

It was then Larry had an idea that would end up consuming a large part of our emotional lives. He emailed Frank—the coolest professor at UND (at least the only one I know with a bobblehead made in his image). Frank teaches "Drugs & Society" and dedicates himself to traveling up and down the Red River Valley talking to folks about harm reduction. To this day, I have met no other teacher with a more blatant selflessness than Frank.

We met in the student newspaper office. I told him about James and the Psychedelic Club, about their success uniting the student body with the administration and campus police. He felt the same and showed us how we might empower ourselves and rally our classmates. He spoke of other students, years ago, excited about the same idea of reducing harm at UND. But like those before them, they graduated, and their ideas disappeared with them into "the real world."

Not this time.

My friends and I guest-lectured in Frank's class a few weeks ago before winter break. We spoke for an hour and a half about those who are gone and what we can do to protect all those who remain. Immediately, we felt the impact of Frank's creation; more than a dozen of his students spoke to us after class about forming a chapter of the Psychedelic Club at UND. We have our first meeting in a couple weeks.

But we can't do it alone. Thankfully, we aren't. Our university is now open, unlike most, to being sincerely responsive to its student community's right to harm reduction. Cara has facilitated candid student discussions with administrators. Frank has given us the gift of self-inspiration. James drafted our new chapter's bylaws.

Meanwhile, Alex is gone. Christian is gone. Elijah is gone. Evan is gone. And so many others.

The moment after we students met with Cara together for the first time, I stepped out into the nighttime rain, thoughts swirling in my head rolling down the slippery street. I walked for 30 minutes along the length of University Avenue on my way home coming in from the cold. In this short time, I passed three different cars pulled over by police on campus. I didn't know if everybody in trouble deserved to be there. I didn't know how every officer were treating their fellow citizens. It felt, in fact, like I knew nothing at all.

As I passed the religious center, I stopped dead in the grass. White banners streamed in the evening breeze. Red, white, and blue police lights flashed across them with a frenzied energy. I'd seen these signs before but never paid enough attention to them.

"ALL ARE WELCOME," read one.

"CHANGE," read another.

That night in bed, I did know what to dream, and decided to dream all I could before it were all gone.

I'm Billy Beaton, a wildlife biology major at the University of North Dakota. The overwhelming passion of my friends and class-mates has helped us create change in our community, and with the support of our instructors we will continue to empower those around us to communicate that which matters to us all. Our web-site, SandbaggerNews.com, will become live later this year.

Technology and Nature Enable Ethanol Abuse
Joel Grossman

Why is it that kids get interested in alcohol relatively early in life? Is the attraction to alcohol some sort of fate residing in the stars, or is there an often-ignored intrinsic biological connection? Perhaps something primordial or prehistoric that left behind clues in the earliest days of human civilization. The ancients would no doubt have first looked to the heavens for answers.

As the new year dawned in 2015, Comet Lovejoy blazed brightly across the sky. Surprisingly, for a comet, it contained water and 5 percent ethanol (ethyl alcohol), the same intoxicating alcohol found in beer, wine, and hard beverages. Though the comet failed the breathalyzer test, this did not mean alien life forms drunkenly driving among the stars and planets. Ethanol forms naturally via pure physical chemistry in outer space. Indeed, an ethanol-laden molecular cloud called Sagittarius B2 lies in the center of our galaxy. Astrophysicists calculated that a distillery in Sagittarius B2 to separate out and condense ethanol would yield over an octillion (a 1 followed by 28 zeros) fifths of 200 proof alcohol; more than humans have fermented in Earth's history (Biver 2015; Zuckerman et al. 1975).

There is no way of completely avoiding ethanol. Rotting fruit ferments and produces ethanol, which may be how our ancestors first developed a taste for alcohol. Animals attracted to fermenting fruit further plant reproduction by spreading seeds. Green plants ferment ethanol inside leaves and roots. Pine, spruce, dogwood, and magnolia trees emit ethanol into the atmosphere when "stressed" (e.g., by drought or flooding), dying, or decaying. Pine beetles and ambrosia beetles attracted to ethanol hone in on weakened trees for the final kill. In other words, ethanol links plant and animal life.

Strangely, yeast and fungal microbes fermenting fruit and grain starch sugars into beer and wine are usually killed before ethanol concentrations reach 15 percent. This may make fermentation microbes the ultimate self-abusers, as they keep at it until poisoning themselves to death. It also makes high proof ethanol a good medical antiseptic or sanitizing weapon against microbes.

Other microbes transform ethanol into vinegar or acetic acid, useful for pickling; and also a controlled spoilage or food preservation process. "Fermentation was not invented, but rather discovered," writes the University of Georgia's Brian Nummer (Nummer 2002). "It not only could preserve foods, but it also created more nutritious foods and was used to create more palatable foods from less than desirable ingredients." For example, rotting bread grain was likely shunted into ancient beer breweries.

"Given the ancient and cosmopolitan reliance on fermented foods and the cultural inheritance of their use, I suggest that humans . . . first encountered high concentrations of ethanol through fermentation processes that were initially fostered for the purpose of food preservation," writes Douglas J. Levey (Levey 2004). "As they discovered the inebriating qualities of some fermented foods, they focused attention on those fermentative processes, ultimately leading to the beer and wine industries of today. . . . Addiction to ethanol may be analogous to addiction to caffeine, nicotine, heroin, or cocaine. All are secondary metabolites that humans have learned to concentrate and that provide a desired physiological response."

Distillation concentrates ethanol, making possible high proof spirits and faster ingestion of higher doses. Medieval monks in monasteries pioneered simple distillations to remove water from wines; boosting ethanol content for brandies, fruit liquors, and medicinal wines. The monks learned distillation techniques from alchemists, secretive "philosopher-chemists" who viewed distillation as a mystical, almost religious quest to obtain the pure spirit or essence of a substance.

Medieval wine distillates, called *aqua vitae* ("water of life") or the *fifth essence* (after earth, air, fire, and water), were more like prescription remedies, often fermented with herbs, like ancient Greek medicinal wines. Aqua vitae was not intended for social drinking, and mood elevation was considered a medicinal benefit. Monasteries of the period were healing centers with medicinal herb gardens, and providers of medical treatment for the poor, along with food, clothing, and other charity.

The Industrial Revolution marked the onset of mass production and consumption of high proof spirits. Political upheaval and revolutions put an end to monastery infirmaries dispensing aqua vitae. Medieval alchemy morphed into modern chemistry. The new idea was multiple or continuous distillation cycles to obtain higher concentrations of ethanol, which was deemed the true essence or spirit of the beverage.

An English naval blockade of imports into France was a catalyst. "Napoleon offered a prize for sugar beet production and fermentation to gain independence from British imports of sugar and alcohol," wrote Professor Norbert Kockmann (Kockmann 2014). "A series of patents on distillation equipment was issued from 1801 to 1818," including "the continuously working distillation patented by Jean-Baptiste Cellier-Blumenthal in 1813." This turned grape wine into purified ethanol, an exceptional solvent for extracting beet sugar as white as pure cane sugar. Plus distillation was economical, as ethanol was purified multiple times and reused. New and improved distillation columns soon enabled new industries and mass production of myriad high proof spirits. By 1873, Germany alone had over 16,000 working distilleries, including one producing a 60–80 percent alcohol potato brandy.

We lack statistics for comparing alcohol abuse by age group in different eras. Suffice it to say, the ancient Greek word "symposium" originally referred to drinking parties featuring intellectual discussions. The ancient world had myriad drinking, cooking, and medicinal wines fermented with Mediterranean herbs. Dioscorides, a founder of modern pharmacy, detailed the subject in his five-volume *De materia medica*.

"Dioscorides described alcoholism" in the first century CE, and cautioned that "one should not drink to the point of inebriation because all drunkenness was harmful, most especially that which was continuous," said medical historian John M. Riddle (Riddle 1985). "There is an exception to the rule about drunkenness: to be moderately drunk for several days can, in some circumstances, actually be helpful because it improves the inner state of the person, purges vapors that annoy the senses, and opens up the pores. If one resorts to this therapy, Dioscorides cautioned, one should drink much water while drinking alcohol and continue to take in water while detoxifying." Clearly, ethanol abuse was a feature of ancient Greek and Roman life.

There is no escape from ethanol, not even in outer space. Human wisdom and détente with the ethanol molecule is the only option.

References

Biver, Nicolas, et al. 2015. "Ethyl Alcohol and Sugar in Comet C/2014 Q2 (Lovejoy)." *Science Advances.* 1(9): e1500863.

Kockmann, Norbert. 2014. "200 Years in Innovation of Continuous Distillation." *ChemBioEng Reviews.* 1(1): 40–49.

Levey, Douglas J. 2004. "The Evolutionary Ecology of Ethanol Production and Alcoholism." *Integrative and Comparative Biology.* 44(4): 284–289.

Nummer, Brian A. 2002. "Historical Origins of Food Preservation." National Center for Home Food Preservation. http://nchfp.uga.edu/publications/nchfp/factsheets/food_pres_hist.html

Riddle, John M. 1985. *Dioscorides on Pharmacy and Medicine.* Austin: University of Texas Press.

Zuckerman, B., et al. 1975. "Detection of Interstellar Trans-Ethyl Alcohol." *The Astrophysical Journal.* 196: L99–L102.

Joel Grossman is a freelance writer and book editor. Read his Biocontrol Beat blog on WordPress.com.

E-Cigarette Vapor versus Cigarette Smoke: Is Vapor Really Safer?
Amber Henning

Electronic cigarettes have gained popularity more rapidly than almost any other contemporary consumer product on the market. The rise in this popularity has been attributed in large part to the claim that e-cigarettes might be able to help one quit smoking while providing a healthier alternative to the traditional form of smoking tobacco.

However, as such a new product on the market, no one can really be sure what the long-term effects of the electronic versions will be. That is the reason that several researchers across the world are working hard to clear up the mystery surrounding the health effects of inhaling e-cigarette vapor.

Researchers in England have been at the forefront of e-cigarette studies that are often considered a benchmark for the industry. Public Health England published an expert independent evidence review in 2015 that purported to show that e-cigarettes are as much as 95 percent less harmful than their combustible predecessors (McNeill 2015).

This was not the first time that researchers made claims of this nature. In fact, research has been piling up that e-cigarette vapor is much less harmful than cigarette smoke, a result that is coming from a variety of sources. Other prominent e-cigarette researchers, such as Robert West and Jamie Brown, outlined the potential benefits of e-cigarettes, stating that e-cigarette vapor contained far less toxins, in fact only about 1/20th that one would find in regular cigarettes (Brown and West 2014).

A 2015 study also made similar comparisons, examining how e-cigarette vapor compared not just with smoke, but also with ambient, indoor air, exhaled tobacco smoke, and regular exhaled breath. The researchers accomplished the comparison by measuring the levels of 156 different volatile organic compounds (VOCs). The researchers tested two e-cigarettes and found 25 VOCs in the vapor of one model and 17 VOCs in the other. Compared to all other kinds of air measured, e-cigarette vapor contained less of these potentially volatile compounds. Normal exhaled breath tested for 36 VOCs, while indoor air tested at 42 VOCs (Marco et al. 2015).

While it seems surprising that e-cigarette vapor contains less VOCs than the regular air one breathes, what is not a shock is how much safer they appear than regular cigarettes, where the smoke measures an astounding 86 VOCs. While not all VOCs are toxic, measuring their levels helps paints a clear picture that e-cigarette emissions really could be much safer than regular tobacco smoke.

A 2014 study also attempted to shed light on the nature of e-cigarette vapor by measuring harmful and potentially harmful constituents, otherwise referred to as HPHCs. They weighed the content of eight HPHCs, to determine the quantity in e-cigarette vapor, as well as ambient air and cigarette smoke.

The weight of the combined HPHCs in the sample size of e-cigarette vapor was recorded at less than 0.17 milligrams. The same researchers also determined that ambient air, which one breathes every day, has a comparable 0.16 milligrams of HPHCs. Again, cigarette smoke produced a staggering amount of HPHCs that measure at an average of 30.6 milligrams of HPHCs. The researchers even state that cigarette smoke "delivered approximately 1500 times more harmful and potentially harmful constituents tested" than the emissions from an e-cigarette aerosol or to the standing air in the room (Tayarah et al. 2014).

Even though the majority of the research appears to be leaning in the direction of e-cigarettes being a safer alternative to smoking, the truth is there is still so much to learn about e-cigarette vapor and, most importantly, its long-term effects.

While e-cigarette vapor does seem to be less harmful than cigarette smoke, there is still question if there is some genuine potential for e-cigarettes to do a certain kind of harm of their own. Since e-cigarettes only first hit the market back in 2007 and 2008, there simply is not the kind of evidence available to support any claims that e-cigarettes could be good, or bad for users in the long-term sense. In addition, many who start using e-cigarettes either discontinue or greatly reduce their nicotine intake along the way, making it even more difficult to gauge long-term effects.

Another area of concern is the addictive nature of nicotine in general. Most e-cigarettes, although not all, do contain some amount of nicotine. Nicotine's addictive qualities make any item that contains nicotine, even those designed for smoking cessation purposes, a potential hazard for users who have struggled with a nicotine addiction. E-liquids used in e-cigarette devices, however, do come in varying nicotine strengths, giving the user the ability to taper off their intake and hopefully curb their addiction altogether.

Everyone wants an easy solution to the cigarette problem, but that simply does not exist. What we can hope is that all the evidence we are receiving is an indicator of the real long-term effect, if there is any at all, from using electronic cigarettes. What we are seeing now, in these studies and many others, is a promising glimpse—that perhaps these e-cigarette devices can provide users with an experience that is close enough to smoking, yet one that is far less dangerous, both to themselves and to others.

References

Brown, R., and J. West. 2014. "E-Cigarettes: Facts and Faction." *British Journal of General Practice.* http://bjgp.org/content/64/626/442.full. Accessed on January 26, 2016.

Marco, E., et al. 2015. "A Rapid Method for the Chromatographic Analysis of Volatile Organic Compounds in Exhaled Breath of Tobacco Cigarette and Electronic Cigarette Smokers." *Journal of Chromatography A.* http://www.sciencedirect.com/science/article/pii/S0021967315010821. Accessed on January 25, 2016.

McNeill, A., et al. 2015. "E-cigarettes: An Evidence Update — A Report Commissioned by Public Health England." Public Health England. https://www.gov.uk/government/uploads/system/uploads/attachment_data/file/457102/Ecigarettes_an_evidence_update_A_report_commissioned_by_Public_Health_England_FINAL.pdf. Accessed on January 26, 2016.

Tayarah, R., et al. 2014. "Comparison of Select Analytes in Aerosol from E-cigarettes with Smoke from Conventional Cigarettes and with Ambient Air." Regulatory Toxicology and Pharmacology. http://www.sciencedirect.com/science/article/pii/S0273230014002505. Accessed on January 25, 2016.

Amber Henning is a freelance writer and editor who is passionate about reporting and researching the truth behind the topics she covers. She holds a bachelor's degree in English and has extensive experience covering the scientific and consumer research behind e-cigarettes, as well as several other health and wellness topics.

The Use of Neurofeedback in Treating Substance Use Disorders in Adolescents
Wanda K. Holloway

Neurofeedback is a neurophysiological clinical intervention that has been used as an alternative technique in the treatment of substance use disorders (SUD), primarily with adults. Although its implications for adolescents are promising, they have not yet been well established or validated. It is an intriguing treatment that has been used for many decades in an effort to regulate the brain in the areas of sleep, emotions, thinking, behaviors, and much more. When an individual is "over-regulated," his or her brain begins to function at a faster pace, creating less impulse control and thus resulting in the inability to modulate emotions, which further intensifies poor decision making. When conducting neurofeedback, also known as brainwave biofeedback or EEG (electroencephalograph) biofeedback, electrodes are placed on the scalp at specific sites identified by the technician using the 10–20 system of placement. The placement of electrodes known as the 10–20 International System of Electrode Placement refers to five key regions of the brain: Frontal (F), Central (C), Temporal (T),

Parietal (P), and Occipital (O). Odd numbers refer to the left hemispheric sites and even numbers to right hemispheric sites. The term "10–20" refers to the placement of electrodes placed 10 percent or 20 percent of the total distance between brain sites. Brainwaves are then displayed on a computer monitor with the goal being the manipulation of the patient's brainwaves through the use of audio-visual feedback, thus informing patients of their success in making changes in brainwaves which results in changes in their physiological system as well.

Goal of Neurofeedback

The goal of neurofeedback is regulation of brainwaves using the slow-wave frequency of alpha-theta training, with either eyes open or eyes closed methods. The alpha wave (8–13 Hz) is indicative of focused relaxation and attentiveness to particular stimuli or visualizations without drowsiness. The theta wave (4–8 Hz) is even slower and is typically seen as a precursor to sleep, but the challenge is to remain deeply relaxed without lapsing into sleep. The goal of beta training is to focus on "down-training" this high-wave frequency and reduce over-stimulation, anxiety, and hyperarousal and encourage an attentive, alert awareness that enhances concentration, attention, motivation, and task completion. Delta training (2–4 Hz) can also be practiced when the goal is the deactivation of high brain-wave activity or overstimulation and focuses instead on the approach to deeper levels of relaxation leading to a restful and restorative level of sleep. Sensory Motor Rhythm (SMR) training (12–15 Hz) is utilized when more specialized training is the goal which can lead to higher levels of attention and concentration, can reduce impulsivity, and can increase performance and productivity.

Research in Neurofeedback

In a 2007 study, the principal investigator William C. Scott reported that "across the country, drug rehab programs have generally achieved a success rate of 20 to 30 percent in relapse prevention one to two years following treatment. In [his] current study, in excess of 50% of experimental subjects remained drug-free a year later." His study involved the use of neurofeedback to teach subjects to control their brainwaves. Scott further stated, "Beyond the scientific implications of this study, which are exciting, the real significance is the hope it offers addicts, their families and our communities. For those who have tried and failed, here is a result that says, 'try again, there are new possibilities.' For families and communities, it's another opportunity to free ourselves from the specter of drugs." In the same study David A. Kaiser, PhD, experimental psychologist who designed the study, noted that "this work complements earlier findings on the efficiency of Neurofeedback in aiding recovery among severe alcoholics, but the present study extends it to opiate abusers, multiple-drug abusers, and users of stimulant-type medications such as methamphetamine and cocaine" (Kaiser and Scott 2007). Further studies have explored the use of neurofeedback for opiate addiction and reported, "Results of this study suggest neurofeedback training may produce additional benefits for increasing mental health in patients addicted to opiates, as well as being feasibly integrated with other methods" (Dehghani-Arani, Rostami, and Nadali 2013). David L. Troudeau noted in *Emerging Brain-Based Interventions for Children and Adolescents* that "neurofeedback is promising as a treatment modality for adolescents, especially those with stimulant abuse and attention and conduct problems. It is attractive as a medication-free, neurophysiologic, and self-actualizing treatment for substance-based, brain-impaired and self-defeating disorder" (Hirshberg, Chiu, and Frazier 2005).

There have been two protocols developed in treating SUD with neurofeedback, the initial being the Peniston Protocol. This is a multimodal intervention integrating alpha-theta neurofeedback, thermal biofeedback, diaphragmatic breathing, autogenic training, emotional catharsis, and guided imagery and visualization. This approach employed independent auditory feedback of two slow brain wave frequencies, alpha (8–13 Hz) and theta (4–8 Hz) in an eyes-closed condition to produce a hypnagogic state. Prior to neurofeedback, the patient was taught to use visualizations that included success imagery (being sober, refusing offers of alcohol, living confidently, and being happy) as they drifted down into an alpha-theta state. Repeated sessions reportedly result in longer-term abstinence and changes in personality testing. An additional approach modified from the Peniston Protocol (Scott-Kaiser modification of the Peniston Protocol) takes into consideration the inability of patients to tolerate over-stimulation too early in the withdrawal process, and has been specifically researched with cannabis and stimulant dependence populations. This protocol involves the use of attention-deficit EEG biofeedback protocols followed by the Peniston Protocol, with substantial improvement in program retention and long-term abstinence rates (Sokhadze, Cannon, and Troudeau 2008).

Research has also elucidated phenotypes in the treatment of addiction. Jay Gunkelman and Curtis Cripe evaluated this distinction and emphasized the identification of "phenotypes" in the treatment of addiction and stated, "The diagnosis of addiction is behavior based, yet current research shows that addictions have a biological base and that this basis has a genetic component." In conclusion the authors stated, "This study is intended to add to the biopsychosocial model the understanding that pheno-type based neurofeedback, done in combination with targeted brain recovery exercises, forms the basis for a tool to assist addiction-related recovery" (Gunkelman and Cripe 2008).

A study conducted by Scott, Kaiser, Othmer and Sideroff in 2005 revealed the following, "The present study employed a Beta-SMR protocol to the alpha-theta protocol previously used in addiction studies. Beta-SMR training previously had been shown to be effective in remediating attentional and cognitive deficits. . . . Testing following the Beta-SMR protocol showed that this procedure improved these test measures for experimental subjects, particularly impulsivity and variability. This result may partly account for the improved treatment retention of this group" (Scott, Kaiser, Othmer and Sideroff 2005).

In conclusion, neurofeedback is an innovative and exciting treatment that is intended to complement other forms of treatment in the SUD population, including medication management, counseling and psychotherapy, 12-step programs, and meditation and relaxation techniques and should be a consideration to enhance long-term successful treatment outcomes for adolescents.

References

Dehghani-Arani, F., R. Rostami, and H. Nadali. 2013. "Neurofeedback Training for Opiate Addiction: Improvement of Mental Health and Craving." *Applied Psychophysiology and Biofeedback*. 38 (2): 133–141.

Gunkelman, J. and C. Cripe. 2008. "Clinical Outcomes in Addiction: A Neurofeedback Case Series." *Biofeedback*. 36(4). 152–156.

Hirshberg, L. M., S. Chiu, and J. Frazier. 2005. "Emerging Brain-Based Interventions for Children and Adolescents: Overview and Clinical Perspective." *Child and Adolescent Psychiatric Clinics of North America*. January 14. 1–19.

Kaiser, D. A., and W. Scott. 2007. "Effect of EEG Biofeedback on Chemical Dependency." www.EEG Info .com. Accessed on January 21, 2016.

Scott, W. C., et al. 2005. "Effects of an EEG Biofeedback Protocol on a Mixed Substance Abusing Population." *American Journal of Drug Alcohol Abuse*. 31(3). 455–469.

Sokhadze, Tato M., R. L. Cannon, and D. L. Troudeau. 2008. "EEG Biofeedback as a Treatment for Substance Use Disorders: Review, Rating of Efficacy, and Recommendation for Further Research." *Applied Psychophysiology Biofeedback*. 33:1–28.

Wanda K. Holloway, PsyD, LPC, CASAC, LCSW, BCB, EMDR Certified, graduated from Forest Institute of Professional Psychology with a Doctor of Psychology. Dr. Holloway is also a licensed professional counselor, certified advanced substance abuse counselor, licensed clinical social worker, certified forensics addictions examiner, and is Board certified in biofeedback and certified in EMDR. She is an outpatient counselor at Burrell Behavioral Health, a large community mental health facility located in the heart of the Ozarks in Springfield, Missouri. She specializes in addictive disorders, eating disorders and obesity, trauma and bio/neurofeedback.

The Demographics of Heroin Abuse Have Shifted Dramatically
Ashley Rekem

In the 1960s heroin abusers were primarily young minority men in cities whose opioid abuse began with heroin, but this stereotypical image of a heroin addict has long been outdated. Today, heroin users are typically older, white, and living in nonurban areas, whose abuse started with prescription for opioid painkillers (Cicero et al. 2014). What is behind the dramatic shift in the demographic of heroin users over the past few decades?

Traditionally, opioids were used largely to treat pain caused by terminal diseases, or in the short term for acute pain, such as after surgery. Starting with Oxycontin in the mid-1990s, the Food and Drug Administration approved numerous opioid medicines and doctors began to accept them as treatments for all kinds of afflictions from back pain to cancer (Cicero et al. 2014). According to the Centers for Disease Control and Prevention (CDC), "Health care providers wrote 259 million prescriptions for painkillers in 2012, enough for every American adult to have a bottle of pills" (CDC 2014).

What is now considered to be overprescribing of this class of drugs contributed in large part to the current opioid addiction crisis (Cicero et al. 2014). "Given that prescription opioids are legal, prescribed by a physician, and thus considered trustworthy and predictable (e.g., the dose is clearly specified on a distinctive tablet or pill), many users viewed these drugs as safer to use than other illicit substances," writes Theodore Cicero, a professor of neuropharmacology at Washington University, in *The Journal of the American Medical Association*. Imagine a suburban mother, an unlikely candidate for drug addiction, going to the doctor complaining of back pain, and months later finding herself addicted to opioids.

An addiction to opioid painkillers is powerfully consuming and poses a unique difficulty in that prescriptions are required to maintain it. Some people found their way to "pill mills"—doctors and clinics more than willing to prescribe continuous rounds of narcotics. Patients who become addicted also have taken to shopping around for new doctors to get these prescriptions, and some have resorted to other means to obtain their high, especially in areas where governments and healthcare providers have tried to curtail narcotic access.

In a study by Cicero et al. (2014), most subjects reported switching to heroin because prescription opioids were harder to obtain and much more expensive. The heroin fix is comparable since it essentially has the same active ingredients as prescription opioids. One survey respondent stated that "heroin is cheaper and stronger than prescription drugs and that the supply is typically pretty consistent. It is also much easier to use intravenously than pills and other prescriptions, which often take more complex methods to break down." Prescription opioids primed people for heroin addiction, and have become the major contributor to heroin initiation (Cicero et al. 2014).

Prescription opioids directed heroin initiation in demographics that have historically had lower rates of heroin use. Today, heroin users tend to be 18–25 years old (CDC 2015). Heroin use has more than doubled among whites, and while men still lead, women aren't far behind. The CDC found, in its recent study of the demographics of heroin abuse from 2002 to 2013, that heroin abuse in women doubled (CDC 2015). The rate of people abusing heroin doubled with a 35.7 percent increase from 2008 to 2010 alone, and this increase paralleled the increase in heroin-related overdose deaths reported since 2010 (CDC 2015). Some 8,200 Americans died of heroin overdoses in 2013 alone (CDC 2015).

The rise of heroin use in whites of rural and suburban America has not stopped short in reaching teenagers. Those aged 12 to 17 years comprise about one quarter of the total population of those with opioid addiction (CDC 2015). While the gateway drugs have been thought to be marijuana and alcohol, a recent New York University study found that three-fourths of high school heroin users are starting with prescription opioids (Palamar 2015). Gaining access to their parents' medicine cabinets, teens are starting to experiment with opioid painkillers like Oxycontin, Percocet, and Vicodin (Palamar 2015). Teens may think they're safe because they're government approved, pharmaceutical grade drugs. They may take opioid pills a couple of times and go unharmed, but many don't realize these pills can be physically addicting (Palamar 2015). Ultimately, a recreational habit becomes a dangerous, full-blown opioid addiction that can quickly transition to heroin addiction.

In *California Watch*'s documentary "Suburban Junkies" about teenage heroin abuse in Orange County, California, one teen explained how he gained access to opioid painkillers through his cancer-stricken grandfather's home. He soon realized that he could obtain the same high through heroin much more cheaply: "I was doing six to seven [pills] a day. It was getting so expensive and I said, I could sell these for like fifty bucks and go buy a gram. One gram of heroin is the price of one pill, and a gram of heroin could last you three or four days. One pill could last you a couple hours," he recounted (Suburban Junkies 2012).

It's certainly time to put aside stereotypes about who's shooting up heroin. The new whiter, more middle-class demographics of heroin abuse have helped change the conversation about drugs in America—galvanizing the drug reform movement's pursuit of treatment-based approaches in lieu of sending drug users to jail and prison.

References

Cicero, Theodore J., et al. 2014. "The Changing Face of Heroin Use in the United States: A Retrospective Analysis of the Past 50 Years." *JAMA Psychiatry*. 71(7): 821–826. Also available online at http://archpsyc.jamanetwork.com/ article.aspx?articleid=1874575.. Accessed on January 5, 2016.

Palamar, Joseph J., et al. 2015. "Nonmedical Opioid Use and Heroin Use in a Nationally Representative Sample of US High School Seniors." *Drug and Alcohol Dependence* 158(8): 132–138. Also available online at http://www .drugandalcoholdependence.com/article/S0376–8716(15) 01747–0/fulltext Accessed on December 15th, 2015.

"Suburban Junkies." 2012. *California Watch.* http://california watch.org/health-and-welfare/ rise-young-painkiller-abuser s-officials-see-more-heroin-overdoses-17550. Accessed on December 15, 2015.

Ashley Rekem has a bachelor's degree in biology from the University of California, Berkeley. Now living and studying in Maine, she writes the Chronic Conditions blog for the Bangor Daily News, *focusing on healthcare and food as medicine.*

The Etiology of Intravenous Heroin Use in Adolescent Girls
Clariza Saint George

Contemporary research has revealed an increase in social and economic problems for female heroin users. The current trend of substance abuse within the adolescent population has been steadily increasing since 1992 and continues today (Eaves 2004; Pugatch et al. 2001). A recent study found 68.75 percent of female participants were introduced to heroin through a male friend or boyfriend, and females are more likely to start using heroin if their romantic partner is currently using (Eaves 2004; Subramaniam and Stitzer 2009). The four sources for the increased use of heroin among adolescents have been identified as: its lower cost and increased availability, drug purity, and the misbelief of the consequences of heroin use (Lambie and Davis 2007; Pugatch et al. 2001). Individuals who snort heroin are more likely to move onto intravenous (henceforth, IV) use of this particular drug. The progression of use of highly addictive substances, such as heroin, by adolescents and emerging adults has been identified as: (1) drinking alcohol; (2) smoking cigarettes; (3) smoking marijuana; and (4) the use of hard narcotics, such as heroin or cocaine (Arnett 2013, 362–391; Subramaniam and Stitzer 2009). Finally, peer influence has contributed to the high rates of addiction within the adolescent population (Pugatch et al. 2001). The available literature surrounding heroin use neglects to acknowledge gender differences between heroin addicts, is outdated, and fails to address current drug trends within the adolescents and emerging adult population.

The gender differences between male and female heroin users range from first-use to intake methods. Female users are more likely to use the drug intravenously, engage in risk-taking behavior, and use the drug more often when compared to their male counterparts (Eaves 2004; Hölscher et al. 2009). The increase of risk-taking behaviors is often manifested as using needles after another injector, sharing needles with a sex partner, and engaging in sexual activities with more than one person when compared to men and similarly aged non-using females (Eaves 2004). Finally, the speed of use to addiction is faster for females: one study revealed that 46.5 percent of women compared to 22.4 percent of men self-reported their onset of addiction within the first three months of heroin use (Eaves 2004).

This progression of heroin use suggests a deeper problem for adolescent girls; although no direct connection has been made to addiction and childhood neglect, recent studies have found that female drug users report poor relationships with their fathers who were often uninvolved or absent (Eaves 2004). Eaves (2004) speculates that females who were introduced to heroin via a male figure are trying to compensate for the lack of a father figure during their developmental years. The impact of a user's childhood on their propensity for substance abuse is a field that needs further exploration, although current studies reflect a causal effect between childhood trauma and/or neglect and future substance abuse (Eaves 2004; Hölscher et al. 2009). Finally, female heroin users are more likely to be diagnosed with psychiatric conditions when compared to male users (Hopfer et al. 2002; Lambie and Davis 2007; Subramaniam and Stitzer 2009). Numerous psychiatric disorders were found in both heroin and prescription opioid users: clinical depression, major depressive episodes and generalized anxiety disorder being the most prevalent; these individuals reported using their "drug of choice" to self-medicate and as a way of managing their emotional and psychological anguish (Hopfer et al. 2002; Lambie and Davis 2007; Subramaniam and Stitzer 2009).

The available body of literature discussing heroin use and adolescent females is considerably lacking. Current literature neglects to address gender differences within addicts and primarily emphasizes the deviant aspect of addiction such as incarceration. The potential causal relationship between childhood trauma and neglect experienced by a female heroin user needs further review. In order to address the epidemic of addiction, exploration of this phenomenon needs to be examined.

References

Arnett, J. J. 2013. *Adolescence and Emerging Adulthood: A Cultural Approach*, 5th ed. Upper Saddle River, NJ: Pearson Prentice Hall.

Eaves, C. 2004. "Heroin Use among Female Adolescents: The Role of Partner Influence in Path of Initiation and Route of Administration." *The American Journal of Drug and Alcohol Abuse*. 30(1): 21–38.

Hölscher, F., et al. 2009. "Differences between Men and Women in the Course of Opiate Dependence: Is There a Telescoping Effect?" *European Archives of Psychiatry and Clinical Neuroscience*. 160: 235–241.

Hopfer, C., et al. 2002. "Adolescent Heroin Use: A Review of the Descriptive and Treatment Literature." *Journal of Substance Abuse Treatment*. 23(3): 231–237.

Lambie, G. W., and K. M. Davis 2007. "Adolescent Heroin Abuse: Implications for the Consulting Professional School Counselor." *Journal of Professional Counseling: Practice, Theory, and Research*. 35(1): 1–17.

Pugatch, D., et al. 2001. "Heroin Use in Adolescents and Young Adults Admitted for Drug Detoxification." *Journal of Substance Abuse*. 13(3): 337–346.

Subramaniam, G. A., and M. A. Stitzer. 2009. "Clinical Characteristics of Treatment-Seeking Prescription Opioid vs Heroin-Using Adolescents with Opioid Use Disorder." *Drug and Alcohol Dependence*. 101(1–2): 13–19.

Clariza Saint George currently works with survivors of sexual violence at Rape Victim Advocates in Chicago, Illinois. Her professional and academic work is focused on interpersonal violence and addiction studies. She is an A.M. candidate at the University of Chicago and earned her BA in psychology from Northeastern Illinois University.

Enhancing Motivation for Therapy: The Importance of the Therapeutic Relationship
Nicole Sciarrino

The therapeutic relationship is often associated with enhancing motivation to change and involves listening, having empathy, and being collaborative and accepting among other facets (Norcross 2010). As a member of a peer group of other teenagers using drugs and alcohol, a desire to seek treatment may not often present due to the normalizing quality of friends who are also using substances. Consequently, when compared to adults, teenagers are less likely to seek treatment for substance use voluntarily (Melnick, De Leon, Hawke, Jainchill, and Kressel 1997). Moreover, per clinical observations in a community mental health program for adolescents seeking therapy for drug and alcohol treatment, the majority of teenagers presenting for therapy do so to appease some external source (e.g., parents, school administration, legal authorities). Therefore, given the external pressures associated with the circumstances surrounding therapy, it is understandable how a strong therapeutic relationship might benefit treatment outcome.

In addition, it seems that there is an assumption that entering a "substance abuse" program denotes that the primary focus of treatment must be abstinence from that substance (i.e., discontinuation of usage). The difficulty here is that substance use often co-occurs with other disorders, such as depression, anxiety, or other psychological difficulties (American Psychiatric Association 2013), as well as problems within the family of origin and peer group. Subsequently, substance use often becomes a form of self-medication and a way of coping with the aforementioned concurrent difficulties. For therapy to concentrate on eliminating substance use would be to overlook other present and underlying issues. Additionally, early therapeutic interventions targeted at drug-related behaviors may undermine the therapeutic relationship depending on the teenager's goals in therapy.

The therapeutic relationship should institute a collaborative process, in which the teenager seeking treatment is directive and actively contributes and agrees upon goals set in therapy (Norcross 2010), for which the client should rank order. In providing the teenager with the freedom to guide the therapeutic process, the initial stages may address daily stressors and ongoing difficulties that the teenager is experiencing, not necessarily substance use. However, this process enhances the therapeutic relationship, thereby impacting the motivation to change. For example, a 17-year-old Caucasian female was referred to treatment by her parents, after having fallen asleep in class due to her recreational use of benzodiazepines. In addition to experimenting with benzodiazepines, the client was a regular cannabis user and presented with persistent depressive disorder. Per the client's report, she did not fit the stereotypical image of an "addict" and did not see her usage as a problem. It became apparent that focusing on reducing and eliminating substance use would be unproductive for therapy and would hinder the development of the therapeutic relationship. Therefore, the therapeutic relationship became fundamental to the process of eliciting change. During her next individual session, the client was asked what she would like to accomplish in session that day. She expressed a desire to reduce the presence of depressive symptoms.

The next three months of therapy implemented interventions aimed at increasing behavioral activation, self-esteem, and emotion regulation. She was forthcoming and attended all scheduled sessions. Further, she successfully maintained long periods of abstinence, as evidenced by self-report and results of urinalysis. In this example, exhibiting empathy for the client's other difficulties and allowing her to learn coping skills for more troubling mental health problems (i.e., depression) allowed her to explore the role that the substance played in coping with daily stressors and maintained other presenting problems.

Employing a motivational interviewing style while establishing the relationship is a commonly used approach that allows individuals to examine the evidence and consequences of their behaviors in a nonjudgmental way, and provides an opportunity for them to arrive at their own conclusions (e.g., Carroll, Libby, Sheehan, and Hyland 2001). This approach facilitates in generating more reasons to stop using and can be accomplished through techniques, such as decisional balance and scaling.

Psychoeducation may also be advantageous by dispelling myths that teenagers possess regarding substances. For example, many teenagers report that they feel more social and outgoing while under the influence of alcohol; however, it is well established that alcohol is a depressant and that long-term use contributes to the presence or exacerbation of depressed mood.

Taken together, teenagers are in a unique situation where they are not always able to remove themselves from people, places, and things that may contribute to urges to use. This may have negative implications for their ability to manage certain stressors, such as family dysfunction or peer difficulties. Although the presence of external pressures may not negatively impact the therapeutic relationship, teenagers who report more reasons for wanting to stop using drugs exhibit better relationships with their therapist (Garner, Godley, and Funk 2008). Research demonstrates the importance of the therapeutic relationship on long-term gains, over and above specific interventions (Norcross 2010). Interventions specifically targeting substances may not be the only way to see improvements in drug-related behaviors. Therefore, the use of a collaborative relationship can facilitate cooperation and enhance motivation for therapy.

References

American Psychiatric Association. 2013. *Diagnostic and Statistical Manual of Mental Disorders*, Fifth Edition, DSM-5.

Carroll, K. M., et al. 2001. "Motivational Interviewing to Enhance Treatment Initiation in Substance Abusers: An Effectiveness Study." *American Journal of Addiction*. 10(4): 335–339.

Garner, B. R., S. H. Godley, and R. R. Funk. 2008. "Predictors of Early Therapeutic Alliance among Adolescents in Substance Abuse Treatment." *Journal of Psychoactive Drugs*. 40(1): 55–65.

Melnick, G., et al. 1997. "Motivation and Readiness for Therapeutic Community Treatment among Adolescents and Adult Substance Abusers." *The American Journal of Drug and Alcohol Abuse*. 23(4): 485–506.

Norcross, J.C. 2010. "The Therapeutic Relationship." In Duncan, B.L., et al., eds. *The Heart and Soul of Change: Delivering What Works in Therapy*. Washington, D.C: APA.

Nicole Sciarrino is a third-year doctoral psychology trainee at Nova Southeastern University (NSU) in Fort Lauderdale, Florida, pursuing a specialization in the program's Trauma Track. In the three years prior to beginning her studies at NSU, she became a certified alcohol and substance abuse counselor (CASAC) in New York State and worked in an outpatient substance use facility where she performed individual and group therapy treatment interventions with an urban population. More recently, Ms. Sciarrino has been working as the clinic coordinator for the Adolescent Drug Abuse Prevention and Treatment (ADAPT) Program and the research coordinator for the Trauma Resolution Integration Program (TRIP) at NSU.

The Myth of the Drug-Habit: Defining Addiction as a Disease
Bryan F. Singer

The *Merriam-Webster* dictionary defines disease as "a condition that prevents the body or mind from working normally" and addiction as a "compulsive need for and use of a habit-forming substance" (*Merriam-Webster Online Dictionary* 2016). In contrast, depression is "a serious medical condition in which a person feels very sad, hopeless, and unimportant and often is unable to live in a normal way." The dictionary makes it clear that depression is a disease. Concerning addiction, it's a bit ambiguous, even though drug abuse prevents the "body or mind from working normally." We need to stop talking about drug abuse as simply a bad habit, and instead start discussing how to treat and prevent addiction as an illness.

How do we change this perception? First, people need to know that addiction, similar to other mental illnesses, often has a partial genetic basis. Not everyone who experiments with drugs becomes an addict, and whether or not a person continues to abuse drugs is dependent on genetics approximately 50 percent of the time. DNA works in combination with environmental factors to alter our susceptibility to addiction. Twin studies are a great example of this: while identical twins who share genetic makeup are much more likely to become addicted to alcohol than non-identical (fraternal) twins, there is still no guarantee that they will become addicts (Enoch and Goldman 2001; Prescott and Kindler 1999). Genes for addiction make us susceptible, but do not pre-determine our fate.

A variety of genes, often in complex combinations, contribute to addiction vulnerability. Genes linked to alcoholism may be different from genes that influence smoking. Importantly, one of many reasons people abuse drugs is for self-medication purposes. A person who has depression may be more likely to abuse alcohol. Not surprisingly these two diseases are thought to share some molecular and genetic underpinnings (Kendler et al. 1995; Plemenitas et al. 2015; Wiers et al. 2015). Treating each of these illnesses individually or in combination (e.g., naltrexone for alcoholism and/or SSRIs for depression) may improve the patient's health.

People sometimes argue that addiction is not a disease because some of the changes that drugs cause in the brain also occur in a healthy individual. Certain regions of the brain are involved in learning, and the brain uses specific proteins and molecules to help us form and retain memories. But healthy memories tend to be different from drug memories. Remembering the act of taking a drug, as well as the sensations associated with drug use, can stir up emotions and evoke an insatiable drive to obtain and consume drugs. A particular chemical messenger in the brain, dopamine, is partially responsible for this. Through unnaturally magnifying dopamine levels in the brain, both drugs and drug-related stimuli initiate craving. By communicating to us via dopamine, addictive substances "bully" people into pursuing drugs, encouraging individuals to obtain them even if it involves performing dangerous behaviors. The loss of control over our actions is a hallmark of the disease.

Drug memories are also long-lasting and difficult to forget; even if an addict is clean for years, memories of drug use may linger. This attribute of memory increases the probability someone will relapse into drug-taking, even after periods of abstinence. Indeed, permanent changes in brain structure, function, and connectivity are visible in individuals who have abused drugs (Seo et al. 2016). So, for a healthy person the sight of a spoon might suggest soup is for dinner, but for someone who previously used crack, seeing the spoon may motivate them to cook and smoke. The spoon does not cause a person to search compulsively for soup, but it has the potential to instigate a relentless hunt for crack. Because this uncontrollable behavior results from disorderly changes in the brain, we consider this addiction a disease.

The body and brain adapt over time to the effects of drugs in a variety of ways. Due to tolerance, some drug effects decrease with repeated administration. Regular alcohol drinkers are less impaired by a single shot of vodka than non-drinkers. In contrast, sensitization results in the increase of other drug effects with repeated dosing. Sensitization may enhance motivation to seek drugs via dopamine, exaggerate a drug's cardiovascular impact, and promote body movement.

Unfortunately, the fickle nature of tolerance and sensitization make them particularly dangerous. For example, learning and memory can alter the degree to which a drug produces tolerance and sensitization. An individual might be tolerant to the effects of heroin at his or her home, but not at a local bar. The amount of heroin the individual needs to get high at home is, therefore, more than the quantity needed at the bar. This is a potentially deadly mistake. Taking the "usual" amount of drug at the bar can result in an overdose where our bodies "forget to breathe" (Gerevich, Bácskai, and Danics 2005). This phenomenon illustrates why drug abuse is not simply a result of "habit-learning" or brain mechanisms of learning gone awry.

By defining drug tolerance as one of several fundamental aspects of drug addiction, we can develop strategies to prevent untimely deaths from overdoses. One way to reverse an overdose of heroin or morphine is to inject the individual with an opioid antagonist. Medications such as Naloxone (Narcan) block the effects of heroin or morphine, potentially allowing the overdosing person to breathe again. Unfortunately, it is unpredictable whether an individual will overdose on a drug because tolerance levels can vary widely. We should, therefore, increase the number of people who are trained to deliver Naloxone. Equipping law enforcement personnel, nurses, and others with this medication will increase the likelihood that overdose patients will survive.

Several pathologies associated with addiction allow for its characterization as a disease. First, addiction runs in families and may have a strong genetic component. Second, addiction hijacks learning processes, uncontrollably motivating our behavior and predisposing us to relapse. Lastly, addiction causes long-lasting changes in the brain which lead to either tolerance or sensitization of specific drug effects. These adaptations are dangerous because they can have unforeseeable consequences, potentially resulting in overdose and death. Importantly though, by identifying at-risk individuals we can take measures to prevent the development of addictions. For those individuals who are addicted, we can both treat the illness and reduce the potential harm the disease causes.

References

Enoch, M. A., and D. Goldman. 2001. "The Genetics of Alcoholism and Alcohol Abuse." *Current Psychiatry Reports.* 3: 144–151.

Gerevich, J., E. Bácskai, and Z. Danics. 2005. "A Case Report: Pavlovian Conditioning as a Risk Factor of Heroin 'Overdose' Death." *Harm Reduction Journal.* 2: 11.

Kendler, K. S., et al. 1995. "The Structure of the Genetic and Environmental Risk Factors for Six Major Psychiatric Disorders in Women. Phobia, Generalized Anxiety Disorder, Panic Disorder, Bulimia, Major Depression, and Alcoholism." *Archives of General Psychiatry.* 52: 374–383.

Merriam-Webster Online Dictionary. <http://www.merriam-webster.com/dictionary/>. Accessed on January 21, 2016.

Plemenitas, A., et al. 2015. "Alcohol Dependence and Genetic Variability in the Serotonin Pathway among Currently and Formerly Alcohol-Dependent Males." *Neuropsychobiology* 72: 57–64.

Prescott, C. A., and K. S. Kendler. 1999. "Genetic and Environmental Contributions to Alcohol Abuse and Dependence in a Population-Based Sample of Male Twins." *American Journal of Psychiatry.* 156: 34–40.

Seo, S., et al. 2015. "Predicting the Future Relapse of Alcohol-Dependent Patients from Structural and Functional Brain Images." *Addiction Biology.* 20(6): 1042–1055.

Wiers, C. E., et al. 2015. "Effects of Depressive Symptoms and Peripheral DAT Methylation on Neural Reactivity to Alcohol Cues in Alcoholism." *Translational Psychiatry* 5: e648.

Bryan F. Singer received his PhD in neurobiology from the University of Chicago and is currently a research fellow in biopsychology at the University of Michigan. His current research aims to understand how individual variation in dopamine neurotransmission contributes to the development of a variety of disorders, including drug addiction.

Substance Abuse and Transgender Youth
Michael Vallario

From 2011 to 2014, I had the great privilege of working at a residential substance abuse and mental health facility in Palm Beach County, Florida. My role there as behavioral health technician (BHT) was much more clinically oriented than other South Florida rehabs, which hired BHTs to simply drive vans and ensure the safety of clients: I facilitated groups, aided in therapeutic interventions, and worked intimately with our patient population. I primarily oversaw our adolescent program as lead tech and was able to help teens 13 to 18 years old from a variety of backgrounds, including two transgender adolescents: one (male-to-female (MTF) and one (female-to-male) FTM, who came to treatment for emotional issues and substance abuse. Both youths stayed under our care for over six months on an inpatient basis, and one continued to attend aftercare for over a year in an outpatient capacity. While our staff was extremely LGBT-friendly (the CEO and head psychiatrist is openly gay), having gender-variant teenage patients presented a unique set of obstacles, exposed our shortcomings as a clinical staff, and provided a rare learning experience to all of us.

One of the first issues I became aware of early on is that as adolescents, the patients I worked with rarely identified as "addicts." Teenagers typically have adults running their lives and are too young to experience the often-devastating consequences of severe, long-term substance abuse compared to adults. Not surprisingly, our adolescent patients were almost invariably forced into treatment by their concerned parents, but did not necessarily meet diagnostic criteria for chemical dependency. Adolescents use substances for a variety of reasons, including "peer pressure, the desire to experiment with something new, to seek independence from parents, or for pleasure" (Jordan 2000). Hence, treating any adolescent—not just gender-variant youths—in a substance abuse setting is complicated because drug use may not be indicative of psychopathology, addiction, or even social deviance. With an estimated 42.5 percent of teens admitting use of illicit drugs and 16.4 percent reporting abuse, attendance in treatment was not a substantiation of addiction (Swendsen et al. 2012). As a treatment team, we focused on providing sufficient psychoeducation, improving coping strategies, and helping to enhance support networks, all in an effort to minimize the likelihood of addiction in adulthood. We were regularly met with resistance and resentment, particularly from our transgender patients, as they believed their parents had simply sent them away to avoid having to accept their gender nonconformity.

Since our adolescent program heavily emphasized 12-step Fellowship for addiction, AA/NA (Alcoholics Anonymous/ Narcotics Anonymous) meetings presented another challenge particularly for our gender-variant teens. Aside from the fact that most of our patients felt they did not belong in an AA meeting, all 12-step–based programs involve sponsorship for members. About half of our teens hailed from areas outside South Florida and intended to return to their families, which meant that obtaining a sponsor in the area would be minimally useful due to their limited time in treatment. Transgender teens had a harder time, as they required a sponsor who would be understanding and accepting of gender variance. For this reason, I sought out AA meetings which were listed as LGBT-friendly; although the people were welcoming and encouraging, they were mostly sexual minorities rather than gender nonconforming. As Benson explained in 2013, "Sexual orientation and gender identity both rely on sex/gender categories" but differ "in that sexual orientation is determined by who a person is attracted to, while gender identity is based on a person's belief about who they are." Unfortunately, our trans adolescents quickly learned that they were as underrepresented among the recovery community as they were with the inpatient population.

Consequently, the most difficult aspect of treating transgender adolescents with substance abuse is the universal and ubiquitous social isolation they experience. Clinicians at my facility were not always able to provide competent care, often using incorrect pronouns when referring to a trans teen and lacking a general knowledge of gender minority issues. Furthermore, the DSM-5 (*Diagnostic and Statistical Manual* of the American Psychiatric Association) still lists "Gender Dysphoria" as a psychiatric disorder, which "pathologizes a minority community, and potentially interferes with their pleas for civil rights and acceptance" (Lev 2013). Our gender-variant adolescents would frequently experience frustration, and rightfully so, stemming from marginalization both intentional and nuanced. There were certainly times when I wondered, had I been "born in the wrong body" (as my teens had described it) and lived through the same painful experiences, would I not also have considered turning to drugs or other self-destructive behaviors at some point? Gender-variant youth are already at a higher risk for suicide and self-harm as a result of social rejection and victimization, so it is not too shocking that drugs and alcohol sometimes serve to help a transgender adolescent temporarily escape a culturally oppressive society (Liu and Mustanski 2012). With so much transphobia and gender-normative thinking, were our gender-variant teens on the road to drug addiction, or were drugs just a manifestation of the emotional turmoil plaguing them? The answer was as convoluted and indecipherable to me then as it is now.

The teenage years are universally regarded as a strenuous time for everyone, across all cultures and identities. Dealing with substance abuse as teen is even more problematic, but coupled with the hardships implicit in the transgender experience, treating gender nonconforming youth is exceptionally difficult. Despite the vast amount of information that has been gleaned in the past several years about the psychological nature of gender identity and about substance abuse, the most appropriate approaches and conceptualizations of addiction treatment for transgender patients will continue to evolve as more is learned and currently leave much to be desired. As challenging and complicated as it may be, it is absolutely quintessential for transgender youth to have an affirming, knowledgeable, and compassionate support network, especially in inpatient settings. Above all, it would be an injustice to the gender-variant, substance-abusing teen to have those entrusted to help them toward wellness and recovery fail to be ever mindful of the intersectionality inherent in their issues.

References

Benson, K. E. 2013. "Seeking Support: Transgender Client Experiences with Mental Health Services." *Journal of Feminist Family Therapy.* 25(1): 17–40.

Jordan, Karen M. 2001. "Substance Abuse among Gay Lesbian, Bisexual, Transgender, and Questioning Adolescents." *School Psychology Review.* 29(2): 201.

Lev, A. I. 2013. "Gender Dysphoria: Two Steps Forward, One Step Back." *Clinical Social Work. Journal.* 41(3): 288–296.

Liu, R. T., and B. Mustanski. 2012. "Suicidal Ideation and Self-Harm in Lesbian, Gay, Bisexual, and Transgender Youth." *American Journal of Preventive Medicine.* 42(3): 221–228.

Swendsen, J., et al. 2012. "Use and Abuse of Alcohol and Illicit Drugs in US Adolescents: Results of the National Comorbidity Survey–Adolescent Supplement." *Archives of General Psychiatry.* 69(4): 390–398.

Michael Vallario is a second-year clinical psychology trainee in the PsyD program at Nova Southeastern University's College of Psychology. He currently works at Fort Lauderdale Hospital as a recreation services specialist. Michael hopes to specialize in treating adolescents and the LGBT population.

Richard Alpert (Ram Dass; 1931–)

During the 1960s, Alpert was involved in research on psycho-active substances at Harvard University, along with his good friend and colleague Timothy Leary. He later spent time study-ing spiritualism in India and devoted the greatest part of his life to studying and teaching about this subject in the United States.

Richard Alpert was born on April 6, 1931, in Newton, Massachusetts. His father was a prominent attorney, president of the New York, New Haven, and Hartford railroad, and a founder of Brandeis University and the Albert Einstein College of Medicine in New York City. Alpert received his BA from Tufts University, his MA in motivation psychology from Wes-leyan University, and his PhD in human development from Stanford University. He then accepted a teaching and research post in the Department of Social Relations and the Gradu-ate School of Education at Harvard University. While at Har-vard, he met Timothy Leary, from whom he learned about the psychoactive effects of a number of substances. Between 1960 and 1961, Alpert and Leary began a series of experiments on psilocybin, using graduate students as their subjects. The direc-tion of these experiments was sufficiently troubling to Harvard

First Lady Nancy Reagan, wife of President Ronald Reagan, discusses her policy to reduce drug use among teens, who should "Just Say No" to drugs and alcohol. Experts disagree as to the extent to which the program was successful in reducing youth substance abuse, if at all. (National Archives)

administrators that both men were dismissed from their academic positions. That move was of little concern to Alpert, who later said that he had already become disillusioned with academics as a "meaningless pursuit."

In 1967, Alpert traveled to India, where he met his spiritual teacher, Neem Karoli Baba, and received his new name, Ram Dass, or "servant of God." He has spent the rest of his life studying a variety of spiritualistic philosophies, including Hinduism, karma, yoga, and Sufism. He is probably best known today not for his early studies of psychoactive substances, but for his 1971 book, *Be Here Now*. His other publications include *The Psychedelic Experience: A Manual Based on the Tibetan Book of the Dead* (with Leary and Ralph Metzner); *Doing Your Own Being* (1973); *The Only Dance There Is* (1974); *Journey of Awakening: A Meditator's Guidebook* (1978); *Compassion in Action: Setting Out on the Path of Service* (with Mirabai Bush; 1991); *Still Here: Embracing Aging, Changing and Dying* (2000); and *Paths to God: Living the Bhagavad Gita* (2004). In 1997, Alpert suffered a stroke that paralyzed the right side of his body and left him with Broca's aphasia, a brain condition that makes speech difficult. Nonetheless, he continues to write, teach, and lecture, as his condition permits.

American Society of Addiction Medicine

The American Society of Addiction Medicine (ASAM) had its origins in the early 1950s, largely through the efforts of Dr. Ruth Fox, who initiated a series of meetings with fellow physicians interested in the research and clinical aspects of alcoholism and its treatment. In 1954, this group formalized its existence by creating the New York Medical Society on Alcoholism (NYMSA). The organization's work was funded primarily by the U.S. Alcohol, Drug Abuse, and Mental Health Administration, predecessor of today's Substance Abuse and Mental Health Services Administration (SAMHSA). In 1967, NYMSA decided to extend its work nationwide and changed its name to the American Medical Society on Alcoholism (AMSA).

As interest in medical aspects of drug abuse and addiction grew in the 1970s, a second organization began operation in California, the California Society for the Treatment of Alcoholism and Other Drug Dependencies (CSTAODD), expanding traditional alcohol treatment programs to include those dependent on or addicted to drugs. Over time, the two groups at opposite ends of the country, AMSA and CSTAODD, began to collaborate with each other, eventually leading to their union in 1983 under AMSA's name. In 1988, AMSA was accepted by the American Medical Association (AMA) as a national medical specialty society and adopted its present name, ASAM. Today, the organization consists of more than 3,200 physicians and related health providers interested primarily in issues of substance abuse. It has state chapters in 36 states and the District of Columbia, along with regional chapters in northern New England and the Northwest that include states that do not have their own separate chapters.

The work carried out by ASAM can be divided into four major categories: education, advocacy, research and treatment, and practice support. The organization's education component is designed to provide physicians and other healthcare workers with the most up-to-date information on basic issues in addiction treatment. In 2015, for example, ASAM offered a review course in addiction medicine and courses on buprenorphine treatment, state of the art in addiction medicine, and opioid risk evaluation and mitigation strategies. The advocacy element in ASAM's program is aimed at influencing state and federal policies involving substance abuse to reflect the organization's goals and objectives. Some examples of the types of action it has taken include pushing for insurance coverage of mental health and addiction disorders, working for the repeal of alcoholism exclusions in insurance policies, expanding treatment for substance abuse among veterans, and regulating the sale of tobacco and alcohol to minors.

The research and treatment feature of ASAM's work aims to provide healthcare providers with a wide range of informational materials on all aspects of addiction and substance abuse. Some of the materials it provides are a Common Threads Conference on Pain and Addiction; clinical updates from the International Association for the Study of Pain; a joint statement on pain and addiction from the American Pain Society, the American Academy of Pain Medicine, and the American Society of Addiction Medicine; and a variety of publications on prescription drug abuse from federal agencies. The area of practice support is designed to provide materials that will help addiction physicians and other providers with the best available information about best practices in the field of addiction medicine. These materials include guidelines and consensus documents, such as the National Practice Guideline for Medications for the Treatment of Opioid Use Disorder; "how to's" and practice resources, such as the Drug Enforcement Agency document, "How to Prepare for a DEA Office Inspection"; standards and performance measures, such as the ASAM Standards of Care for the Addiction Specialist Physician Document; and "ASAM Criteria," a comprehensive set of guidelines for placement, continued stay, and transfer/discharge of patients with addiction and co-occurring conditions.

ASAM produces and provides a wide variety of print and electronic publications for the addiction physician and healthcare worker, such as the books *Principle of Addiction Medicine* and *The ASAM Essentials of Addiction Medicine; Journal of Addiction Medicine*, the association's official peer-reviewed journal; *ASAMagazine*, a publication containing news and commentary; and *ASAM Weekly*, an online publication intended for both members and nonmembers who are interested in issues of addiction medicine.

Harry J. Anslinger (1892–1975)

Anslinger was appointed the first commissioner of the Federal Bureau of Narcotics when it was established in 1930. He held that office for 32 years, one of the longest tenures of any federal official in modern history. He was consistently a strong advocate for severe penalties against the manufacture, distribution, sale, and use of certain drugs, especially marijuana.

Harry Jacob Anslinger was born in Altoona, Pennsylvania, on May 20, 1892, to Robert J. and Rosa Christiana Fladt Anslinger, immigrants from Switzerland and Germany, respectively. Upon completing high school, Anslinger attended the Altoona Business College before taking a job with the Pennsylvania Railroad. He received a leave of absence from the railway that allowed him to matriculate at Pennsylvania State College (now Pennsylvania State University), where he received his two-year associate degree in engineering and business management. From 1917 to 1928, Anslinger worked for a number of private and governmental agencies on problems of illegal drug use, a job that took him to a number of countries around the world. He has been credited with helping to shape drug policies both in the United States and in a number of foreign countries where he worked or consulted.

In 1929, Anslinger was appointed assistant commissioner in the U.S. Bureau of Prohibition, a position he held only briefly before being selected as the first commissioner of the newly created Federal Bureau of Narcotics in 1930. He assumed that post at a time when state and federal officials were debating the need (or lack of need) for regulations of hemp and marijuana. Both hemp and marijuana are obtained from plants in the genus Cannabis, the former with many important industrial applications, and the latter used almost exclusively as a recreational drug. Historians have discussed the motivations that may have driven Anslinger's attitudes about the subject, but his actions eventually demonstrated a very strong opposition to the growing, processing, distribution, and use of all products of the Cannabis plant. He was instrumental in formulating federal policies and laws against such use that developed during the 1930s.

Anslinger remained in his post until 1970, staying on even after his 70th birthday until a replacement was found. He then served two more years as U.S. representative to the United Nations Narcotic Convention. By the end of his tenure with the convention, he was blind and suffered from both angina and an enlarged prostate. He died in Hollidaysburg, Pennsylvania, on November 14, 1975, of heart failure.

Bill W. (1895–1971)

Bill W. was cofounder with Dr. Bob of Alcoholics Anonymous (AA), an organization devoted to helping alcoholics attain sobriety. He had his last alcoholic drink on December 11, 1934, shortly after cofounding AA, and maintained his sobriety ever after that time.

Bill W. is the name much preferred by William Griffith Wilson because it reflects and emphasizes the anonymity that AA asks of and offers to its members as they fight their battle against alcohol addiction. He was born on November 26, 1895, in East Dorset, Vermont, to Gilman Barrows Wilson, a womanizer and heavy drinker, and Emily Griffith Wilson, a strong-willed and abusive mother. His father abandoned the family in 1905, and his mother decided to do the same, choosing to study for a career in osteopathic medicine. Bill W. then became the ward of his maternal grandparents, with whom he spent the rest of his childhood.

After graduating from high school, Bill entered Norwich University, but remained for only a short time, partly because of his shyness and lack of social skills, and partly because of his own misconduct and that of other classmates. It was during these years that he had his first drink, before rapidly becoming an alcoholic with many "lost weekends" in his life. He eventually was readmitted to Norwich, from which he graduated with a degree in electrical engineering in 1917. He then served as a second lieutenant in the U.S. Army, a time during which his drinking became even more of a problem. When he returned at the end of World War I, he took a job in the insurance department of the New York Central Railroad, while attending the Brooklyn Law School at night. He earned his law degree in 1920, but is said to have been too drunk to pick up his diploma. Over the next decade, Bill worked as a field investigator for a number of financial firms, traveling over most of the United States to complete his assignments. Eventually, his drinking problem became so severe that he was unable to hold a job and he was admitted to the Charles B. Towns Hospital for Drug and Alcohol Addictions in New York City.

Bill experienced his first, short-lived recovery in 1934 when he met an old drinking friend, Ebby Thacher, and learned that he (Thacher) had become sober largely through the efforts of an evangelical Christian organization known as the Oxford Group. Bill's own efforts to achieve a similar result failed, however, and he was returned to the Towns Hospital a second time. Finally, in May 1935, on a business trip to Akron, Ohio, Bill met another alcoholic who was going through struggles similar to his own, Robert Holbrook Smith ("Dr. Bob"), with whom he developed plans for a new group to help themselves and other alcoholics like themselves. That organization eventually grew to become the largest and most successful group for the treatment of alcoholism in the world. Bill spent the rest of his life serving in one role or another in AA. In 2009, *Time* magazine named Bill one of the 100 most important people of the twentieth century.

Hale Boggs (1914–1972/1973)

Boggs was a Democratic member of the U.S. House of Representative from Louisiana's Second Congressional District from 1947 to 1973. He was majority whip of the House from 1962 to 1971 and House Majority Leader from 1971 to 1973. In the years following the end of World War II, Boggs was one of the leading spokespersons for a more rigorous approach to sentencing for drug-related crimes. His position on the topic reflected that of many legislators, law enforcement officers, and members of the general public who believed that the use of illegal drugs had begun to skyrocket after the end of the war, and that some judges were treating the "drug epidemic" much too casually with overly generous fines and prison sentences. In 1951, Boggs submitted a bill to the Congress that dramatically increased the penalties for drug use and drug trafficking and, for the first time in U.S. history, applied those penalties equally to both narcotic drugs and marijuana. It also imposed mandatory sentencing for individuals convicted of drug-related crimes more than once. In 1956, Boggs also sponsored the Narcotic Control Act, which increased penalties even further.

Thomas Hale Boggs Sr. was born on February 15, 1914, in Long Beach, Mississippi. He attended public and parochial schools in Jefferson Parish, Louisiana, before matriculating at Tulane University, in New Orleans, from which he received his bachelor's degree in journalism in 1934 and his law degree in 1937. He established his own law practice in New Orleans, but soon became interested in politics. He ran for the U.S. House of Representatives from the Second District of Louisiana in 1941 and was elected, but failed to receive his party's nomination for the same post a year later. He then returned to his law practice in New Orleans before enlisting in the U.S. Naval Reserve in November 1943, after which he was assigned to the Potomac River Naval Command. He was discharged from the service in January 1946, ran for Congress again, and was once more elected to the U.S. House of Representatives. He served in that body until October 16, 1972, when he was lost on a flight from Anchorage to Juneau, Alaska, working for the campaign of Representative Nick Begich. Neither the wreckage of the plane itself, nor any of its passengers were ever found, and Boggs was declared legally dead on January 3, 1973, to allow the election of his successor, who, it turned out, was his wife, Lindy Boggs. Mrs. Boggs was then re-elected eight more times, serving in the House until 1991.

Community Anti-Drug Coalitions of America

Community Anti-Drug Coalitions of America (CADCA) was founded in 1992 on the suggestion of Jim Burke, then chair of

the President's Drug Advisory Council, as a possible mechanism for dealing with the growing problem of substance abuse
throughout the United States. Today, CADCA claims to be "the
premier membership organization representing those working
to make their communities safe, healthy and drug-free." It works
with more than 5,000 local communities to prevent tobacco
use among youth, underage drinking of alcohol, and the use
of illicit drugs. The coalition carries out its work in cooperation with about 30 partners from government, nonprofit organizations, the business world, and international associations
and organizations. Some of those partners are the Centers for
Disease Control and Prevention; Drug Enforcement Administration; and Departments of Education, Health and Human
Services, Homeland Security, Justice, Labor, and State; National
Institute on Drug Abuse; international drug prevention groups,
such as FEBRAE (Brazil), MENTOR and SURGIR (Colom-
bia), FUNDASALVA (El Salvador), SECCATID (Guatemala),
ANCOD (Honduras), CEDRO and CRESER (Peru), and
SANCA AND TASC (South Africa); the American College of
Pediatrics; National Association of Counties; National Sheriffs
Association; Students against Destructive Decisions; Consumer
Healthcare Products Association; DIRECTV; Krispy Kreme;
M&T Bank; the Robert Wood Johnson Foundation; and Xerox.

CADCA offers seven types of core services to communities:
public policy and advocacy, training and technical assistance,
research dissemination and evaluation, special events and conferences, communications, international programs, and youth
programs. In the area of policy and advocacy, the group works
with its partners to promote legislation and rulemaking that
promotes drug prevention efforts that it supports. Recently,
it has encouraged members and the general public to write
letters to members of the U.S. Congress in support of four
pieces of legislation, the Comprehensive Addiction and Recovery Act (CARA); Drug-Free Communities Program (DFC);
Preventing Abuse of Cough Treatments (PACT) Act; and
Sober Truth on Preventing (STOP) Underage Drinking Act.
The CADCA training program has resulted in the training of

more than 13,000 individuals from over 900 coalition members and over 150 coalition graduates from the organization's year-long National Coalition Academy. The coalition has also conducted more than 1,200 technical assistance sessions for its member coalitions. In addition to the National Coalition Academy, CADCA holds three other major training sessions, the Mid-Year Training Institute, National Leadership Forum, and National Youth Leadership Initiative.

Some of the organization's priority efforts are organized into ongoing events, programs, and campaigns on very specific topics. Some of the recent topics have been 17th Annual Drug-Free Kids Campaign Awards Dinner, Annual Survey of Coalitions, Drug-Free Kids Campaign, GOT OUTCOMES!, National Medicine Abuse Awareness Month, Tobacco Initiatives, and VetCorps. In connection with its efforts related to prescription drug abuse, CADCA has produced the "Prevent Rx Abuse" toolkit. The toolkit consists of four elements, the most basic of which is Prevention Strategies, seven methods of prevention that make use of access to information, enhancement of skills, provision of support, changes in access and barriers, changes in consequences, changes in physical design, and modification and change in policies. (Additional detailed information about the toolkit is available online at http://www.preventrxa buse.org/.)

The CADCA website is a rich source of reference materials on virtually every aspect of alcohol and drug prevention. These materials can be accessed by way of an interactive index at http://www.cadca.org/resources.

The primary element of the CADCA research function is the organization's Annual Survey of Coalitions, which attempts to identify coalitions around the country and learn more about what they are doing to address substance abuse problems in their communities. One result of the survey is the selection of a handful of local coalitions that have been most successful in achieving position outcomes in their communities. These results are published in a publication called GOT OUTCOMES!

In 2005, CADCA began to expand its work to others parts of the world and has since that date helped to establish 130 community antidrug coalitions in 22 countries, including most of Central and South America, the Cape Verde Islands, Italy, Senegal, South Africa, Ghana, Kenya, Tanzania, Kyrgyzstan, Tajikistan, Iraq, and the Philippines. The organization offers essentially the same training, research, resource, and other services provided to domestic coalitions.

A useful overview of the structure and work of the coalition is available in its "Handbook for Community Anti-Drug Coalitions," which can be accessed online at http://www.cadca .org/sites/default/files/files/coalitionhandbook102013.pdf.

Thomas De Quincey (1785–1859)

De Quincey was an English author best known for his autobiographical work, *Confessions of an Opium Eater*. He also wrote a number of other works, including novels, essays, critical reviews, and additional autobiographical sketches.

Thomas De Quincey was born on August 15, 1785, in Manchester, England. After his father died in 1796, De Quincey's mother moved the family to Bath, where he was enrolled in King Edward's School. He was an outstanding scholar, able to read Greek and compose poems in the language as a teenager. His home life was difficult, however, and he ran away to Wales at the age of 17, with the blessings and minimal financial support of his mother and uncle. Eventually he found his way to London, where he nearly died of starvation and survived only because of the kindness of a 15-year-old prostitute whom we now know of only as "Anne of Oxford Street."

In 1804, he was found by friends in London and returned to his family, who arranged for him to enroll at Worcester College, Oxford. It was at Oxford that he first took opium, in the form of laudanum, for a painful and persistent toothache. He soon became addicted to the drug, an addiction that persisted to a greater or lesser degree for the rest of his life. He describes his years of addiction in *Confessions*, as well as its effects on his life and writing and his efforts to overcome his addiction. From time to time, he was able to withdraw from use of the drug but, a point noted by some of his biographers, the quantity and quality of his literary work suffered significantly during these periods of abstinence.

In 1816, De Quincey married Margaret Simpson, who was eventually to bear him eight children. She has been described as the "anchor" in his life, and, after her death in 1837, De Quincey's use of opium increased significantly.

Drug Free America Foundation Inc.

Drug Free American Foundation Inc. (DFAF) is a 501(c)(3) nonprofit organization which, according to its mission statement, is "committed to developing, promoting and sustaining global strategies, policies and laws that will reduce illegal drug use, drug addiction, drug-related injury and death." The organization was founded by Mr. and Mrs. Mel Sembler in 1995. Mr. Sembler was chairman of the board of the Sembler Company, a developer and manager of shopping centers. He also served as U.S. ambassador to Italy and to Australia and Nauru. Mrs. Sembler is listed as founder and chair of the organization in the DFAF 2010 Annual Report.

Mr. and Mrs. Sembler couple originally founded the organization known as Straight, Inc., in 1976, as a nonprofit drug treatment program that claims to have treated more than 12,000 young people with substance abuse problems in eight cities in the United States. Straight Inc. was long the subject of intense scrutiny for alleged abusive practices used in its drug treatment programs. It later changed its name to Straight Foundation Inc. and spun off a number of drug treatment programs, such as the Seed, Kids Helping Kids, Pathway Family Center, Life, Growing Together, KIDS (of various cities and regions), SAFE, and Alberta Adolescent Recovery Center (AARC). Drug Free America Foundation is reputed to be one of the Straight Inc.

spinoffs. The DFAF website makes little or no mention of this alleged connection.

Most of DFAF's work is carried out through six divisions:

- The Institute on Global Drug Policy is an alliance of physicians, scientists, attorneys, and drug specialists who advocate for the adoption of public policies that curtail the use of illicit and misuse of licit drugs and alcohol. A major activity of the institute is co-sponsorship of *The Journal of Global Drug Policy and Practice* with another division of DFAF, the International Scientific and Medical Forum on Drug Abuse. Relatively little information is available online about the organization, membership, or activities of the institute. In a statement announcing formation of the division, its mission was described as "creating and strengthening international laws that hold drug users and dealers criminally accountable for their actions. It will vigorously promote treaties and agreements that provide clear penalties to individuals who buy, sell or use harmful drugs. It will push for a uniform legal requirement that marijuana and other addictive drugs must meet the same scientific standards as other drugs to be deemed therapeutic for medical conditions."

- The International Scientific and Medical Forum on Drug Abuse is described by DFAF as a "brain trust" of researchers and physicians concerned about substance abuse who have an interest in dispelling incorrect depictions of the consequences of drug use among the general public. The division is a co-sponsor of *The Journal of Global Drug Policy and Practice* with the Institute on Global Drug Policy.

- The International Task Force on Strategic Drug Policy is a network of professionals in the field of substance abuse and community leaders who work together to develop and implement drug reduction principles around the world. The task force convenes meetings in cooperation with other divisions of the DFAF to train individuals in methods of drug reduction principles. The task force reports having held eight such conferences of about 60–130 individuals since 2001 in locations such as London, Buenos Aires, Tampa, and Guayaquil, Ecuador.

- The Drug Prevention Network of the Americas (DPNA) is a cooperative effort of nongovernmental agencies in North, South, and Central America working to reduce demand for illegal substances through conferences, training seminars, and Internet communications.

- Students Taking Action Not Drugs (STAND) is a student-based organization whose goal it is to distribute on campuses accurate scientific information about the effects of taking illegal drugs.

- National Drug-Free Workplace Alliance (NDWA) is a division attempting to develop drug-free work environments in the state of Florida and, working with other agencies and organizations, throughout the United States.

The organization's web page provides its views on a broad array of drug topics including marijuana, overcoming addiction, prescription drug abuse, drug policy, drug testing, prevention of substance abuse, and international drug policy. Associated with each topic is a PDF file or other attachment that provides more detail on the subject, such as PDF files on federal and state laws dealing with medical marijuana, "the truth" about marijuana, and how to get rich by suing a doctor who prescribes marijuana for medical purposes. The organization's web site also contains the Otto and Connie Moulton Library for Drug Prevention, which contains more than 2,100 books and other media dealing with substance abuse issues, which visitors to the site are invited to access. In addition to three position statements on substance abuse (on harm reduction, student drug testing, and medical marijuana), DFAF offers a small number of DVDs dealing with substance abuse issues, including "True Compassion–About Marijuana," "Real View Mirror: Looking at Your Future, Leaving the Drug Culture Behind," "In Focus: A Clear Message about Drugs," and "Deadly Indifference: The Price of Ignoring the Youth Drug Epidemic."

Drug Policy Alliance

The Drug Policy Alliance (DPA) was created in July 2000 as a result of the merger of the Lindesmith Center (TLC) and the Drug Policy Foundation (DPF). The Lindesmith Center, in turn, had been formed in 1994 as a think-tank for the consideration of alternatives to existing policies and practices for dealing with drug issues, while the Drug Policy Foundation had been established in 1987, an organization established to work for drug reform, largely through the provision of grants to advance further studies on drug policies. The DPA now claims to be "the world's leading drug policy reform organization of people who believe the war on drugs is doing more harm than good." The organization currently claims to have nearly 30,000 members, with an additional 70,000 individuals receiving its online e-newsletter and action alerts.

DPA organizes its work under the rubric of about a half dozen major issues: Reforming Marijuana Laws, Fighting Injustice, Reducing Drug Harm, Protecting Youth, Defending Personal Liberty, and Making Economic Sense. Each of these general topics is further divided into more specific issues. The Reforming Marijuana Laws topic, for example, covers issues such as developing a legal regulatory market for marijuana, helping individuals who have been arrested for marijuana possession, and providing information about the potential health and social effects of marijuana use. The topic of Protecting Youth is further divided into efforts to deal with drug testing in schools and zero-tolerance policy in some school districts, as well as providing information and materials on "reality-based" drug education. The Making Economic Sense topic deals in more detail with subjects such as problems of supply and demand for marijuana, the problem of drug prohibition and violence, and the economic benefits of legalizing and taxing the sale of marijuana.

An important part of the DPA efforts on behalf of marijuana issue is a series of Action Alerts, through which members and friends of the association are encouraged to contact legislators, administrative officials, and other stakeholders about specific issues of concern to the organization. During 2012, for example, DPA sponsored Action Alerts on protection of medical marijuana patients directed to members of the U.S. Senate, a campaign to influence President Barack Obama to work harder to protection of medical marijuana patients, efforts to lobby members of the U.S. Congress to end criminalization of marijuana use and possession, and a campaign to encourage the Congress to reduce federal sending on the enforcement of existing marijuana laws.

The DPA publishes a number of reports, factsheets, and other print and electronic materials on the topic of marijuana legalization. Members receive the tri-annual newsletter *The Ally*, which provides information on the organization's current activities and successes. Other publications include *Safety First: A Reality-Based Approach to Teens and Drugs*, a tool designed to help parents evaluate and discuss strategies for protecting teenagers from drug abuse; *Crime and Punishment in New Jersey: The Criminal Code and Public Opinion on Sentencing*, a report on the legal status of marijuana in that state; *Drug Courts Are Not the Answer: Toward a Health-Centered Approach to Drug Use*, an analysis of existing laws on marijuana possession; *Overdose: A National Crisis Taking Root in Texas*, a report on the growing number of overdose deaths in that state and the United States; *Arresting Latinos for Marijuana in California: Possession Arrests in 33 Cities, 2006–08*, a report on the special risk faced by Latinos in California for marijuana offenses; and *Healing a Broken System: Veterans Battling Addiction and Incarceration*, dealing with the special problems of marijuana use faced by veterans returning from service in Iraq and Afghanistan.

DPA also provides an excellent resource dealing with drug facts on its website. Some of the topics covered on this page include fundamental facts about marijuana and other drugs, some new solutions for dealing with the nation's drug problems, the relevance of federal and state drug laws for individuals, a summary of individual rights in connection with existing drug laws, statistical information about the nation's war on drugs, and drug laws around the world.

European Monitoring Centre for Drugs and Drug Addiction

The concept of an all-European agency to deal with the growing problem of substance abuse on the continent was first proposed by French president Georges Pompidou in the late 1960s. That idea languished for about two decades before it was raised once more in 1989 by French president François Mitterrand in 1989. Mitterrand suggested a seven-step program that would involve establishing a common method for analyzing drug addiction in the European states; harmonizing national policies for substance abuse; strengthening controls and improving cooperation among states; finding ways of implementing the 1988 UN Convention Against Illicit Traffic in Narcotic Drugs and Psychotropic Substances; coordinating policies and practices between producing and consuming countries; developing a common policy dealing with drug-related money laundering; and designating a single individual in each country responsible for antidrug actions within that country.

Mitterrand's suggestion led to a series of actions within the European community that eventually resulted in 1993 in the creation of the European Monitoring Centre for Drugs and Drug Addiction (EMCDDA) under Council Regulation (EEC) no. 302/93. The general administrative structure was established the following year, consisting of an executive director, a management board, and a scientific committee. The management board is the primary decision-making body for EMCDDA. It meets at least once a year and is composed of one representative from each member state of the European Union, two representatives from the European Commission, and two representatives from the European Parliament. The board adopts an annual work program and a three-year work program that guides the organization's day-to-day operations. The three-year program is developed with input from a wide variety of sources, including the general public (through the organization's website). The 2010–12 program focused on topics such as refining methodologies to allow better identification and monitoring of new and established substances; developing a framework for monitoring illegal drug supply, drug markets, and drug-related crimes; improving methods for estimating and describing dependence and drug problems in non-opiate populations; and developing guidelines and good practice standards for interventions and the development and dissemination of quality standards.

The scientific committee consists of 15 members appointed by the management board for the purpose of advising the board on scientific issues related to substance abuse. The first meeting of the management board was held in April 1994 at its Lisbon headquarters, where its administrative offices remain until today. Much of the work of EMCDDA takes place within eight units of the scientific committee. The eight units focus on prevalence, consequences, and data management; supply reduction and new trends; interventions, best practice, and scientific partners; policy, evaluation, and content coordination; Reitox and international cooperation; communication; information and communication technology; and administration. Reitox is the name given to a network of human and computer links among the 27 nations that make up the EMCDDA operation.

The EMCDDA website is one of the richest resources available on nearly every aspect of substance abuse issues in the world. It contains information on a wide variety of topics, such as health consequences (deaths and mortality, infectious diseases, treatment demand, and viral hepatitis); prevalence and epidemiology (general population surveys, drug trends in youth, problem drug use, key indicators, and wastewater analysis); best practice (prevention, treatment, harm reduction, standards, and guidelines); Exchange on Drug Demand Reduction Action (EDDRA) and Evaluation Instruments Bank (EIB); drug profiles (amphetamine, barbiturates, benzodiazepines, BZP and other piperazines, cannabis, cocaine and crack, fentanyl, hallucinogenic mushrooms, heroin, khat, LSD, MDMA, methamphetamine, *Salvia divinorum*, synthetic cannabinoids and "Spice," synthetic cathinones, synthetic cocaine derivatives, and volatile substances); health and social interventions (harm reduction, prevention of drug use, social reintegration, and treatment of drug use); policy and law (EU policy and law, laws, and public expenditure); new drugs and trends (action on new drugs); supply and supply reduction (interventions against drug supply, interventions against diversion of chemical precursors, interventions against money-laundering activities, supply reduction, markets, and crime and supply reduction indicators); resources by drug (cannabis thematic page, cocaine and crack thematic page, and opioids and heroin thematic page); drugs and society (crime, driving, social exclusion, women and gender issues, and young people); and science and research (addiction medicine, neuroscience, and research in Europe).

Over the decades, EMCDDA has produced a plethora of publications on virtually every imaginable aspect of substance abuse, including all possible topics related to cannabis. Among the 2011 publications are national reports for the 27 EU countries plus Croatia and Turkey; "selected issues" reports on "Guidelines for the Treatment of Drug Dependence: A European Perspective"; "Mortality Related to Drug Use in Europe" and "Cost and Financing of Drug Treatment Services in Europe"; "Summary Report from EMCDDA Trendspotter Meeting 18–19 October 2011" (reports of scientific Research); "Pilot Study on Wholesale Drug Prices in Europe" (a thematic paper); and "ECDC and EMCDDA Guidance. Prevention and Control of Infectious Diseases among People Who Inject Drugs" (a joint publication with the European Centre for Disease Prevention and Control). One of EMCDDA's most valuable publications is its annual *General Report of Activities*, which describes in some detail the work undertaken and completed by the organization during the preceding year. The publication is available online at http://www.emcdda.europa.eu/attachements.cfm/att_136906_EN_TDAB11001ENN_FINAL_Web.pdf.

Francis B. Harrison (1873–1957)

Harrison is probably best known today as author of the Harrison Narcotics Tax Act of 1914, an act that was passed, somewhat ironically, only after Harrison himself had left office. The act did not specifically prohibit any illegal substance, but it provided for the registration and taxation of "all persons who produce, import, manufacture, compound, deal in, dispense, sell, distribute, or give away opium or coca leaves, their salts, derivatives, or preparations, and for other purposes." Law enforcement officers and the courts immediately began to interpret the law as restricting physicians from writing prescriptions for the nonmedical use of opiates, and they began arresting, prosecuting, and convicting individuals for such activities. To a significant extent, then, the Harrison Act marked the beginning of a national campaign against the use of certain substances for other than medical uses.

Francis Burton Harrison was born in New York City on December 18, 1873, to Burton Harrison, an attorney and private secretary to Jefferson Davis, president of the Confederate States, and Constance Cary Harrison, a novelist and social activist. He attended the Cutler School in New York City, and Yale University, from which he received his BA in 1895. He then earned his LLB at New York Law School in 1897. Harrison was elected to the U.S. Congress from New York's 13th District, but resigned after one term to run (unsuccessfully) for lieutenant governor of New York. After a brief hiatus in the private practice of law, he ran for Congress again in 1907, this time from New York's 20th district, and was elected. He served for three terms in Congress before accepting an appointment as governor general of the Philippine Islands, where he remained until 1921. Following his service in the Philippines, Harrison essentially retired from public life, spending extended periods of time in Scotland and Spain. He returned to the Philippines on a number of occasions, however, as consultant and advisor, especially when the islands were granted their independence in 1934. Harrison was married six times, with five of those marriages ending in divorce. He died in Flemington, New Jersey, on November 21, 1957.

Albert Hofmann (1906–2008)

Hofmann discovered the psychedelic compound lysergic acid diethylamide (LSD) and experienced its hallucinogenic effects in 1943. He later studied chemicals present in so-called magic mushrooms also responsible for hallucinogenic effects and synthesized the most important of these, psilocybin.

Albert Hofmann was born in Baden, Switzerland, on January 11, 1906, to Adolf Hofmann, a toolmaker, and Elisabeth Schenk Hofmann. He attended Zürich University, from which he received his bachelor's degree in chemistry in 1929 and his doctorate in the same subject in 1930. He then accepted an appointment as research chemist at Sandoz Pharmaceuticals, a company with which he remained for the rest of his professional career.

The event in Hofmann's life for which he is best known and that has now been recounted endlessly occurred on April 16, 1943. At the time, Hofmann was involved in a long-term study of some naturally occurring psychedelic plants, including the fungus ergot and the herb squill. He was working in particular with a chemical found in a number of these plants, known in German as Lysergsäure-diethylamid, and in English as lysergic acid diethylamide (LSD). In particular, he was studying LSD-25, that is, the 25th preparation of the substance. During his research, Hofmann spilled a small amount of LSD-25 on his hands and, before long, began to feel mentally disoriented. After a period of time, he found he could no longer continue working and jumped on his bicycle to ride home. That bicycle ride, as Hofmann has recounted the event on a number of occasions, was such a bizarre experience that he thought for some time that he had perhaps lost his mind. After about six hours of "extremely stimulated imagination . . . a dreamlike state . . . and an uninterrupted stream of fantastic pictures, extraordinary shapes with intense, kaleidoscopic play of colors" (as he later described the experience), Hofmann returned to normal, but with a desire to learn more about the compound he had discovered.

Much of Hofmann's career was devoted to further studies of LSD and other psychedelic compounds, research that was supported and encouraged by Sandoz because of its potential for application in the treatment of psychological disorders. In 1962, for example, Hofmann and his wife traveled to Mexico to collect the psychoactive herb Ska Maria Pastora (*Salvia divinorum*) for study and analysis. He also identified the most important active agent in another psychedelic plant, the Mexican morning glory (*Rivea corymbosa*), a close relative of LSD, lysergic acid amide. Hofmann retired from Sandoz in 1971 but continued a career of writing, public speaking, and participation in a variety of professional organizations. Perhaps his most popular book is his own account of his research on LSD and its psychedelic effects, *LSD: My Problem Child* (1980). Hofmann died on April 29, 2008, in the village of Burg im Leimental, near Basel, Switzerland, at the age of 102.

Hon Lik (1951–)

Hon Lik (also Han Li) is a pharmacist and inventor, known internationally as the inventor of the modern e-cigarette. He pursued the concept of a tobacco-free cigarette in the early twenty-first century partly over concerns of his own high levels of smoking (two packs a day) and partly because of his own father's fate, death from lung cancer arising out of his addiction to cigarette smoking also. Hon decided that there had to be a technical means for enjoying the pleasures of tobacco smoking without actually burning tobacco and producing the host of harmful components it contains. By 2004 he had developed such a device and applied for a patent for an "electronic atomization cigarette." The device works by vaporizing a solution that contains nicotine and other components in a small cartridge. The user then inhales the vapor produced (a process that has come to be called *vaping*) to enjoy the stimulus provided by nicotine along with artificial flavors and aromas that have been added to the cartridge solution. Hon eventually received a Chinese, European, and U.S. patent for this device.

Hon and others founded the Ruyan company in China to market his invention which, at first, was a huge success (it being the only company in China to manufacture such a device). Before long, however, Ruyan's business began to decline, a trend that Hon later attributed to resistance by Chinese tobacco and cigarette firms that worried about competition from the e-cigarette. Eventually Ruyan's sales fell from a near-monopoly of the Chinese market to about 5 percent. Throughout all his travails, Hon has remained optimistic. "From the day my invention worked," Hon told a reporter from the French newspaper *Libération* in 2013, "where I could satisfy my nicotine without ruining my health, I realized that I opened a great debate. For my invention is a turning point for the hundreds of millions of smokers and for the future of the global tobacco industry" (in translation). Rights to the e-cigarette are now owned by the British firm of Imperial Tobacco, although Hon has yet to see any royalties from sales of the product.

Hon Lik was born on September 26, 1951, in Shenyang, Liaoning, China. He attended the Liaoning College of Traditional Chinese Medicine, where he majored in pharmacy. After graduation, he joined the Liaoning Academy of Traditional Chinese Medicine, where he focused on the study of the ginseng plant, a popular aphrodisiac. As a result of this line of research, Hon was able to found his own company, Chenlong Baoling Longevity Ginseng products, to patent and sell his discoveries. In 1990, he was also appointed vice superintendent for technology development at the Liaoning Academy. In order to commercialize his invention of the e-cigarette, Hon founded the Golden Dragon company in 2005, where he served as chief executive officer until 2013. He then was appointed head of the Chinese Research and Development team of Fontem Ventures, a division of Imperial Tobacco focusing on the development and sales of e-cigarettes.

Lloyd D. Johnston (1940–)

The early 1970s were a period of great concern to Americans and others around the world who were concerned about growing statistics for substance abusers. The U.S. Congress had just passed the Controlled Substances Act of 1970 and President Richard M. Nixon had announced a "war on drugs" in order to deal with this problem. Meanwhile, a group of researchers at the Institute for Social Research at the University of Michigan were especially interested in substance abuse among younger Americans. They were hoping to find funds to carry out a large study of substance use among high school seniors in the United States. The researchers were Jerald Bachman, Robert Kahn, and Lloyd D. Johnston.

At first these men were met with disinterest for their proposal. Granting agencies such as the Carnegie Corporation were unimpressed with their research plans. Almost ready to give up, Bachman, Kahn, and Johnston had one last idea: talking to the leader of the nation's newest drug agency, the National Institute on Drug Abuse, Robert DuPont. When they presented their ideas to DuPont, he was enthusiastic about the contribution that such a study could make to the nation's understanding of adolescent substance abuse and the steps that might be helpful in dealing with that issue. He arranged for a $3 million grant for five years to get the project started and, as they say, the rest was history.

"The rest" has been the ongoing Monitoring the Future (MTF) study first conceived by the Michigan researcher which, in 2015, published its 40th report on the use of and attitudes toward substances such as marijuana, cocaine, heroin, alcohol, and smoking among twelfth graders and, since 1991, eight and tenth graders. The study is now recognized worldwide as one of the most important pieces of research on substance abuse, at *any* age, anywhere in the world. The latest report still carries the name of Lloyd D. Johnston as lead author, along with that of Bachman and other researchers who have joined the project since its inception.

Lloyd Douglas Johnston was born in Boston, Massachusetts, on April 18, 1940. He attended Williams College, in Williamstown, Massachusetts, from which he received his bachelor's degree in economics in 1962. He then continued his studies at Harvard University, where he earned his MBA in organizational behavior in 1965 before continuing his work at Harvard and the Massachusetts Institute of Technology (MIT) in psychology and human relations. He then moved on to the University of Michigan, in Ann Arbor, where he earned his MA and PhD in social psychology in 1971 and 1973, respectively. He then accepted an offer to join the university's Institute for Social Research (ISR) as assistant research scientist and senior study director at the institute. His primary responsibility there became development and conduct of the MTF.

Johnston has remained at Michigan throughout his academic career, serving as senior research scientist at ISR and program director from 1978 to 1998 and then research professor and distinguished research scientist at ISR from 1998 to the present. Since 2011, Johnston has also been Angus Campbell Collegiate Research Professor at Michigan. In addition to his work with MTF, Johnston has been involved in studies of value and lifestyle orientations, risk and protection factors related to HIV/AIDS, obesity in adolescents and young adults, and international and comparative studies on these topics.

Johnston is author or coauthor of more than 300 peer-reviewed articles, most of which deal with some aspect of substance abuse in young adults and children. He is the recipient of a number of honors and awards, including the National Pacesetter

Award in research of the National Institute on Drug Abuse; the University of Michigan Regent's Award for Distinguished Public Service; the Sir Alister McIntyre Distinguished Award of the University of the West Indies, University of Technology, Jamaica, and Northern Caribbean University; the Collegiate Research Professorship Award of the regents of the University of Michigan; and the Lifetime Achievement Award of the Community Anti-Drug Coalitions of America. He is listed in *Who's Who in the World*; *Who's Who in America*; *Who's Who in Medicine and Health Care*; *Who's Who in American Education*, and is listed as among the top 0.5 percent of the most highly cited authors in the social sciences by the Institute for Scientific Information.

National Council on Alcoholism and Drug Dependence Inc.

The National Council on Alcoholism and Drug Dependence Inc. (NCADD) was founded in 1944 by Marty Mann, the first woman who is said to have achieved sustained sobriety through the Alcoholic Anonymous program. Inspired by the work of reformer Dorothea Dix, who had developed a breakthrough program in mental health care, Mann wondered if she could create a similar program for alcoholics, like herself. She was able to obtain a modest grant from the Yale University Center of Alcohol Studies to establish such an organization, which she called the National Committee for Education on Alcoholism (NCEA). Over the years, the organization evolved into a variety of formats, eventually becoming the National Council on Alcoholism and, in 1990, adding "and Drug Dependence" to its name, to reflect an emphasis that had been added to the organization's mission three years earlier.

Mann created the NCEA on three simple principles, which continue to guide the organization's work today:

• Alcoholism is a disease and the alcoholic is a sick person.
• The alcoholic can be helped and is worth helping.

• This is a public health problem and therefore a public responsibility.

In its literature today, NCADD points out that it was formed at a time when the public perception of alcoholism and drug dependence was very different, one in which the attitude was one of "let[ting] the existing population of alcoholics and addicts die off and prevent the creation of future alcoholics and addicts by legally prohibiting the sale of alcohol and legally control-ling the distribution of opium, morphine and cocaine." Mann's approach, of course, was entirely different from that view, and it is one that continues to inspire the organization today.

The mission of the NCADD focuses on a half dozen major themes, the most important of which is the message to alcohol-ics and drug addicts to "get help," an offer that is fleshed out by the organization with a number of specific suggestions for deal-ing with one's addiction. Additional themes focus on becoming educated about the nature of alcohol and drugs, with special recommendations for parents, youth, friends and family, and those in recovery. The organization's website contains a very useful section on prescription drug abuse, which talks about the types of drugs most commonly abused and their character-istic features and effects, the nature of the problem for various age groups, methods of prevention and treatment, and useful resources on the topic.

National Institute on Drug Abuse

The origins of the National Institute on Drug Abuse (NIDA) date to 1935 when the U.S. Public Health Service (USPHS) established a research facility on drug abuse in Lexington, Ken-tucky. In 1948, that facility was officially renamed the Addiction Research Center. Research on drug abuse was facilitated in the site of the original facility, called "Narco," which was adjacent to a prison that held drug offenders and was run cooperatively with the Federal Bureau of Prisons. The federal government's interest in drug abuse was expanded in 1971 when President Richard M. Nixon established the Special Action Office of Drug Abuse Prevention within the White Office. A year later, the Special Action Office initiated two programs, the Drug Abuse Warning Network (DAWN) and the National Household Survey on Drug Abuse (NHSDA), both of which continue today. DAWN is a public health surveillance system that monitors emergency department drug-related admissions. It is now a part of the Substance Abuse and Mental Health Services Administration (SAMHSA). NHSDA is now known as the National Survey on Drug Use and Health (NSDUH) and is also located in SAMHSA. Its function is to provide national and state-level data on the use of illegal drugs, tobacco, alcohol, and mental health to researchers and the general public.

The NIDA itself was created by the act of Congress in 1974 for the purpose of promoting research, treatment, prevention, training, services, and data collection on the nature and extent of drug abuse. In general, the activities of the NIDA can be classified into one of two major categories: the conduct and support of research on a variety of issues related to drug abuse and dissemination of this information both for the purposes of future research and to improve programs of prevention and treatment of drug abuse, as well as to inform decisions by state, local, and the federal governments on drug abuse policies and practices. The agency's organizational charts reflect the way in which these activities are organized. Three of the main NIDA offices deal with extramural affairs (funding of outside research), science policy and communications, and management. The agency also consists of a number of divisions that deal with intramural research (research within the agency); basic neuroscience and behavioral research; clinical research and behavioral research; epidemiology, services, and prevention research; and pharmacotherapies and medical consequences of drug abuse. Special programs, working groups, consortia, and interest groups focus on more specific topics, such as HIV/AIDS; childhood and adolescence issues; community epidemiology;

women and sex/gender differences; nicotine and tobacco; neu-
rosciences; and genetic issues.

The direction of NIDA activities over the period 2010–2015
has been laid out in the agency's *Strategic Plan*, published in
September 2010. That report describes in detail the elements of
the agency's four-pronged program over the coming five years:
prevention, treatment, HIV/AIDS, and crosscutting priorities,
activities that involve the interaction of drug abuse issues with
other questions of international, national, and local concerns.
This publication is available online at http://www.drugabuse
.gov/sites/default/files/stratplan.pdf.

The NIDA budget has remained relatively constant over the
first decade of the twenty-first century. It rose slightly from 2011
($1,048,776) to 2012 ($1,052,114) to 2013 ($1,054,001)
with also a relatively constant number of full-time employee
equivalents (386, 386, and 382, respectively). About 90 percent of that budget goes for extramural research ($902,696 in
2013), with the largest fraction of that designated for basic and
clinical neuroscience and behavior research ($478,902).

As indicated earlier, dissemination of information is a major
focus of the work carried out by the NIDA. Its publications
include educational curricula, factsheets, guidelines and manuals, journals, administrative and legal documents, posters,
presentations, promotional materials, and reports. These publications can be reviewed on the agency's website at http://www
.drugabuse.gov/publications by audience (students, teachers,
parents, researchers, and health and medical professionals), by
drug of abuse (e.g., alcohol, amphetamines, club drugs, LSD,
marijuana, and steroids), by drug topic (e.g., addiction science,
comorbidity, criminal justice, drugged driving, medical consequences, and relapse and recovery), by series (among which are
Addiction Science and Clinical Practice, Brain Power, Drug-
Facts, Mind over Matter, and Research Reports), and by type.

The NIDA website also provides links to a number of
resources for additional information about the subject of drug
abuse and about the agency itself, including sections on NIDA

in the News, NIDA Notes, meetings and events related to drug abuse topics, news releases, podcasts of NIDA-related programs, and electronic newsletters. The website is also available in a Spanish-language edition.

Albert Niemann (1834–1861)

During his short life, Niemann made two important discoveries. The first was the active ingredient in coca leaves responsible for their psychoactive properties, a compound that he named cocaine. The second was a powerful gas produced by reacting ethylene (C_2H_4) with sulfur dichloride (SCl_2). The product became known as mustard gas, a chemical agent used widely during World War I.

During the late 1850s, Niemann was studying for his doctoral degree in chemistry at the University of Göttingen under the great chemist Friedrich Wöhler. For some years, Wöhler had been interested in the chemical composition of coca leaves brought back to Germany from South America, but had been unable to find the active ingredient for the plant's extraordinary psychoactive properties. When he received a shipment of fresh leaves in 1859, he assigned to Niemann the task of analyzing the natural product. Niemann responded successfully to this assignment, extracting from the leaves a white powder which he described as having a bitter taste (like other alkaloids, of which this compound was an example), promoting the flow of saliva, and having a numbing effect on the tongue. Niemann gave the name of *cocaine* to the new substance, a combination of the plant name from which it came ("coca") and the traditional suffix used by chemists for all alkaloids ("-ine"). Niemann's research on cocaine earned him his PhD from Göttingen in 1860. In the same year, Niemann described his research on mustard gas (chemically, 1,1'-thiobis[2-chloroethane]; also known as sulfur mustard). He said that the gas caused terrible burns that festered for a long period of time and were very painful.

Following his research on mustard gas, Niemann's health deteriorated rapidly, and he returned to his home in Goslar,

Germany, where he died on January 19, 1861, at the age of 26. Although some uncertainty surrounds the circumstances of his death. some historians believe that his exposure to mustard gas may have been a contributing factor. Two years after his death, a colleague at Göttingen, Wilhelm Lossen, determined the chemical formula for cocaine.

Office of Adolescent Health

The Office of Adolescent Health (OAH) was created in 2010 as a division of the U.S. Department of Health and Human Services. The agency's objectives are to provide information to adolescents, their parents, health professionals, and the general public that will improve the health and general well-being of adolescents, with the objective of helping them to become healthy and productive adults.

A major focus of the agency's work is the administration and conduct of a number of grantee and technical assistance programs, including the Teen Pregnancy Prevention Program, the Pregnancy Assistance Fund, and the National Resource Center for HIV/AIDS Prevention among Adolescents. Much of its work is centered around five major adolescent health issues: reproductive health, mental health, physical health and nutrition, healthy relationships, and substance abuse. In the field of substance abuse, OAH provides information and resources in four fields: alcohol, tobacco, illicit and licit drugs, and state practices. In each of these areas, the OAH website offers basic information on the topic, as well as a number of links to additional assistance for adolescents and their parents. The "In the States" section is particularly interesting because it provides detailed statistics about substance use and abuse in each of the 50 states and the District of Columbia.

Office of National Drug Control Policy

The Office of National Drug Control Policy (ONDCP) was established in 1989 as a provision of the Anti-Drug Abuse Act of 1988. Attached to the Director's Office are a number of administrative units, including the offices of the Legal Counsel, Research and Data Analysis, Legislative Affairs, Management and Administration, Public Affairs, Performance and Budget, and Intergovernmental Public Liaison. The three programmatic offices attached to the Director's Office deal with demand reduction; supply reduction; and state, local, and tribal affairs. In its 2011 budget, ONDCP requested a staff of 98 full-time employees, of whom about two-thirds would be employed at pay grades of GS-14, GS-15, or SES with a minimum salary of $105,211 per year. The office's mission is to advise the president on drug-control issues, coordinate drug-control activities and related funding across the federal government, and produce the annual National Drug Control Strategy. This document outlines efforts by the federal government to reduce illicit drug use, manufacturing and trafficking, drug-related crime and violence, and drug-related health consequences.

Under the administration of President Barack Obama, ONDCP has taken a somewhat different approach to the nation's drug control problem than has that of earlier administrations. It is, according to its website, focusing on "renewed emphasis on community-based prevention programs, early intervention programs in healthcare settings, aligning criminal justice policies and public health systems to divert non-violent drug offenders into treatment instead of jail, funding scientific research on drug use, and, through the Affordable Care Act, expanding access to substance abuse treatment."

Much of the office's work is organized under one of about a half dozen initiatives and key policies areas. They are: ONDCP is focused on a number of ongoing initiatives and key policy areas, including prescription drug abuse, drugged driving, community-based drug, prevention, healthcare, marijuana, methamphetamine, and public lands. The office takes among the strongest and most aggressive stands on the use of marijuana of any American organization. It warns that marijuana is "addictive and unsafe," especially for adolescents. Cannabis contains, the office warns, chemicals that "can change the way the brain works," and is associated with a host of mental and physical disorders, including "addiction, respiratory and mental illness, poor motor performance, and cognitive impairment." The office also campaigns strongly against the use of smoked marijuana for medical purposes. It acknowledges that, although some orally administered components of cannabis may have medical value, "smoking marijuana is an inefficient and harmful method for delivering the constituent elements that have or may have medicinal value." It also reiterates the fact that, while a number of states have legalized the use of marijuana for medical purposes, possession and use of the drug are illegal under federal law, and anyone who uses marijuana for medical purposes in any part of the nation is liable for arrest and prosecution under the Controlled Substances Act of 1970.

ONDCP has also developed a number of programs for populations that it regards as being at special risk for drug abuse: military, veterans, and families; women, children, and families; colleges and universities; and Native Americans and Alaskan Natives. The office argues, for example, that men and women who have served in the military services are at special risk for drug abuse both while they are in active service and after they have been discharged. They point to the high proportion of veterans who are currently serving prison terms (60 percent of 140,000 men and women) who are "struggling with substance abuse." The office reminds members of the military service and veterans of the host of services available for assistance with substance abuse, such as the Substance Abuse Treatment Facility Locator of the Substance Abuse and Mental Health Services Administration (SAMHSA); the U.S. Department of Veterans Affairs; the National Association of Drug Court Professionals Veterans Treatment Courts Clearinghouse of the U.S. Department of Justice; the Veterans Suicide Prevention Hotline of SAMHSA; the "Dealing With Effects of Trauma" self-help guide provided by SAMHSA and the federal government's Veterans Employment Website of the Office of Personnel Management.

President Obama's emphasis on prevention and treatment is reflected in a number of well-developed programs for the general public in these areas. The major focus of the ONDCP's National Youth Anti-Drug Media Campaign, for example, is a program called Above the Influence, which includes both national-level advertising and targeted efforts at the local community level. A similar program is the ONDCP's Drug-Free Communities Support Program, which provides federal grants to community-based coalitions working to prevent and reduce youth substance abuse. The other prong of President Obama's approach to substance abuse is treatment, with an emphasis on getting young substance abusers into treatment programs rather than prison systems. A host of existing federal and state services, as well as a number of new programs, are available to achieve this objective.

The two primary components of supply reduction efforts by the office are a number of international agreements and a strong enforcement program. The international programs involve agreements with Afghanistan, the Andean Region, Canada, the Caribbean, Central America, Europe, Mexico, and Russia to reduce the production, processing, and distribution of illegal substances within and through these countries and areas. The enforcement aspect of ONDCP's work focuses on the whole range of activities through which illegal substances are distributed in the United States. One of the major programs in this area is the High Intensity Drug Trafficking Area (HIDTA) Program which targets regions where the transport and distribution of illegal substances is especially high.

ONDCP's most important publication is probably its *National Drug Control Strategy*, an annual publication that reviews the current status of substance abuse in the United States along with the federal government's plans for dealing with various aspects of that issue.

Quanah Parker (ca. 1845–1911)

Parker was the last chief of the Quahadi Comanche Indian tribe and a leading proponent of the melding of Christian and

Native American Church movements, in which peyote is incorporated into traditional forms of worship. His most famous commentary is probably his comment that "the White Man goes into his church and talks about Jesus. The Indian goes into his Tipi and talks with Jesus."

The details of Quanah Parker's birth, as well as some other aspects of his life, are somewhat unclear. He is thought to have been born in the mid-1840s somewhere in the present state of Oklahoma. He himself claimed to have been born on Elk Creek, south of the Wichita Mountains, although other places have also been mentioned as a probable birthplace. His parents were Comanche warrior Noconie (also known by the Indian name of Tah-con-ne-ah-pe-ah and called Peta Nocona by the whites) and Cynthia Ann Parker (later given the Indian name of Nadua, or "the found"), who had been captured by the Comanche during a raid on Fort Parker in Texas. Parker apparently grew up in a traditional Native American community, replete with tribal customs. After his father was killed in 1860, Parker took shelter with a subgroup of the Comanches, the Quahadi tribe. Over time, he grew in respect and responsibility within the tribe and became its leader. From the mid-1860s to the mid-1870s, Parker fought against surrender to or assimilation by whites who were committed to taking over Native American lands and property. He eventually lost that fight at the battle of Adobe Walls, and was resigned to retiring to the reservation to which his tribe had been assigned.

Parker's connection with peyote is reputed to stem from 1884, when he fell very ill from an infection. Although he had, by then, become thoroughly absorbed by white culture, the medicines available to him from white practitioners were of no use. Only when he was provided with a concoction of peyote did he recover. The experience proved to be life-changing for him, convincing him of the value of native traditions (and native drugs) even in the modern world of the reservation. He spent much of the rest of his life in developing and promoting the National American Indian church movement, which incorporates elements of both white Christianity and traditional

Native American beliefs and practices. Largely through his efforts, the modern Native American church still includes the use of peyote in its rituals.

Nancy Reagan (1921–2016)

Reagan was the widow of former president Ronald Reagan. She was First Lady during the Reagan presidential administration, from 1981 to 1989. Among the accomplishments for which she is most famous is her "Just Say No" antidrug campaign, initiated in 1982.

Reagan was born in New York City on July 6, 1921, as Anne Francis Robbins. Her father was a car salesman, Kenneth Seymour Robbins, and her mother, Edith Luckett, an actress. After her parents were divorced shortly after her birth, she was raised for six years by an aunt and uncle in Bethesda, Maryland. When her mother remarried in 1929, the family moved to Chicago, where Nancy attended the Girls' Latin School of Chicago. After graduation, she enrolled at Smith College in Northampton, Massachusetts, where she majored in drama and English. She was awarded her bachelor's degree from Smith in 1943 and returned to Chicago, where she held a series of jobs in retail. Partially through her mother's influence, she was able to find work in the entertainment industry, with roles on Broadway, in traveling shows, and, eventually, in Hollywood films. In November 1949, she met Ronald Reagan, then president of the Screen Actors' Guild. They were married in March 1952.

As First Lady, Reagan was the subject of considerable admiration and disdain, both for her political views and for her personal beliefs and actions. She was widely criticized in 1988, for example, when President Reagan wrote about his wife's use of astrologers to make public and private decisions. She was also widely applauded and criticized for her "Just Say No" campaign against drug abuse. The campaign had its beginnings when Nancy Reagan visited the Longfellow Elementary School in Oakland, California, in 1982. When a girl in the classroom she was visiting asked what she should do if she were offered drugs, Reagan responded by saying, "Just say no." That phrase soon became a slogan for a national, and eventually, international, campaign to combat drug abuse. Reagan appeared on a number of television programs, spoke widely across the country, worked with a number of national organizations, and visited many drug treatment and prevention programs to spread her message. Experts disagree as to the effectiveness of the campaign. Some point to an apparent decline in drug use during the Reagan administration and suggest that "Just Say No" was an important contributor to that trend. Others believe that sloganeering had only a limited effect on substance abuse patterns.

Following President Reagan's death in 2004, Nancy Reagan remained visible and active on the national scene. Perhaps her most important efforts were on behalf of stem cell research, attempting to convince then-president George W. Bush to change his mind and extend opportunities for research in this field, an effort in which she was not successful. Nancy Reagan died in Los Angeles on March 6, 2016.

Friedrich Sertürner (1783–1841)

While still a young pharmacist's apprentice, Sertürner isolated the psychoactive agent morphine from the opium plant. His accomplishment is especially important because it was not only the first such agent extracted from opium, but also the first alkaloid obtained from any plant. Sertürner named his new discovery after the Greek god of dreams, Morpheus, for its powerful analgesic and sedative properties.

Friedrich Wilhelm Adam Ferdinand Sertürner was born in Neuhaus, Prussia, on June 19, 1783. His parents were in service to Prince Friedrich Wilhelm, who was also his godfather. When both his father and the prince died in 1794, he was left without means of support and, therefore, was apprenticed to a court apothecary by the name of Cramer. One of the topics in which he became interested in his new job was the chemical composition of opium, a plant that had long been known for its powerful analgesic and sedative properties. By 1803, he had extracted from opium seeds a white crystalline powder clearly responsible for the pharmacological properties of the plant. He named the new substance morphine and proceeded to test its properties, first on stray animals available at the castle, and later on his friends and himself. His friends soon withdrew from the experiments because, while pleasurable enough in its initial moderate doses, the compound ultimately caused unpleasant physical effects, including nausea and vomiting. Sertürner continued, however, to test the drug on himself, unaware of its ultimate addictive properties.

Sertürner was awarded his apothecary license in 1806 and established his own pharmacy in the Prussian town of Einbeck. In addition to operating his business, he continued to study the chemical and pharmacological properties of morphine for a number of years. His work drew little attention from professional scientists, however, and he eventually turned his attention to other topics, including the development of improved firearms and ammunition. During the last few years of his life, he became increasingly depressed about his failure to interest the scientific community in his research on opium. He withdrew into his own world and turned to morphine for comfort against his disillusionment with what he saw as the failure of his life. He did receive some comfort in 1831 when he was awarded a Montyon Prize by the Académie Française, sometimes described as the forerunner of the Nobel Prizes, with its cash award of 2,000 francs. By the time of his death in Hamelin, Prussia, on February 20, 1841, however, the scientific world in general had still not appreciated the enormous significance of his research on morphine.

Alexander "Sasha" Shulgin (1925–2014)

Shulgin was arguably the best known and most highly regarded advocates of so-called designer drugs within the scientific community. He is thought to have synthesized and tested more than

200 psychoactive compounds in his life and wrote a number of important books and articles on the properties and potential benefits of such substances.

Alexander Shulgin, widely known as "Sasha," was born in Berkeley, California, on June 17, 1925. He graduated from high school at the age of 16 and received a full scholarship to Harvard University. His tenure at Harvard was cut short, however, with the beginning of World War II, during which he served with the U.S. Navy in both the North Atlantic and the Pacific campaigns. After the war, he returned to Berkeley, where he eventually earned his BA in chemistry at the University of California in 1949 and his PhD in biochemistry at 1954. He completed his postdoctoral studies at the University of California at San Francisco (UCSF) in pharmacology and psychiatry. After working for a year at the BioRad Laboratories company, he took a position with Dow Chemical, where he was a research scientist from 1955 to 1961 and senior research chemist from 1961 to 1966.

Shulgin's most significant accomplishment at Dow was to develop a pesticide known as physostigmine, a substance that was to become one of Dow's best-selling products. In appreciation of Shulgin's work, Dow provided him with a laboratory of his own where he was allowed to work on projects that were of special interest to him. One of those projects turned out to be the synthesis and study of psychedelic compounds. Shulgin later reported that his interest in psychedelics was prompted by his first experience in taking mescaline in 1960. As a result of that experience, he told an interviewer from *Playboy* magazine in 2004, he had found his "learning path," the direction he wanted the rest of his career to go.

In 1965, Shulgin decided to leave Dow in order to enter medical school at UCSF. He left that program after only two years, however, to pursue his interest in psychedelics. That decision posed a problem for both Shulgin and the U.S. Drug Enforcement Administration (DEA), the federal agency responsible for control of illegal drug use in the United States. Although its primary function is to discourage the development and use of illegal drugs, the DEA apparently saw some benefit in Shulgin's work, and they agreed to a special dispensation that allowed him to synthesize and study a number of otherwise illegal substances. That relationship eventually worked out well for both partners, as it permitted Shulgin to pursue the studies in which he was most interested and provided the DEA with invaluable information on substances about which it might otherwise have little or no information. In 1988, for example, he wrote *Controlled Substances: Chemical & Legal Guide to Federal Drug Laws*, a book that has become a standard reference for DEA employees.

Shulgin's special relationship with the DEA ended in 1994 when the agency raided his Berkeley laboratory and withdrew his license to conduct research on illegal substances, claiming that he had failed to keep proper records. Some observers believe, however, that the agency's actions were prompted by a book that Shulgin and his wife Ann had written a few years earlier, *PiHKAL: A Chemical Love Story*. (The PiHKAL of the title stands for "phenylethylamines I have known and loved.") The Shulgins later wrote a second book about another group of psychedelic substances, *TiHKAL: The Continuation*. In this case, the title word TiHKAL stands for "tryptamines I have known and loved." One of Shulgin's most recent book was somewhat more technically oriented, *The Simple Plant Isoquinolines* (with Wendy E. Perry). In 2008, his first two laboratory books were scanned and placed online. He published his final work, *The Shulgin Index*, originally planned to appear in two volumes, in 2011. By the time of his death on June 2, 2014, at his home in Lafayette, California, the second volume had not appeared, nor has it since his death.

Substance Abuse and Mental Health Services Administration

The Substance Abuse and Mental Health Services Administration (SAMHSA) was created in 1992 during the reorganization of the federal government's agencies responsible for mental health services. It assumed most of the responsibilities of the Alcohol, Drug Abuse, and Mental Health Administration (ADAMHA), which was disbanded in the reorganization. The organization is charged with developing and supporting programs that improve the quality and availability of prevention, treatment, and rehabilitation for abusers of both legal and illegal drugs. As of 2015, it had about 660 employees and a budget of about $3.7 billion. Its headquarters are in Rockville, Maryland, and it maintains four primary research centers there, the Center for Behavioral Health Statistics and Quality, Center for Mental Health Services, Center for Substance Abuse Prevention, and Center for Substance Abuse Treatment.

From time to time, SAMHSA selects a small number of strategic initiatives on which it focuses its efforts over a specific and limited period of time. Currently those initiatives are:

- Prevention of Substance Abuse and Mental Health, the current form of an ongoing effort to make use of existing research knowledge to reduce the risk of substance abuse and mental health among Americans, especially high-risk populations of transition-age youth; college students; American Indian/Alaska Natives; ethnic minorities experiencing health and behavioral health disparities; service members, veterans, and their families; and lesbian, gay, bisexual, and transgender (LGBT) individuals.

- Health Care and Health Systems Integration, designed to make the best available therapies available to all individuals in the areas of both substance abuse and mental health.

- Trauma and Justice, an effort to increase the availability of mental health and substance abuse services to individuals in the criminal justice and juvenile justice systems.

- Recovery Support, which focuses on providing assistance to individuals who are in recovery from both mental health and substance abuse disorders.

- Health Information Technology, designed to promote the use of existing technology, such as electronic health records, to transform the fundamental nature of behavioral health care.
- Workforce Development, an effort to train more workers in methods for using modern technology to address the behavioral health needs of the nation.

More detailed information about these initiatives is available at http://store.samhsa.gov/shin/content//PEP14-LEADCHANGE2/PEP14-LEADCHANGE2.pdf.

In addition to its specialized strategic initiatives, SAMHSA maintains a large number of ongoing programs and campaigns on specific issues within the areas of substance abuse and mental health. Some of these topics are Behavioral Health Equity, the Buprenorphine Information Center, the Center for Application of Prevention Technologies, National Prevention Week, the Partners for Recovery Initiative, the Recovery to Practice program, the Safe Schools/Healthy Students Initiative, the Disaster Technical Assistance Center, the Division of Workplace Programs, the Fetal Alcohol Spectrum Disorders Center, the Homelessness Resource Center, the SAMHSA Knowledge Applications Project, and the Tribal Training and Technical Assistance Center.

The SAMHSA website is one of the best resources for information on virtually all aspects of substance abuse. This information is organized under about two dozen rubrics, including alcohol, tobacco, and other drugs; behavioral health treatments and services; criminal and juvenile justice; data, outcomes, and quality; disaster preparedness, response, and recovery; health care and health systems integration; health disparities; health financing; health information technology; HIV, AIDS, and viral hepatitis; homelessness and housing; laws, regulations, and guidelines; mental and substance use disorders; prescription drug misuse and abuse; prevention of substance abuse and mental illness; recovery and recovery support; school and campus health; specific populations; state and local government partnerships; suicide prevention; trauma and violence; tribal affairs; underage drinking; veterans and military families; wellness; and workforce. The Prescription Drug Abuse page provides basic information obtained from a number of essential studies, such as the 2013 National Survey on Drug Use and Health, a 2011 analysis by the Centers for Disease Control and Prevention, a 2008 report by the Coalition Against Insurance Fraud, and the 2014 National Drug Control Strategy. Other sections of this part of the website deal with additional issues such as types of commonly misused or abused drugs, specific populations and prescription drug misuse and abuse, SAMHSA's efforts to fight prescription drug misuse and abuse, grants related to prescription drug misuse and abuse, and publications and resources on prescription drug misuse and abuse. SAMHSA also maintains an extensive library of brochures, pamphlets, reports, toolkits, digital downloads, comic books, guidelines, manuals, and other publications on the range of topics in which it is interested and involved.

Luther L. Terry (1911–1985)

Terry was the ninth surgeon general of the United States. He was appointed to the office by President John F. Kennedy, and he served through Kennedy's incomplete first term in office and the first year of Lyndon B. Johnson's first term. He is probably best known today for the first report issued by the U.S. Public Health Service on the health effects of smoking, *Smoking and Health: Report of the Advisory Committee to the Surgeon General*, released in 1964. Among the many findings in that report, some of the most outstanding were that the mortality rate was 70 percent higher for smokers than for nonsmokers of a comparable age, that moderate smokers were 9 to 10 times more likely (and heavy smokers 20 times more likely) to develop cancer than nonsmokers, and that health risks rose and fell consistently with increases and decreases, respectively, in the amount of smoking.

Luther Leonidas Terry was born in Red Level, Alabama, on September 15, 1911, to James Edward and Lula M. (Durham) Terry. He attended Birmingham Southern College, from which he received his BA degree in 1931, and the Tulane Medical School, which awarded his MD in 1935. Terry completed his internship at the Hillman Hospital in Birmingham and his residency at City Hospitals in Cleveland. In 1938, he served an additional internship in pathology at Washington University, in St. Louis. In 1940, he accepted an appointment as instructor at the University of Texas, Galveston, where he remained for four years. He then moved to the Johns Hopkins University Medical School in Baltimore, while also holding an appointment at the Public Health Service Hospital in Baltimore. In 1950, he accepted an appointment as Chief of General Medicine and Experimental Therapeutics at the National Heart Institute in Bethesda in 1950. The position was, at first, a part-time appointment, but it became a full-time post three years later when his division was transferred to the newly established National Institutes of Health Clinical Center. In 1958, Terry was appointed assistant director of the National Heart Institute, and, three years later, became surgeon general of the United States.

Shortly after assuming his post as surgeon general, Terry appointed a committee to study the health effects of smoking. His action was motivated to a large extent by a similar study that had just been completed and announced by the Royal College of Physicians in Great Britain, in which strong evidence for somewhat dramatic health effects as a result of smoking had been reported. Terry decided that a similar report for the United States was needed, although it would almost certainly be controversial and economically risky. The final report, issued on January 11, 1964, summarized the findings of more than 7,000 scientific articles and the expert testimony of more than 130 witnesses before Terry's committee.

After his retirement as surgeon general in 1965, Terry took a post as vice president for medical affairs and professor of medicine and community medicine at the University of Pennsylvania. He maintained his affiliation with Pennsylvania until 1982, and then accepted a position as corporate vice president for medical affairs and, later, as consultant to ARA Services Inc. Terry died in Philadelphia on April 29, 1985.

United Nations Office on Drugs and Crime

The United Nations Office on Drugs and Crime (UNODC) was created in 1997 as the Office for Drug Control and Crime Prevention by the merger of two preexisting United Nations (UN) organizations, the United Nations International Drug Control Programme and the Crime Prevention and Criminal Justice Division of the United Nations office at Vienna, Austria. The organization's name was changed to its present name in 2002. UNODC is one of 32 funds, programs, agencies, departments, and offices that make up the United Nations Development Group (UNDG) and whose goal it is to provide more effective and more efficient support to nations attempting to achieve certain internationally agreed-upon development goals. A few other members of the UNDG are the United Nations Children's Fund, United Nations Population Fund, World Food Programme, Office of the High Commissioner for Human Rights, Joint United Nations Programme on HIV/ AIDS, and the World Health Organization.

UNODC lists three main "pillars" that underlie its work. The first pillar is research and analysis aimed at improving the world's knowledge about drugs and crime with the aim of providing an accurate basis for the development of policies and legislation. The second pillar is assistance to nations in the development of international treaties and domestic legislation designed to fight drug abuse, crime, and terrorism. The third pillar is field-based cooperative projects that improve the ability of nations to counteract substance abuse, crime, and terrorism. In order to accomplish these goals, UNODC is divided administratively into four major divisions: Division for Operations,

Division for Treaty Affairs, Division for Policy Analysis and Public Affairs, and Division of Management. The Division for Operations is responsible for programs such as HIV/AIDS; drug prevention, treatment, and rehabilitation; sustainable livelihoods; and justice. The Division for Treaty Affairs deals with activities such as organized crime and illicit trafficking; corruption and economic crime; and terrorism prevention. The Division for Policy Analysis and Public Affairs is concerned with laboratory and scientific studies; statistics and surveys; studies and threat analysis; strategic planning; and advocacy. The Division of Management is responsible for in-house management issues, such as human resources and information technology.

In order to facilitate its services to member states of the United Nations, UNODC has developed a Menu of Services which clearly and succinctly outline the ways in which the organization can assist individual nations and regions in dealing with problems of illicit drugs, crime, and terrorism. That Menu of Services is available in print and electronic form, the latter at the agency's website at http://www.unodc.org/docu ments/frontpage/MoS_book11_LORES.pdf. Some of the services that are listed and described in the Menu of Services publication are the following:

- research and threat analysis;
- cross-border cooperation and knowledge sharing;
- statistic expertise;
- quantitative and qualitative trends;
- research and survey reports and threat assessments;
- capacity development assessment;
- expert advice;
- specialized training;
- legal assistance;
- model laws and legislation;

- scientific and forensic services; and
- awareness raising campaigns and initiatives.

As a way of carrying out its general program, UNODC has developed a number of specific focus areas within which to conduct its day-to-day work. Currently these focus areas include alternative development; corruption; crime prevention and criminal justice; drug prevention, treatment, and care; drug trafficking; HIV and AIDS; human trafficking and migrant smuggling; money laundering; organized crime; piracy; terrorism prevention; and wildlife and forest crime. An example of the work conducted under these focus topics is the program on drug prevention, treatment, and care. For many years, UNODC has been working to identify the best practices in achieving progress in these three areas of substance abuse. As a result of these efforts, it has developed two programs, Global Youth Network against Drug Abuse and the Global Initiative on Primary Prevention of Substance Abuse. The former program is intended to provide a mechanism by which young adults are able to disseminate knowledge about programs that they have developed throughout the international community. The program's "Taking Action" page describes some of these programs on topics such as Preventing the Use of Amphetamine-Type Stimulants among Young People, Putting the Right Message across to Youth, Prevention in School, Working with Families, Alternative Activities, Working with Vulnerable Populations, and Violence Prevention: The Evidence. The Global Initiative on Primary Prevention of Substance Abuse was a collaborative project between UNODC and the World Health Organization (WHO), funded by the government of Norway. The program involved identifying successful drug prevention programs in various countries around the world and then providing those programs with training and financial and technical support. One result of this effort was the development of a set of good practices that have been found to be successful in reducing substance abuse.

UNODC has developed a number of tools for use in its campaign against illicit drugs, crime, and terrorism, such as campaigns (World Drug Day, International Day against Drug Abuse and Illicit Trafficking, and International Anti-Corruption Day); commissions (Commission on Narcotic Drugs, Commission on Crime Prevention and Criminal Justice, and Governance and Finance Working Group); an annual Congress on Crime Prevention and Criminal Justice; data and analysis tools (*World Drug Report, Global Report on Trafficking in Persons*, statistical reports, transnational organized crime threat assessments, and studies and journals); legal tools (e.g., the Legal Library, Human Trafficking Case Law Database, collection of international drugs control conventions and commentaries, Directories of Competent National Authorities, Mutual Legal Assistance Request Writer Tool, and model laws and treaties); and laboratory and forensic science services (which include information on drug analysis and forensic science laboratories; criminal justice system and law enforcement authorities; regulatory and health authorities, quality assurance support; manuals, guidelines and publications; partnerships; news and events; and synthetic drugs).

UNODC produces a very large number of publications that are generally available in both print and electronic formats. A few of the most important of those publications are the *Bulletin of Narcotics*, which was published between 1949 and 2008; the *Forum on Crime and Society*, which was published between 2001 and 2006; and *World Drug Report*, which has been published annually since 1999 and is one of the best resources on drug statistics currently available.

U.S. Drug Enforcement Administration

The U.S. government has had a succession of agencies designed to deal with substance abuse problems in general, and marijuana, in particular. The earliest of those agencies was the Narcotics Division, established in the Bureau of Internal Revenue in 1921. The agency was created to carry out mandates of the

Harrison Narcotic Act of 1914. A year later, a second agency was created, the Federal Narcotics Control Board, whose mandate it was to make and publish regulations concerning the import and export of narcotic substances. These two agencies were consolidated in 1930 to form the Bureau of Narcotics in the U.S. Department of the Treasury. In yet another reorganization act, the Bureau of Narcotics and the Bureau of Drug Abuse Control (created in the Food and Drug Administration in 1965) were combined to form the Bureau of Narcotics and Dangerous Drugs within the Department of Justice. The final step in this sequence of events occurred on July 28, 1973, when President Richard Nixon signed the Reorganization Plan No. 2 of 1973, bringing under one roof all agencies in the federal government with some responsibility for substance abuse, including the Bureau of Narcotics and Dangerous Drugs and a number of smaller agencies in a variety of cabinet departments. The new agency, which still exists today, was the Drug Enforcement Administration (DEA). The first administrator of the DEA was John R. Bartels Jr., a former federal prosecutor. The current DEA administrator is Chuck Rosenberg, formerly chief of staff to the director of the FBI.

As specified on its website, the mission of the DEA is "to enforce the controlled substances laws and regulations of the United States and bring to the criminal and civil justice system of the United States, or any other competent jurisdiction, those organizations and principal members of organizations, involved in the growing, manufacture, or distribution of controlled substances appearing in or destined for illicit traffic in the United States; and to recommend and support non-enforcement programs aimed at reducing the availability of illicit controlled substances on the domestic and international markets."

DEA activities fall into one of about 20 major categories, including:

• Organized Crime Drug Enforcement Task Forces (OCDETF): This program involves the participation of a number of federal agencies to attack major drug trafficking and money-laundering activities related to the importation and sale of illegal drugs to the United States.

- Demand reduction: In addition to apprehending and prosecuting substance abusers and their enablers, the agency works to reduce the use of illegal drugs by working with state, regional, and local agencies to help individuals understand the dangers posed by substance abuse and to find ways of avoiding involvement in drug activities.

- Asset forfeiture: Federal law provides that profits from drug-related activities collected by drug enforcement activities are forfeited to the government and may be used to support worthy causes through the Asset Forfeiture Fund.

- Aviation program: Since 1971, the DEA has provided air support for ground activities of the agency's agents, helping to detect, locate, identify, and assess narcotics-related trafficking activities.

- Diversion control: This program is aimed at monitoring and controlling the illegal use of prescription drugs, the fastest-growing substance abuse problem in the United States today. The program involves the arrest of physicians who sell prescriptions to drug dealers, pharmacists who falsify records and sell prescription drugs to dealers, employees who steal from inventories and/or falsify records, and individuals who obtain prescription drugs by illegal activities.

- Forensic sciences: The DEA forensic science laboratory provides assistance to prosecutors who need evidence for the conduct of criminal cases involving the use of illegal substances.

- Foreign cooperative investigations. Since almost all illegal substances (except for marijuana) are grown or produced outside the United States, cooperation with foreign government where drugs are produced is an essential feature of the U.S. drug control program.

The DEA's Domestic Cannabis Eradication/Suppression Program (DCE/SP) is of special interest largely because marijuana is the only major Schedule I grown in the United States. One of the major goals of DCE/SP, then, is to eliminate the supply of marijuana in the United States by finding and destroying farms where the cannabis plant is being grown. In 2010, for example, DEA agents identified and eradicated a total of 23,622 outdoor marijuana growing sites with an estimated total of 9,866,766 individual plants. In addition, 4,721 indoor sites were identified and eradicated, with a loss of 462,419 plants. Total estimated value of all the destroyed plants was $34,311,819. In addition to plant destruction, DEA agents made 9,687 arrests of individuals associated with plant growth and collected 5,081 weapons.

Each year, the DEA schedules a number of special operations to carry out the agency's mission. In 2011, for example, those operations included Operation Fire and Ice, a five-year investigation of an international drug trafficking organization called La Oficina de Envigado, based in Medellín, Colombia; Operation Pill Nation, which involved the arrest of 22 individuals and the seizing of more than $2.2 million in cash from a number of rogue pain clinics in South Florida; and the 38th Street Gang Roundup, in which federal agents seized more than seven kilograms of cocaine, one pound of methamphetamine, and about $250,000 cash from a notorious gang located in south Los Angeles.

DEA makes available on its website a number of valuable print and electronic publications including the biweekly electronic newsletter, *Dateline DEA*; a set of 33 "Drug Facts" informational sheets; an annual report *Drugs of Abuse*; a publication especially designed for state and local law enforcement officials, environmental protection groups, and public health agencies, *Guidelines for Law Enforcement for the Cleanup of Clandestine Drug Laboratories*; a document dealing with the decriminalization of currently illegal drugs, *Speaking Out against Drug Legalization*; and two technical publications, *Microgram Bulletin* and *Microgram Journal*.

R. Gordon Wasson (1898–1986)

Wasson was a wealthy New York City banker with a lifelong intense interest in mushrooms. He conducted a number of original studies on all varieties of mushrooms, put forth an attempt to prove that psychedelic mushrooms were integrally involved in the development of many religions, and provided financial assistance to a number of researchers in the field of psychoactive studies, including Timothy Leary and Richard Alpert.

Robert Gordon Wasson was born in Great Falls, Montana, on September 22, 1898. His father was an Episcopalian priest with a strong interest in languages, being fluent in Latin and Greek and conversant in Icelandic, Hebrew, and Sanskrit. His mother has been described as a "vivacious woman," who was also learned and one of six women selected to organize the Columbia University Library. When the senior Wasson accepted an appointment at a small parish in Newark, New Jersey, the family reestablished its home on the East Coast. During his childhood, Gordon was apparently subjected to serious instruction in language, the arts, and theology. Biographers note that he and his brother had each read the Bible completely through three times before the age of 13.

After three years of high school, Gordon joined his older brother Thomas Campbell Wasson, and the two young men spent the early war years traveling through Europe. Gordon then enlisted in the U.S. Army in 1917, serving in France as a radio operator. After the war, he enrolled at Columbia University, from which he received his bachelor's degree in literature in 1920. After working as a reporter and an editor for various newspapers and magazines, including the New Haven *Register*, *The New York Herald Tribune*, and *Current Opinion*, for eight years, he decided to pursue a career in finance. He joined the Guaranty Company of New York in 1928, where he was given a number of international assignments, before moving to the J. P. Morgan Company in 1934. He remained affiliated with Morgan for the rest of his career, retiring in 1963.

Wasson's interest in mushrooms can be traced to a honeymoon trip to the Catskill Mountains that he and his wife took in 1925. On that trip, the couple found a number of species of mushrooms that Mrs. Wasson (the former Valentina Pavlovna Guercken) recognized from her native Russia. Over the years, the couple continued their research not only on the scientific aspects of mushrooms, but also on their involvement in other fields, including literature, history, theology, mythology, art, and archaeology. In 1953, Wasson visited Mexico, where he was introduced to the so-called magic mushrooms widely used in religious ceremonies there. He is credited with having brought back the first herbarium samples of those mushrooms, and having made his experience famous by means of an article in the May 17, 1957 edition of *Life* magazine, entitled "The Discovery of Mushrooms That Cause Strange Visions." Wasson was the author or coauthor of a number of scholarly articles and 11 books on psychedelic mushrooms, including *Persephone's Quest: Entheogens and the Origins of Religion* (1986), *The Wondrous Mushroom: Mycolatry in Mesoamerica* (1980), *The Road to Eleusis: Unveiling the Secret of the Mysteries* (1978), *Maria Sabina and Her Mazatec Mushroom Velada* (1976), and *Soma: Divine Mushroom of Immortality* (1968). Wasson died in Danbury, Connecticut, on December 23, 1986.

Hamilton Wright (1867–1917)

Wright has been described as the "father of drug laws" in the United States because of his strong objections to the use of illegal drugs and his vigorous efforts to have laws passed against the manufacture, transport, sale, and consumption of illegal substances. Although he was not a member of Congress at the time, he is generally regarded as the author of the Harrison Narcotics Tax Act of 1914, which instituted taxes on opiates for the first time in U.S. history.

Hamilton Wright was born in Cleveland, Ohio, on August 2, 1867. After graduating from high school in Boston, he enlisted in the U.S. Army, where he served in the 7th Fusiliers in the Reale Rebellion, earning a medal for his valor during the war. He then attended McGill University in Montréal, Canada, from which he received his MD in 1895. From 1895 to 1908, he was engaged in a variety of research projects at a number of sites around the world, studying tropical diseases such as beri-beri, plague, and malaria. His work took him to China, Japan, Malaya, Great Britain, Germany, and France. In 1908, President Teddy Roosevelt appointed Wright the nation's first commissioner on international opium, a capacity in which he represented the United States at the International Opium Conference held at The Hague, the Netherlands, in 1911. He spent the rest of his life campaigning against opium use in the United States, which, as he wrote in a 1911 article for *The New York Times*, had the highest proportion of opium users of any country in the world.

Wright is known today for his willingness to use inflammatory, often inaccurate statements about the dangers posed by opium. He was especially critical of blacks and Chinese Americans for their use of the drug, suggesting at one point that "one of the most unfortunate phases of the habit of smoking opium in this country is the large number of women who have become involved and are living as common-law wives or cohabiting with Chinese in the Chinatowns of our various cities." He also railed against cocaine use, suggesting at one time that "cocaine is often the direct incentive to the crime of rape by the Negroes of the South and other sections of the country."

Wright was very successful in pushing his anti-opium agenda both domestically and internationally. At home, his greatest achievement was the adoption of the Harrison Act in 1914; overseas, it was the adoption of the International Opium Convention in 1912. In both cases, Wright had pushed for even broader, more comprehensive control over drugs other than opium, especially marijuana, but without success. Wright died at his home in Washington, D.C., on January 9, 1917, as a result of complications resulting from an automobile accident in France two years earlier. He was assisting in U.S. relief efforts in that country following the conclusion of World War II.

Introduction

Useful information about the status of youth substance abuse in the United States and the rest of the world can often be gleaned from national, state, and local laws; court cases dealing with the topic; and statistics and data about the use of various substances by youth. This chapter provides some of this basic information.

Data

Table 5.1 Alcohol Involvement among Young Drivers (Age 15 to 20) Involved in Fatal Crashes, by Year and Driver Status, 2003 and 2012

Driver Status	Total Number of Drivers	BAC = .01–.07		BAC = .08 +		BAC = .01+	
		Number	Percentage	Number	Percentage	Number	Percentage
			2003				
Survived	4,262	178	4	543	13	721	17
Did not survive	3,675	219	6	917	25	1,136	31
Total	7,937	397	5	1,460	18	1,857	23
			2012				
Survived	2,408	88	4	304	13	392	16
Did not survive	1,875	75	4	459	24	534	28
Total	4,283	163	4	763	18	926	22

Source: "Young Drivers." 2014. Traffic Safety Facts. National Highway Safety Transportation Administration. http://www-nrd.nhtsa.dot.gov/Pubs/812019.pdf. Accessed on January 8, 2016.

Carnival goers dance at the start of the Electric Daisy Carnival in Las Vegas. The Electric Daisy Carnival is one of the world's largest electronic music festivals, with 26 carnival rides, music from hit DJs, and a reputation for wild drug use. (AP Photo/Julie Jacobson)

Table 5.2 Trends in Lifetime Prevalence of Use of Various Drugs for Grades 8, 10, and 12 (percentage of respondents)

Drug	1991	1992	1993	1994	1995	1996	1997	1998	1999	2000	2001	2002	2003	2004	2005	2006	2007	2008	2009	2010	2011	2012	2013	2014
A	30.4	29.8	32.1	35.7	38.9	42.2	43.3	42.3	41.9	41.0	40.9	39.5	37.5	36.4	35.7	34.0	32.7	32.6	33.2	34.4	34.7	34.1	36.0	34.9
B	22.7	21.1	23.4	27.8	31.6	35.6	37.8	36.5	36.4	35.3	35.3	34.0	32.4	31.4	30.8	28.9	27.9	27.9	29.0	30.4	31.0	30.7	32.0	30.5
C	17.0	16.9	18.2	18.6	19.4	19.1	18.6	18.1	17.5	16.4	15.3	13.6	13.4	13.7	14.1	13.7	13.5	13.1	12.5	12.1	10.6	10.0	8.9	8.8
D	6.1	6.3	7.0	7.7	8.9	10.0	10.2	9.5	9.0	8.5‡	9.2	7.6	6.9	6.3	5.9	5.7	5.8	5.6	5.3	5.8	5.7	5.0	5.0	4.3
E	5.5	5.7	6.5	6.9	8.1	8.9	9.1	8.3	7.9	7.2	6.5	5.0	3.7	3.0	2.6	2.5	2.6	2.7	2.5	2.8	2.7	2.5	2.6	2.4
F	2.4	2.5	2.7	3.6	3.9	4.8	4.9	4.8	4.4	4.5‡	6.7	6.0	5.8	5.6	5.4	5.2	5.1	4.8	4.7	5.0	4.9	4.3	4.1	3.5
G	–	–	–	–	–	4.9	5.2	4.5	5.3	7.2	8.0	6.9	5.4	4.7	4.0	4.3	4.5	4.1	4.6	5.5	5.5	4.6	4.7	3.5
H	4.6	4.0	4.1	4.5	5.1	6.0	6.6	7.0	7.2	6.5	5.9	5.7	5.3	5.5	5.5	5.3	5.2	4.8	4.2	3.8	3.4	3.3	3.1	2.9
I	2.0	1.9	2.0	2.5	2.8	3.2	3.4	3.8	3.8	3.5	3.2	3.2	2.9	2.9	2.8	2.6	2.5	2.2	2.0	1.9	1.6	1.5	1.5	1.3
J	4.1	3.5	3.6	3.9	4.2	5.2	5.9	6.1	6.3	5.6	5.1	4.8	4.5	4.7	4.7	4.7	4.6	4.1	3.7	3.4	3.1	2.9	2.7	2.5
K	1.1	1.3	1.3	1.6	1.9	2.1	2.1	2.2	2.2	2.1	1.7	1.7	1.5	1.5	1.5	1.4	1.4	1.3	1.4	1.4	1.2	1.0	1.0	0.9
L	12.9	12.5	13.8	14.3	15.2	15.5	15.2	14.5	14.0	13.5	13.9	13.1	11.8	11.2	10.3	10.1	9.5	8.6	8.6	8.9	8.6	8.3	10.5	9.7
M	5.5	5.3	5.4	5.5	5.8	6.5	6.6	6.9	7.0	6.9‡	7.9	7.9	7.3	7.1	6.8	7.0	6.7	6.3	6.5	6.6	6.0	5.8	5.2	5.3
N	80.1	79.2‡	68.8	68.4	68.2	68.4	68.8	67.4	66.4	66.6	65.5	62.7	61.7	60.5	58.6	57.0	56.3	55.1	54.6	53.6	51.5	50.0	48.4	46.4
O	53.5	53.0	54.0	54.6	55.8	57.8	57.4	56.0	54.5	51.8	49.1	44.2	40.8	39.6	37.4	35.0	33.3	31.3	31.2	30.9	28.7	27.0	25.6	22.9
P	26.2	25.6	26.3	26.0	25.7	22.7	21.1	19.4	17.9	16.6	15.2	14.1	–	13.6	13.8	13.3	12.9	12.3	13.5	14.5	13.8	13.5	12.8	12.1
Q	1.9	1.8	1.8	2.1	2.1	1.8	2.1	2.3	2.8	3.0	3.3	3.3	3.0	2.5	2.1	2.0	1.8	1.6	1.5	1.5	1.5	1.4	1.5	1.4

A = Any illicit drug

B = Marijuana/hashish

C = Inhalants

D = Hallucinogens

E = LSD

F = Hallucinogens other than LSD

G = Ecstasy (MDMA)

H = Cocaine

I = Crack

J = Other cocaine

K = Heroin

L = Amphetamines

M = Tranquilizers

N = Alcohol

O = Cigarettes

P = Smokeless tobacco

Q = Steroids

‡ = Change in phrasing of question(s)

Source: "Trends in Lifetime Prevalence of Use of Various Drugs for Grades 8, 10, and 12 Combined." Johnston, L.D., P. M. O'Malley, R.A. Miech, J.G. Bachman, and J.E. Schulenberg. (2015). *Monitoring the Future National Survey Results on Drug Use: 1975–2014: Overview, Key Findings on Adolescent Drug Use.* Ann Arbor: Institute for Social Research, The University of Michigan. Table 1, page 5.

Table 5.3   Trends in Annual Prevalence of Use of Various Drugs for Grades 8, 10, and 12 Combined (percentage)

Drug	1991	1992	1993	1994	1995	1996	1997	1998	1999	2000	2001	2002	2003	2004	2005	2006	2007	2008	2009	2010	2011	2012	2013	2014
A	20.2	19.7	23.2	27.6	31.0	33.6	34.1	32.2	31.9	31.4	31.8	30.2	28.4	27.6	27.1	25.8	24.8	24.9	25.9	27.3	27.6	27.1	28.6	27.2
B	15.0	14.3	17.7	22.5	26.1	29.0	30.1	28.2	27.9	27.2	27.5	26.1	24.6	23.8	23.4	22.0	21.4	21.5	22.9	24.5	25.0	24.7	25.8	24.2
C	7.6	7.8	8.9	9.6	10.2	9.9	9.1	8.5	7.9	7.7	6.9	6.1	6.2	6.7	7.0	6.9	6.4	6.4	6.1	6.0	5.0	4.5	3.8	3.6
D	3.8	4.1	4.8	5.2	6.6	7.2	6.9	6.3	6.1	5.4‡	6.0	4.5	4.1	4.0	3.9	3.6	3.8	3.8	3.5	3.8	3.7	3.2	3.1	2.8
E	3.4	3.8	4.3	4.7	5.9	6.3	6.0	5.3	5.3	4.5	4.1	2.4	1.6	1.6	1.5	1.4	1.7	1.9	1.6	1.8	1.8	1.6	1.6	1.7
F	1.3	1.4	1.7	2.2	2.7	3.2	3.2	3.1	2.9	2.8‡	4.0	3.7	3.6	3.6	3.4	3.3	3.3	3.2	3.0	3.3	3.1	2.7	2.5	2.1
G	–	–	–	–	–	3.1	3.4	2.9	3.7	5.3	6.0	4.9	3.1	2.6	2.4	2.7	3.0	2.9	3.0	3.8	3.7	2.5	2.8	2.2
H	2.2	2.1	2.3	2.8	3.3	4.0	4.3	4.5	4.5	3.9	3.5	3.7	3.3	3.5	3.5	3.5	3.4	2.9	2.5	2.2	2.0	1.9	1.8	1.6
I	1.0	1.1	1.2	1.5	1.8	2.0	2.1	2.4	2.2	2.1	1.8	2.0	1.8	1.7	1.6	1.5	1.5	1.3	1.2	1.1	1.0	0.9	0.8	0.7
J	2.0	1.8	2.0	2.3	2.8	3.4	3.7	3.7	4.0	3.3	3.0	3.1	2.8	3.1	3.0	3.1	2.9	2.6	2.1	1.9	1.7	1.7	1.5	1.5
K	0.5	0.6	0.6	0.9	1.2	1.3	1.3	1.2	1.3	1.3	0.9	1.0	0.8	0.9	0.8	0.8	0.8	0.8	0.8	0.8	0.7	0.6	0.6	0.5
L	7.5	7.3	8.4	9.1	10.0	10.4	10.1	9.3	9.0	9.2	9.6	8.9	8.0	7.6	7.0	6.8	6.5	5.8	5.9	6.2	5.9	5.6	7.0	6.6
M	2.8	2.8	2.9	3.1	3.7	4.1	4.1	4.4	4.4	4.5‡	5.5	5.3	4.8	4.8	4.7	4.6	4.5	4.3	4.5	4.4	3.9	3.7	3.3	3.4
N	67.4	66.3‡	59.7	60.5	60.4	60.9	61.4	59.7	59.0	59.3	58.2	55.3	54.4	54.0	51.9	50.7	50.2	48.7	48.4	47.4	45.3	44.3	42.8	40.7
Q	1.2	1.1	1.0	1.2	1.3	1.1	1.2	1.3	1.7	1.9	2.0	2.0	1.7	1.6	1.3	1.3	1.1	1.1	1.0	0.9	0.9	0.9	0.9	0.9

A = Any illicit drug

B = Marijuana/hashish

C = Inhalants

D = Hallucinogens

E = LSD

F = Hallucinogens other than LSD

G = Ecstasy (MDMA)

H = Cocaine

I = Crack

J = Other cocaine

K = Heroin

L = Amphetamines

M = Tranquilizers

N = Alcohol

O = Cigarettes

P = Smokeless tobacco

Q = Steroids

‡ = Change in phrasing of question(s)

Source: "Trends in Lifetime Prevalence of Use of Various Drugs for Grades 8, 10, and 12 Combined." Johnston, L.D., P. M. O'Malley, R.A. Miech, J.G. Bachman, and J.E. Schulenberg. (2015). *Monitoring the Future National Survey Results on Drug Use: 1975-2014: Overview, Key Findings on Adolescent Drug Use.* Ann Arbor: Institute for Social Research, The University of Michigan. Table 2, page 56.

Table 5.4   Trends in 30-Day Prevalence of Use of Various Drugs for Grades 8, 10, and 12 Combined (percentage)

Drug	1991	1992	1993	1994	1995	1996	1997	1998	1999	2000	2001	2002	2003	2004	2005	2006	2007	2008	2009	2010	2011	2012	2013	2014
A	10.9	10.5	13.3	16.8	18.6	20.6	20.5	19.5	19.5	19.2	19.4	18.2	17.3	16.2	15.8	14.9	14.8	14.6	15.8	16.7	17.0	16.8	17.3	16.5
B	8.3	7.7	10.2	13.9	15.6	17.7	17.9	16.9	16.9	16.3	16.6	15.3	14.8	13.6	13.4	12.5	12.4	12.5	13.8	14.8	15.2	15.1	15.6	14.4
C	3.2	3.3	3.8	4.0	4.3	3.9	3.7	3.4	3.3	3.2	2.8	2.7	2.7	2.9	2.9	2.7	2.6	2.6	2.5	2.4	2.1	1.7	1.5	1.4
D	1.5	1.6	1.9	2.2	3.1	2.7	3.0	2.8	2.5	2.0‡	2.3	1.7	1.5	1.5	1.5	1.3	1.4	1.4	1.3	1.4	1.3	1.1	1.1	1.0
E	1.3	1.5	1.6	1.9	2.8	2.1	2.4	2.3	2.0	1.4	1.5	0.7	0.6	0.6	0.6	0.6	0.6	0.7	0.5	0.7	0.7	0.5	0.6	0.6
F	0.5	0.5	0.7	1.0	1.0	1.2	1.2	1.2	1.1	1.1‡	1.4	0.7	1.4	1.2	1.3	1.2	1.1	1.1	1.1	1.0	1.2	1.0	0.9	0.8
G	–	–	–	–	–	1.5	1.3	1.2	1.6	2.4	2.4	1.8	1.0	0.9	0.9	1.0	1.1	1.2	1.2	1.5	1.4	0.8	1.0	0.8
H	0.8	0.9	0.9	1.2	1.5	1.7	1.8	1.9	1.9	1.7	1.5	1.6	1.4	1.6	1.6	1.6	1.4	1.3	1.0	0.9	0.8	0.8	0.8	0.7
I	0.4	0.5	0.5	0.7	0.8	0.9	0.8	1.0	0.9	0.9	0.9	1.0	0.8	0.8	0.8	0.7	0.7	0.6	0.5	0.5	0.5	0.4	0.4	0.4
J	0.7	0.7	0.8	1.1	1.2	1.3	1.5	1.6	1.7	1.4	1.3	1.3	1.2	1.4	1.3	1.4	1.1	1.1	0.8	0.8	0.7	0.7	0.6	0.6
K	0.2	0.3	0.3	0.4	0.6	0.6	0.6	0.6	0.6	0.6	0.4	0.5	0.4	0.5	0.5	0.4	0.4	0.4	0.4	0.4	0.4	0.3	0.3	0.3
L	3.0	3.3	3.9	4.0	4.5	4.8	4.5	4.3	4.2	4.5	4.7	4.4	3.9	3.6	3.3	3.0	3.2	2.6	2.7	2.7	2.8	2.5	3.2	3.2
M	1.1	1.1	1.1	1.3	1.6	1.7	1.7	1.9	1.9	2.1‡	2.3	2.4	2.2	2.1	2.1	2.1	2.0	1.9	1.9	1.9	1.7	1.5	1.5	1.5
N	39.8	38.4‡	36.3	37.6	37.8	38.8	38.6	37.4	37.2	36.6	35.5	33.3	33.2	32.9	31.4	31.0	30.1	28.1	28.4	26.8	25.5	25.9	24.3	22.6
O	20.7	21.2	23.4	24.7	26.6	28.3	28.3	27.0	25.2	22.6	20.2	17.7	16.6	16.1	15.3	14.4	13.6	12.6	12.7	12.8	11.7	10.6	9.6	8.0
P	–	9.2	9.1	9.7	9.6	8.5	8.0	7.0	6.3	5.8	6.1	5.2	5.3	5.1	5.3	5.1	5.2	4.9	6.0	6.5	5.9	5.6	5.7	5.4
Q	0.6	0.6	0.6	0.7	0.6	0.5	0.7	0.7	0.9	0.9	0.9	1.0	0.9	0.9	0.7	0.7	0.6	0.6	0.6	0.6	0.5	0.5	0.6	0.5

A = Any illicit drug

B = Marijuana/hashish

C = Inhalants

D = Hallucinogens

E = LSD

F = Hallucinogens other than LSD

G = Ecstasy (MDMA)

H = Cocaine

I = Crack

J = Other cocaine

K = Heroin

L = Amphetamines

M = Tranquilizers

N = Alcohol

O = Cigarettes

P = Smokeless tobacco

Q = Steroids

Source: "Trends in Lifetime Prevalence of Use of Various Drugs for Grades 8, 10, and 12 Combined." Johnston, L.D., P. M. O'Malley, R.A. Miech, J.G. Bachman, and J.E. Schulenberg. (2015). *Monitoring the Future National Survey Results on Drug Use: 1975–2014: Overview, Key Findings on Adolescent Drug Use*. Ann Arbor: Institute for Social Research, The University of Michigan, Table 3, page 57.

Table 5.5   Trends in Use of Certain Specific Drugs, Grades 8, 10, and 12 (percentage)

Drug	2000	2002	2004	2006	2008	2010	2012	2014
PCP								
Grade 12	2.3	1.1	1.3	0.7	1.1	1.0	0.9	0.8
Salvia								
Grade 8	–	–	–	–	–	1.7	1.4	0.6
Grade 10	–	–	–	–	–	3.7	2.5	1.8
Grade 12	–	–	–	–	–	5.5	4.4	1.8
Nitrites								
Grade 12	0.6	1.1	0.8	0.5	0.6	–	–	–
Ecstasy								
Grade 8	3.1	2.9	1.7	1.4	1.7	2.4	1.1	0.9
Grade 10	5.4	4.9	2.4	2.8	2.9	4.7	3.0	2.3
Grade 12	8.2	7.4	4.0	4.1	4.3	4.5	3.8	3.6
OxyContin								
Grade 8	–	1.3	1.7	2.6	2.1	2.1	1.6	1.0
Grade 10	–	3.0	3.5	3.8	3.6	4.6	3.0	3.0
Grade 12	–	4.0	5.0	4.3	4.7	5.1	4.3	3.3
Vicodin								
Grade 8	–	2.5	2.5	3.0	2.9	2.7	1.3	1.0
Grade 10	–	6.9	6.2	7.0	6.7	7.7	4.4	3.4
Grade 12	–	9.6	9.3	9.7	9.7	8.0	7.5	4.8
Adderall								
Grade 8	–	–	–	–	–	2.3	1.7	1.3
Grade 10	–	–	–	–	–	5.3	4.5	4.6
Grade 12	–	–	–	–	–	6.5	7.6	6.8
"Bath Salts"								
Grade 8	–	–	–	–	–	–	0.8	0.5
Grade 10	–	–	–	–	–	–	0.6	0.9
Grade 12	–	–	–	–	–	–	1.3	0.9
OTC Cough/Cold Medications								
Grade 8	–	–	–	4.2	3.6	3.2	3.0	2.0
Grade 10	–	–	–	5.3	5.3	5.1	4.7	3.7
Grade 12	–	–	–	6.9	5.5	6.6	5.6	4.1

Drug	2000	2002	2004	2006	2008	2010	2012	2014
Rohypnol								
Grade 8	0.5	0.3	0.6	0.5	0.5	0.5	0.4	0.3
Grade 10	0.8	0.7	0.7	0.5	0.4	0.6	0.5	0.5
Grade 12	0.8	1.6	1.6	1.1	1.3	1.5	1.5	0.7
GHB								
Grade 8	1.2	0.8	0.7	0.8	1.1	0.6	–	–
Grade 10	1.1	1.4	0.8	0.7	0.5	0.6	–	–
Grade 12	1.9	1.5	2.0	1.1	1.2	1.4	1.4	1.0
Ketamine								
Grade 8	1.6	1.3	0.9	0.9	1.2	1.0	–	–
Grade 10	2.1	2.2	1.3	1.0	1.0	1.1	–	–
Grade 12	2.5	2.6	1.9	1.4	1.5	1.6	1.5	1.5

Source: "Trends in Lifetime Prevalence of Use of Various Drugs for Grades 8, 10, and 12 Combined." Johnston, L.D., P. M. O'Malley, R.A. Miech, J.G. Bachman, and J.E. Schulenberg. (2015). Monitoring the Future National Survey Results on Drug Use: 1975–2014: Overview, Key Findings on Adolescent Drug Use. Ann Arbor: Institute for Social Research, The University of Michigan, Table 6, pages 63–67.

Table 5.6 Percentage of High School Students Who Ever Took Steroids and Who Ever Took Prescription Drugs, by Sex, Race/ethnicity, and Grade

	Ever Took without a Doctor's Prescription					
	Steroids			Prescription Drugs		
Category	Female	Male	Total	Female	Male	Total
Race/Ethnicity						
White	1.8	3.8	2.8	18.0	19.4	18.7
Black	1.3	3.3	2.3	11.1	15.7	13.3
Hispanic	3.6	5.0	4.2	19.9	18.5	19.2
Grade						
9	2.3	3.5	2.9	14.0	10.9	12.4
10	2.8	3.5	3.2	16.9	17.6	17.3
11	2.4	4.0	3.1	19.5	22.3	20.8
12	1.2	5.1	3.1	18.6	24.0	21.3
Total	2.2	4.0	3.2	17.2	18.3	17.8

Source: "Youth Risk Behavior Surveillance." Centers for Disease Control and Prevention. http://www.cdc.gov/mmwr/pdf/ss/ss6304.pdf Table 59.

Table 5.7   Trends in Disapproval of Substance Use (percentage)

	Grade 8		Grade 10		Grade 12	
Behavior	2000	2014	2000	2014	2000	2014
Trying marijuana once or twice	72.5	70.5	54.9	53.8	52.5	48.0
Smoking marijuana occasionally	80.6	77.7	67.2	62.9	65.8	56.7
Smoking marijuana regularly	85.3	82.2	79.1	74.6	79.7	73.4
Trying LSD once or twice	66.7	52.8	77.0	67.8	82.4	85.0
Trying LSD regularly	69.3	54.8	82.1	73.3	94.2	94.7
Trying ecstasy once or twice	69.0[1]	61.0	72.6[1]	74.4	81.0	83.1
Trying ecstasy regularly	73.6[1]	54.1	81.0[1]	84.0	–	–
Trying crack cocaine once or twice	85.4	88.0	87.1	90.6	87.5	89.3
Trying crack cocaine occasionally	88.8	89.8	90.9	92.4	91.9	91.9
Trying powder cocaine once or twice	84.8	87.7	84.8	88.9	84.1	85.5
Trying powder cocaine occasionally	88.8	89.1	89.9	91.9	90.3	90.4
Trying heroin once or twice (no needle)	87.2	87.1	90.1	91.9	93.0	94.7
Trying heroin regularly (no needle)	88.9	88.1	92.3	92.7	96.6	97.1
Taking 1 or 2 drinks of alcohol a day	48.7	53.3	33.4	40.7	25.2	29.2
Taking 1 or 2 drinks of alcohol often	77.8	79.6	73.8	77.9	70.0	71.7
Taking 5 or more drinks of alcohol on weekends	81.2	84.9	68.2	79.5	65.2	72.6
Smoking 1–5 cigarettes a day	79.1	–	69.1	–	–	–
Smoking a pack of cigarettes a day	81.9	87.5	76.7	88.0	70.1	85.0
Using electronic cigarettes regularly	–	58.4	–	54.6	–	–
Taking steroids	79.2	80.2	–	–	88.8	87.5

[1] 2001 data

Source: "Trends in Lifetime Prevalence of Use of Various Drugs for Grades 8, 10, and 12 Combined." Johnston, L.D., P. M. O'Malley, R.A. Miech, J.G. Bachman, and J.E. Schulenberg. (2015). *Monitoring the Future National Survey Results on Drug Use: 1975–2014: Overview, Key Findings on Adolescent Drug Use*. Ann Arbor: Institute for Social Research, The University of Michigan, Tables 12, 13, 14, pages 83–86.

Documents

Eighteenth Amendment to the
U.S. Constitution (1919)

On December 17, 1917, the U.S. House of Representatives took the first step in amending the U.S. Constitution to prohibit the use of alcoholic beverages in the United States. The U.S. Senate approved the same act the following day. The proposed amendment was then submitted to the separate states, where it was finally approved by the required number of states (36) on January 16, 1919. Ultimately, only two states defeated the proposed amendment, Connecticut and Rhode Island. On January 26, 1919, acting secretary of state Frank L. Polk certified adoption of the amendment. The amendment did not specifically prohibit the use of alcohol beverages in the United States, although it made it very difficult to obtain such beverages legally. The text of the amendment is as follows.

Amendment XVIII

Section 1. After one year from the ratification of this article the manufacture, sale, or transportation of intoxicating liquors within, the importation thereof into, or the exportation thereof from the United States and all territory subject to the jurisdiction thereof for beverage purposes is hereby prohibited.

Section 2. The Congress and the several states shall have concurrent power to enforce this article by appropriate legislation.

Section 3. This article shall be inoperative unless it shall have been ratified as an amendment to the Constitution by the legislatures of the several states, as provided in the Constitution, within seven years from the date of the submission hereof to the states by the Congress.

Source: National Archives. U.S. Constitution. http://www.archives.gov/exhibits/charters/constitution_amendments_11–27.html. Accessed on November 19, 2015.

Twenty-First Amendment to the U.S. Constitution (1933)

After more than a decade of Prohibition in the United States, many people were convinced that the great experiment to control the use of alcohol in this country was a failure. In response to that feeling, the U.S. Congress on February 20, 1933, adopted an act initiating the repeal of the Eighteenth Amendment by the adoption of a new amendment to the Constitution, the Twenty-First Amendment, which abrogated the earlier amendment. On December 5, 1933, the 36th state, Utah, ratified the amendment, and it was certified on the same date. Only one state, South Carolina, rejected the proposed amendment, although eight other states never took action on the amendment. The text of the amendment is as follows.

Amendment XXI

Section 1. The eighteenth article of amendment to the Constitution of the United States is hereby repealed.

Section 2. The transportation or importation into any state, territory, or possession of the United States for delivery or use therein of intoxicating liquors, in violation of the laws thereof, is hereby prohibited.

Section 3. This article shall be inoperative unless it shall have been ratified as an amendment to the Constitution by conventions in the several states, as provided in the Constitution, within seven years from the date of the submission hereof to the states by the Congress.

Source: National Archives. U.S. Constitution. http://www .archives.gov/exhibits/charters/constitution_amendments_ 11–27.html. Accessed on November 19, 2015.

Controlled Substances Act (1970)

The cornerstone of the U.S. government's efforts to control substance abuse is the Controlled Substances Act of 1970, now a part of the U.S. Code, Title 21, Chapter 13. That act established the system of "schedules" for various categories of drugs that is still used by agencies of the U.S. government today. It also provides extensive background information about the domestic and international status of drug abuse efforts. Some of the most relevant sections for the domestic portion of the act are reprinted here. Section 801 of the act presents Congress's findings and declarations about controlled substances, with special mention in Section 801a of psychotropic drugs.

§ 801. Congressional findings and declarations: controlled substances

The Congress makes the following findings and declarations:

(1) Many of the drugs included within this subchapter have a useful and legitimate medical purpose and are necessary to maintain the health and general welfare of the American people.

(2) The illegal importation, manufacture, distribution, and possession and improper use of controlled substances have a substantial and detrimental effect on the health and general welfare of the American people. . . .

(7) The United States is a party to the Single Convention on Narcotic Drugs, 1961, and other international conventions designed to establish effective control over international and domestic traffic in controlled substances.

§ 801a. Congressional findings and declarations: psychotropic substances

The Congress makes the following findings and declarations:

(1) The Congress has long recognized the danger involved in the manufacture, distribution, and use of certain psychotropic substances for nonscientific and nonmedical purposes, and has provided strong and effective legislation to

control illicit trafficking and to regulate legitimate uses of psychotropic substances in this country. Abuse of psychotropic substances has become a phenomenon common to many countries, however, and is not confined to national borders. It is, therefore, essential that the United States cooperate with other nations in establishing effective controls over international traffic in such substances.

(2) The United States has joined with other countries in executing an international treaty, entitled the Convention on Psycho-tropic Substances and signed at Vienna, Austria, on February 21, 1971, which is designed to establish suitable controls over the manufacture, distribution, transfer, and use of certain psychotropic substances. The Convention is not self-executing, and the obligations of the United States thereunder may only be performed pursuant to appropriate legislation. It is the intent of the Congress that the amendments made by this Act, together with existing law, will enable the United States to meet all of its obligations under the Convention and that no further legislation will be necessary for that purpose. . . .

Section 802 deals with definitions used in the act, and section 803 deals with a minor housekeeping issue of financing for the act. Section 811 deals with the Attorney General's authority for classifying and declassifying drugs and the manner in which these steps are to be taken. In general:

§ 811. Authority and criteria for classification of substances

(a) Rules and regulations of Attorney General; hearing

The Attorney General shall apply the provisions of this subchapter to the controlled substances listed in the schedules established by section 812 of this title and to any other drug or other substance added to such schedules under this subchapter. Except as provided in subsections (d) and (e) of this section, the Attorney General may by rule—

(1) add to such a schedule or transfer between such schedules any drug or other substance if he—

    (A) finds that such drug or other substance has a potential for abuse, and

    (B) makes with respect to such drug or other substance the findings prescribed by subsection (b) of section 812 of this title for the schedule in which such drug is to be placed; or

(2) remove any drug or other substance from the schedules if he finds that the drug or other substance does not meet the requirements for inclusion in any schedule. . . .

Section (b) provides guidelines for the evaluation of drugs and other substances. The next section, (c), is a key element of the act.

(c) Factors determinative of control or removal from schedules

In making any finding under subsection (a) of this section or under subsection (b) of section 812 of this title, the Attorney General shall consider the following factors with respect to each drug or other substance proposed to be controlled or removed from the schedules:

(1) Its actual or relative potential for abuse.

(2) Scientific evidence of its pharmacological effect, if known.

(3) The state of current scientific knowledge regarding the drug or other substance.

(4) Its history and current pattern of abuse.

(5) The scope, duration, and significance of abuse.

(6) What, if any, risk there is to the public health.

(7) Its psychic or physiological dependence liability.

(8) Whether the substance is an immediate precursor of a substance already controlled under this subchapter.

Section (d) is a lengthy discussion of international aspects of the nation's efforts to control substance abuse. Sections (e) through (h) deal with related, but less important, issues of the control of substance abuse. Section 812 is perhaps of greatest interest to the general reader in that it establishes the system of classifying drugs still used in the United States, along with the criteria for classification and the original list of drugs to be included in each schedule (since greatly expanded):

§ 812. Schedules of controlled substances

(a) Establishment

There are established five schedules of controlled substances, to be known as schedules I, II, III, IV, and V. Such schedules shall initially consist of the substances listed in this section. The schedules established by this section shall be updated and republished on a semiannual basis during the two-year period beginning one year after October 27, 1970, and shall be updated and republished on an annual basis thereafter.

(b) Placement on schedules; findings required

Except where control is required by United States obligations under an international treaty, convention, or protocol, in effect on October 27, 1970, and except in the case of an immediate precursor, a drug or other substance may not be placed in any schedule unless the findings required for such schedule are made with respect to such drug or other substance. The findings required for each of the schedules are as follows:

(1) Schedule I.—

(A) The drug or other substance has a high potential for abuse.

(B) The drug or other substance has no currently accepted medical use in treatment in the United States.

(C) There is a lack of accepted safety for use of the drug or other substance under medical supervision.

(2) Schedule II.—

  (A) The drug or other substance has a high potential for abuse.

  (B) The drug or other substance has a currently accepted medical use in treatment in the United States or a currently accepted medical use with severe restrictions.

  (C) Abuse of the drug or other substances may lead to severe psychological or physical dependence.

(3) Schedule III.—

  (A) The drug or other substance has a potential for abuse less than the drugs or other substances in schedules I and II.

  (B) The drug or other substance has a currently accepted medical use in treatment in the United States.

  (C) Abuse of the drug or other substance may lead to moderate or low physical dependence or high psychological dependence.

(4) Schedule IV.—

  (A) The drug or other substance has a low potential for abuse relative to the drugs or other substances in schedule III.

  (B) The drug or other substance has a currently accepted medical use in treatment in the United States.

  (C) Abuse of the drug or other substance may lead to limited physical dependence or psychological dependence relative to the drugs or other substances in schedule III.

(5) Schedule V.—

  (A) The drug or other substance has a low potential for abuse relative to the drugs or other substances in schedule IV.

(B) The drug or other substance has a currently accepted medical use in treatment in the United States.

(C) Abuse of the drug or other substance may lead to limited physical dependence or psychological dependence relative to the drugs or other substances in schedule IV.

(c) Initial schedules of controlled substances

Schedules I, II, III, IV, and V shall, unless and until amended [1] pursuant to section 811 of this title, consist of the following drugs or other substances, by whatever official name, common or usual name, chemical name, or brand name designated.
[List of drugs under each Schedule follow.]

Source: "Controlled Substances Act." U.S. Food and Drug Administration. http://www.fda.gov/regulatoryinformation/legislation/ucm148726.htm. Accessed on November 19, 2015.

Controlled Substance Analogue Enforcement Act of 1986

For at least four decades, drug control agencies in the United States and other parts of the world have been engaged in a "cat and mouse" game with a small group of chemists seeking to discover or invent new psychoactive substances for use by recreational drug users that are not prohibited by federal law. In 1986, the U.S. Congress attempted to take a proactive stance on this problem by declaring in advance that any product made for such a person was automatically declared to be prohibited under terms of the 1970 Controlled Substances Act. The action was taken essentially by redefining what that act meant by a "controlled substance."

SEC. 1202. Treatment of Controlled Substance Analogues.

Part B of the Controlled Substances Act is amended by adding at the end the following new section:

"Treatment of Controlled Substance Analogues

"SEC. 203. A controlled substance analogue shall, to the extent intended for human consumption, be treated, for the purposes of this title and title III as a controlled substance in schedule I.".

SEC. 1203. Definition.

Section 102 of the Controlled Substances Act (21 U.S.C. 802) is amended by adding at the end thereof the following:

"(32)(A) Except as provided in subparagraph (B), the term 'controlled substance analogue' means a substance—

"(i) the chemical structure of which is substantially similar to the chemical structure of a controlled substance in Schedule I or II;

"(ii) which has a stimulant, depressant, or hallucinogenic effect on the central nervous system that is substantially similar to or greater than the stimulent [sic], depressant, or hallucinogenic effect on the central nervous system of a controlled substance in schedule I or II; or

"(iii) with respect to a particular person, which such person represents or intends to have a simulant [sic], depressant, or hallucinogenic effect on the central nervous system that is substantially similar to or greater than the stimulant, depressant, or hallucinogenic effect on the central nervous system of a controlled substance in schedule I or II.

"(B) Such term does not include—

"(i) a controlled substance;

"(ii) any substance for which there is an approved new drug application;

"(iii) with respect to a particular person any substance, if an exemption is in effect for investigational use, for that person, under section 505 of the Federal

Food, Drug, and Cosmetic Act (21 U.S.C. 355) to the extent conduct with respect to such substance is pursuant to such exemption; or

"(iv) any substance to the extent not intended for human consumption before such an exemption takes effect with respect to that substance."

Source: Public Law 99–570. U.S. Statutes. https://www.gpo.gov/fdsys/pkg/STATUTE-100/pdf/STATUTE-100-Pg3207.pdf. Accessed on January 8, 2016.

Vernonia v. Acton, 515 U.S. 646 (1995)

The U.S. Supreme Court has had very little to say about the legal issues surrounding substance misuse and abuse by adolescents specifically. One of the most important exceptions to that statement involved a 1995 case, Vernonia v. Acton. *In that case, the school board of the Vernonia (Oregon) school district decided that any student wishing to play athletics at the school had to sign an agreement to take a drug test. One student who declined to do so, James Acton, declined to agree to such a test, and was prohibited from joining the school's seventh-grade football team. Ultimately, his parents brought suit against the school district on his behalf, claiming that suspicionless drug testing was unconstitutional. The case worked its way through the courts, with each side recording at least one favorable ruling along the way, until it reached the U.S. Supreme Court in 1995, at which time the Court ruled for the school district by a vote of 6 to 3. The syllabus for this case summarizes the main points contained in the Court's decision, as written by Justice Antonin Scalia.*

Held: The Policy is constitutional under the Fourth and Fourteenth Amendments. Pp. 652–666.

(a) State-compelled collection and testing of urine constitutes a "search" under the Fourth Amendment. Skinner v. Railway

Labor Executives' Assn., 489 U.S. 602, 617. Where there was no clear practice, either approving or disapproving the type of search at issue, at the time the constitutional provision was enacted, the "reasonableness" of a search is judged by balancing the intrusion on the individual's Fourth Amendment interests against the promotion of legitimate governmental interests. Pp. 652–654.

(b) The first factor to be considered in determining reasonableness is the nature of the privacy interest on which the search intrudes. Here, the subjects of the Policy are children who have been committed to the temporary custody of the State as schoolmaster; in that capacity, the State may exercise a degree of supervision and control greater than it could exercise over free adults. The requirements that public school children submit to physical examinations and be vaccinated indicate that they have a lesser privacy expectation with regard to medical examinations and procedures than the general population. Student athletes have even less of a legitimate privacy expectation, for an element of communal undress is inherent in athletic participation, and athletes are subject to preseason physical exams and rules regulating their conduct. Pp. 654–657.

(c) The privacy interests compromised by the process of obtaining urine samples under the Policy are negligible, since the conditions of collection are nearly identical to those typically encountered in public restrooms. In addition, the tests look only for standard drugs, not medical conditions, and the results are released to a limited group. Pp. 658–660.

(d) The nature and immediacy of the governmental concern at issue, and the efficacy of this means for meeting it, also favor a finding of reasonableness. The importance of deterring drug use by all this Nation's schoolchildren cannot be doubted. Moreover, the Policy is directed more narrowly to drug use by athletes, where the risk of physical harm to the user and other players is high. The District Court's conclusion that the District's concerns were immediate is not clearly erroneous, and it is self-evident that a drug problem largely caused by athletes, and of particular danger to athletes, is effectively addressed by ensuring that athletes do not use drugs. The Fourth Amendment does not require that the "least intrusive" search be conducted, so respondents' argument that the drug testing could be based on suspicion of drug use, if true, would not be fatal; and that alternative entails its own substantial difficulties. Pp. 660–664

Source: *Vernonia School District 47J, Petitioner V. Wayne Acton, et ux., etc.* 515 U.S. 646 (1995).

Ecstasy Anti-Proliferation Act of 2000

The U.S. Congress has considered a large number of bills dealing with the manufacture, distribution, use, and control of a variety of specific illegal and/or dangerous substances over the past three decades. A small number of these bills become law in and of themselves, while the majority are appended to other legislation that may or may not have any relevance to the issue of substance abuse itself. Such is the case with a bill that began life as the Ecstasy Anti-Proliferation Act of 2000, introduced into the Senate by Senator Bob Graham (D-FL) in May 2000. After passing the House and Senate, the bill was later incorporated into a much larger piece of legislation, the Children's Health Act of 2000. The relevant portion of that act (Sections 3661 to 3665, 3671–3672, and 5068) is summarized here. The bill begins with a list of its "findings" about the use of ecstasy, the fourth of which is as follows:

(4) Greater emphasis needs to be placed on—
   (A) penalties associated with the manufacture, distribution, and use of Ecstasy;
   (B) the education of young people on the negative health effects of Ecstasy, since the reputation of Ecstasy as

a "safe" drug is the most dangerous component of Ecstasy;

(C) the education of State and local law enforcement agencies regarding the growing problem of Ecstasy trafficking across the United States;

(D) reducing the number of deaths caused by Ecstasy use and the combined use of Ecstasy with other "club" drugs and alcohol; and

(E) adequate funding for research by the National Institute on Drug Abuse to—

   (i) identify those most vulnerable to using Ecstasy and develop science-based prevention approaches tailored to the specific needs of individuals at high risk;

   (ii) understand how Ecstasy produces its toxic effects and how to reverse neurotoxic damage;

   (iii) develop treatments, including new medications and behavioral treatment approaches;

   (iv) better understand the effects that Ecstasy has on the developing children and adolescents; and

   (v) translate research findings into useful tools and ensure their effective dissemination.

SEC. 3663. Enhanced Punishment of Ecstasy Traffickers.

(a) Amendment to Federal Sentencing Guidelines.—Pursuant to its authority under section 994(p) of title 28, United States Code, the United States Sentencing Commission (referred to in this section as the "Commission") shall amend the Federal sentencing guidelines regarding any offense relating to the manufacture, importation, or exportation of, or trafficking in—

(1) 3,4-methylenedioxy methamphetamine;

(2) 3,4-methylenedioxy amphetamine;

(3) 3,4-methylenedioxy-N-ethylamphetamine;

(4) paramethoxymethamphetamine (PMA); or

(5) any other controlled substance, as determined by the Commission in consultation with the Attorney General, that is marketed as Ecstasy and that has either a chemical structure substantially similar to that of 3,4-methylenedioxy methamphetamine or an effect on the central nervous system substantially similar to or greater than that of 3,4-methylenedioxy methamphetamine, including an attempt or conspiracy to commit an offense described in paragraph (1), (2), (3), (4), or (5) in violation of the Controlled Substances Act (21 U.S.C. 801 et seq.), the Controlled Substances Import and Export Act (21 U.S.C. 951 et seq.), or the Maritime Drug Law Enforcement Act (46 U.S.C. 1901 et seq.). . . .

(d) Sense of the Congress.—It is the sense of the Congress that—

(1) the base offense levels for Ecstasy are too low, particularly for high-level traffickers, and should be increased, such that they are comparable to penalties for other drugs of abuse; and

(2) based on the fact that importation of Ecstasy has surged in the past few years, the traffickers are targeting the Nation's youth, and the use of Ecstasy among youth in the United States is increasing even as other drug use among this population appears to be leveling off, the base offense levels for importing and trafficking the controlled substances described in subsection (a) should be increased.

Source: Public Law 106–310. 106th Congress. http://www.gpo .gov/fdsys/pkg/PLAW-106publ310/html/PLAW-106publ310 .htm. Accessed on November 24, 2015. The new sentencing guidelines mandated in this act can be found at http:// www.ussc.gov/sites/default/files/pdf/news/congressional-testimony-and-reports/drug-topics/200105_RtC_MDMA_ Drug_Offenses.pdf, accessed on November 24, 2015.

Combat Methamphetamine Epidemic Act of 2005

By the mid-2000s, one of the most serious substance abuse problems in the United States involved the manufacture, sale, and use of methamphetamine, also known by a number of common names, such as "meth," "ice," "crystal," and "crank." One of the problems in dealing with the methamphetamine epidemic was the ready availability of the raw materials needed to produce the drug in a simple home-based laboratory. In order to deal with this problem, and issues related to the misuse of the drug, Senator James Talent (R-MO) introduced Senate Bill S 103 in the 109th Congress. The bill was referred to committee, but never acted on in its original form. Instead, it was incorporated into the USA PATRIOT Improvement and Reauthorization Act of 2005, which was passed by Congress and signed by President George W. Bush on March 9, 2006. Perhaps the most important part of the methamphetamine control portion of the bill was the limitations it placed on the sale of a number of widely used cough and cold products whose ingredients included raw materials from which meth can be made. The core provisions of the act in this respect are to be found in Section (b) of Section 711 of Title VII of the main act, as follows:

(b) Restrictions on Sales Quantity; Behind-the-Counter Access; Logbook Requirement; Training of Sales Personnel; Privacy Protections—

    (1) IN GENERAL- Section 310 of the Controlled Substances Act (21 U.S.C. 830) is amended by adding at the end the following subsections:

Section (c) is Absent from the Final Version of the Bill.

(d) Scheduled Listed Chemicals; Restrictions on Sales Quantity; Requirements Regarding Nonliquid Forms— With respect to ephedrine base, pseudoephedrine base, or phenylpropanolamine base in a scheduled listed chemical product—

(1) the quantity of such base sold at retail in such a product by a regulated seller, or a distributor required to submit reports by subsection (b)(3) may not, for any purchaser, exceed a daily amount of 3.6 grams, without regard to the number of transactions; and

(2) such a seller or distributor may not sell such a product in nonliquid form (including gel caps) at retail unless the product is packaged in blister packs, each blister containing not more than 2 dosage units, or where the use of blister packs is technically infeasible, the product is packaged in unit dose packets or pouches.

(e) Scheduled Listed Chemicals; Behind-the-Counter Access; Logbook Requirement; Training of Sales Personnel; Privacy Protections—

(1) Requirements Regarding Retail Transactions—

(A) IN GENERAL- Each regulated seller shall ensure that, subject to subparagraph (F), sales by such seller of a scheduled listed chemical product at retail are made in accordance with the following:

(i) In offering the product for sale, the seller places the product such that customers do not have direct access to the product before the sale is made (in this paragraph referred to as "behind-the-counter" placement). For purposes of this paragraph, a behind-the-counter placement of a product includes circumstances in which the product is stored in a locked cabinet that is located in an area of the facility involved to which customers do have direct access.

(ii) The seller delivers the product directly into the custody of the purchaser.

(iii) The seller maintains, in accordance with criteria issued by the Attorney General, a written or electronic list of such sales that identifies the products by name, the quantity sold, the names and addresses of purchasers, and the dates and times of the sales (which list is referred to in this subsection as the "logbook"), except that such requirement does not apply to any purchase by an individual of a single sales package if that package contains not more than 60 milligrams of pseudoephedrine.

(iv) In the case of a sale to which the requirement of clause (iii) applies, the seller does not sell such a product unless-

    (I) The Prospective Purchaser-

        (aa) presents an identification card that provides a photograph and is issued by a State or the Federal Government, or a document that, with respect to identification, is considered acceptable for purposes of sections 274a.2(b)(1)(v)(A) and 274a.2(b)(1)(v)(B) of title 8, Code of Federal Regulations (as in effect on or after the date of the enactment of the Combat Methamphetamine Epidemic Act of 2005); and

        (bb) signs the logbook and enters in the logbook his or her name, address, and the date and time of the sale; and

    (II) The Seller—

        (aa) determines that the name entered in the logbook corresponds to the name provided on such identification and that the date and time entered are correct; and

        (bb) enters in the logbook the name of the product and the quantity sold.

    (v) The logbook includes, in accordance with criteria of the Attorney General, a notice to purchasers that entering false statements or misrepresentations in the logbook may subject the purchasers to criminal penalties under section 1001 of title 18, United States Code, which notice specifies the maximum fine and term of imprisonment under such section.

    (vi) The seller maintains each entry in the logbook for not fewer than two years after the date on which the entry is made.

    (vii) In the case of individuals who are responsible for delivering such products into the custody of purchasers or who deal directly with purchasers by obtaining payments for the products, the seller has submitted to the Attorney General a self-certification that all such individuals have, in accordance with criteria under subparagraph (B)(ii), undergone training provided by the seller to ensure that the individuals understand the requirements that apply under this subsection and subsection (d).

    (viii) The seller maintains a copy of such certification and records demonstrating that individuals referred to in clause (vii) have undergone the training.

    (ix) If the seller is a mobile retail vendor:

        (I) The seller complies with clause (i) by placing the product in a locked cabinet.

        (II) The seller does not sell more than 7.5 grams of ephedrine base, pseudoephedrine base, or phenylpropanolamine base in such products per customer during a 30-day period.

(B) ADDITIONAL PROVISIONS REGARDING CERTIFICATIONS AND TRAINING-

    (i) IN GENERAL—A regulated seller may not sell any scheduled listed chemical product at retail unless the seller has submitted to the Attorney General the self-certification referred to in subparagraph (A)(vii). The certification is not effective for purposes of the preceding sentence unless, in addition to provisions regarding the training of individuals referred to in such subparagraph, the certification includes a statement that the seller understands each of the requirements that apply under this paragraph and under subsection (d) and agrees to comply with the requirements.

The remainder of this long section describes in detail the process by which a retailer obtains a certificate of the kind described earlier.

Remaining sections of Title 7 deal with topics such as certain types of regulated transactions (§712), authority to sell production quotas (§713), penalties (§714), importation and legal uses of otherwise restricted products (§715), importation and exportation of restricted materials (§716), and a variety of "housekeeping" issues.

Source: Public Law 109–177. 109th Congress. http://www.gpo.gov/fdsys/pkg/STATUTE-120/pdf/STATUTE-120-Pg192.pdf. Accessed on November 19, 2015.

Morse, et al. v. Frederick (2007)

Teenage substance abuse is seldom an issue litigated before state or federal courts. One interesting exception involved a case brought by Deborah Morse, principal of Juneau-Douglas High School in Juneau, Alaska, against one of her former students, Joseph Frederick. During an Olympic Torch Relay held in Juneau on January 24, 2002, Frederick and friends unfurled a 20-foot long banner reading "BONG HiTS FOR JESUS," which Morse took to be an endorsement for marijuana smoking. She suspended Frederick for violating school policy prohibiting the promotion of illegal drug use in school or at campus events, a case that eventually worked its way to the U.S. Supreme Court. Frederick's defense of his action *was that he was simply exercising his First Amendment rights of expressing his views of a subject of interest to him, illegal drug use. Although Frederick won earlier rounds of this process, markedly in the Ninth Circuit Court of Appeals, the Supreme Court sided with Morse. Writing for the majority, Chief Justice John Roberts based the Court's decision on three basic points (An asterisk, *, indicates the omission of citations):*

(a) Frederick's argument that this is not a school speech case is rejected. The event in question occurred during normal school hours and was sanctioned by Morse as an approved social event at which the district's student-conduct rules expressly applied. Teachers and administrators were among the students and were charged with supervising them. Frederick stood among other students across the street from the school and directed his banner toward the school, making it plainly visible to most students. Under these circumstances, Frederick cannot claim he was not at school.

(b) The Court agrees with Morse that those who viewed the banner would interpret it as advocating or promoting illegal drug use, in violation of school policy. At least two interpretations of the banner's words—that they constitute an imperative encouraging viewers to smoke marijuana or, alternatively, that they celebrate drug use—demonstrate that the sign promoted such use. This pro-drug interpretation gains further plausibility from the paucity of alternative meanings the banner might bear.

(c) A principal may, consistent with the First Amendment, restrict student speech at a school event, when that speech is reasonably viewed as promoting illegal drug use. In Tinker v. Des Moines Independent Community School Dist., 393 U.S. 503, the Court declared, in holding that a policy prohibiting high school students from wearing antiwar armbands violated the First Amendment, * that student expression may not be suppressed unless school officials reasonably conclude that it will "materially and substantially disrupt the work and discipline of the school." * The Court in Bethel (*) however, upheld the suspension of a student who delivered a high school assembly speech employing "an elaborate, graphic, and explicit sexual metaphor," *. Analyzing the case under Tinker, the lower courts had found no disruption, and therefore no basis for discipline. * This Court reversed, holding that the school was "within its permissible authority in imposing sanctions . . . in response to [the student's] offensively lewd and indecent speech." * Two basic principles may be distilled from Fraser. First, it demonstrates that "the constitutional rights of students in public school are not automatically coextensive with the rights of adults in other settings." * Had Fraser delivered the same speech in a public forum outside the school context, he would have been protected. * In school, however, his First Amendment rights were circumscribed "in light of the special characteristics of the school environment." * Second, Fraser established that Tinker's mode of analysis is not absolute, since the Fraser Court did not conduct the "substantial disruption" analysis. Subsequently, the Court has held in the Fourth Amendment context that "while children assuredly do not 'shed their constitutional rights . . . at the schoolhouse gate,' . . . the nature of those rights is what is appropriate for children in school," *, and has recognized that deterring drug use by schoolchildren is an "important—indeed, perhaps compelling" interest, *. Drug abuse by the Nation's youth is a serious problem. For example, Congress has declared that part of a school's job is educating students about the dangers of drug abuse, see, e.g., the Safe and Drug-Free Schools and Communities Act of 1994, and petitioners and many other schools have adopted policies aimed at implementing this message. Student speech celebrating illegal drug use at a school event, in the presence of school administrators and teachers, poses a particular challenge for school officials working to protect those entrusted to their care. The "special characteristics of the school environment," *, and the governmental interest in stopping student drug abuse allow schools to restrict student expression that they reasonably regard as promoting such abuse.*

Source: *Morse, et al. v. Frederick,* 551 U.S. 393 (2007). http://www.supremecourt.gov/opinions/06pdf/06-278.pdf. Accessed on November 24, 2015.

Sottera, Inc. v. Food and Drug Administration (No. 10-5032; 627 F.3d 891) (2010)

One of the most significant changes in the use of substances for recreational purposes in recent history has been the development of electronic cigarettes (e-cigarettes), devices for the delivery of tobacco-like products (especially nicotine) by means of a battery-operated vaporizer. Considerable dispute has developed over the safety and usefulness of e-cigarettes, producing, as expected, a number of court cases dealing with their manufacture, distribution, and use. One of the most important of those cases arose out of a decision by the U.S. Food and Drug Administration (FDA) to begin regulating e-cigarettes under the authority granted it by the Federal Food, Drug, and Cosmetic Act of 1938 (FDCA). Some e-cigarette makers argued that the appropriate regulatory power was not the FDCA, but the Tobacco Control Act of 2009 (TCA), which provided different standards for the tobacco products that the FDA could regulate. A district court agreed with the e-cigarette companies and, when the FDA appealed to the U.S. Circuit Court of Appeals for the District of Columbia, that court agreed with the lower court's decision. As a consequence, e-cigarettes are currently not regulated by any federal statute or regulation. The appeal court's ruling was as follows (asterisks [*] represent omitted citations):

Under the FDCA, the FDA has authority to regulate articles that are "drugs," "devices," or drug/device combinations. 21 U.S.C.

§ 321(g)(1) defines drugs to include (B) articles intended for use in the diagnosis, cure, mitigation, treatment, or prevention of disease in man or other animals; and (C) articles (other than food) intended to affect the structure or any function of the body of man or other animals.

*

Until 1996, the FDA had never attempted to regulate tobacco products under the FDCA (with one exception, irrelevant for reasons discussed below) unless they were sold for therapeutic uses, that is, for use in the "diagnosis, cure, mitigation, treatment, or prevention of disease" under § 321(g)(1) (B). * But in that year, the FDA changed its long-held position, promulgating regulations affecting tobacco products as customarily marketed, i.e., ones sold without therapeutic claims. * The agency asserted that nicotine is a drug that affects the structure or function of the body under § 321(g)(1)(C) and that cigarettes and smokeless tobacco were therefore drug/device combinations falling under the FDA's regulatory purview, even absent therapeutic claims. *

In *FDA v. Brown & Williamson*, the Supreme Court rejected the FDA's claimed FDCA authority to regulate tobacco products as customarily marketed. Looking to the FDCA's "overall regulatory scheme," the "tobacco-specific legislation" enacted since the FDCA, and the FDA's own frequently asserted position, it held that Congress had "ratified . . . the FDA's plain and resolute position that the FDCA gives the agency no authority to regulate tobacco products as customarily marketed." *

To fill the regulatory gap identified in *Brown & Williamson*, Congress in 2009 passed the Tobacco Act, Pub. L. No. 111-31, 123 Stat. 1776, 21 U.S.C. §§ 387 et seq., providing the FDA with authority to regulate tobacco products. The act defines tobacco products so as to include all consumption products derived from tobacco except articles that qualify as drugs, devices, or drug-device combinations under the FDCA:

(rr) (1) The term "tobacco product" means any product made
or derived from tobacco that is intended for human
consumption, including any component, part, or
accessory of a tobacco product . . .

(2) The term "tobacco product" does not mean an article
that is a drug under [the FDCA's drug provision],
a device under [the FDCA's device provision], or a
combination product described in [the FDCA's combination product provision]

*[The court then discusses in detail the history of tobacco legisla-
tion and its implications for this particular case. They conclude
that:]*

. . . *Brown & Williamson* interprets the six statutes [passed
by Congress] not as a particular carve-out from the FDCA for
cigarettes and smokeless tobacco (plus any additional products covered in the six statutes, which the FDA briefs make no
effort to itemize), but rather as "a distinct regulatory scheme to
address the problem of tobacco and health"—one that Congress intended would "preclude [] any role for the FDA" with
respect to "tobacco absent claims of therapeutic benefit by the
manufacturer." * In doing so, Congress also "persistently acted
to preclude a meaningful role for any administrative agency
in making policy on the subject of tobacco and health." * As
customarily marketed, tobacco products were to remain the
province of Congress.

[The Court's Opinion Then Concludes With:]

As we have already noted, the FDA has authority to regulate customarily marketed tobacco products—including
ecigarettes—under the Tobacco Act. It has authority to regulate therapeutically marketed tobacco products under the
FDCA's drug/device provisions. And, as this decision is limited
to tobacco products, it does not affect the FDA's ability to regulate other products under the "structure or any function" prong
defining drugs and devices in 21 U.S.C.§ 321 (g) and (h), as
to the scope of which—tobacco products aside—we express no

opinion. Of course, in the event that Congress prefers that the FDA regulate e-cigarettes under the FDCA's drug/device provisions, it can always so decree.

The Judgment of the District Court is
Affirmed.

Source: *Sottera, Inc., Doing Business as Njoy, Appellee v. Food & Drug Administration,* et al., Appellants. (No. 10-5032; 627 F.3d 891). https://www.cadc.uscourts.gov/internet/opinions.nsf/ D02F9D2CA50299F0852577F20070BCC2/$file/10-5032- 1281606.pdf. Accessed on November 25, 2015.

House Bill No. 682 (The General Assembly of Pennsylvania) (2015)

Possibly the most startling news about changes in substance use by teenagers in the past decade has been the explosive growth of interest in e-cigarettes. Recent studies show that the popularity of these products more than tripled in a single year, from 2013 to 2014, among middle and high school students surveyed. The number of users of e-cigarettes in 2014 among high school students exceeded two million and among middle school students, it was greater than 450,000. This change has caught legislative bodies and regulatory agencies at the federal and state levels unprepared to deal with laws and rules for the use of e-cigarettes. The FDA has proposed regulating the use of e-cigarettes in a fashion similar to the rules used for regular cigarettes, but has been prevented from doing so by the courts. Some states have begun to consider legislation that would classify e-cigarettes in the same category as regular cigarettes, imposing substantial restrictions and limitations on their use. An example of this approach is a bill submitted to the Pennsylvania legislature in late 2015. As of April 2016, no action has been taken on this bill.

An act regulating smoking in this Commonwealth; imposing powers and duties on the Department of Health and local boards of health; providing penalties; preempting local action; and making a related repeal," amending the title; further providing for definitions; further prohibiting smoking in public places; further providing for signage, for 8enforcement, for penalties and for administration; *[and for other purposes]*

. . .

Section 2. Definitions.

. . .

"E-cigarette." Any electronic oral device, such as one composed of a heating element, battery or electronic circuit, which provides a vapor of nicotine or any other substances and the use or inhalation of which simulates smoking. The term shall include any such device, whether manufactured, distributed, marketed or sold as an e-cigarette, e-cigar or e-pipe or under any other product name or descriptor. . . .

"Smoking." [The carrying by a person of a lighted cigar, cigarette, pipe or other lighted smoking device.] Inhaling, exhaling, burning or carrying any lighted or heated cigar, cigarette or pipe or any other lighted or heated tobacco plant product intended for inhalation, in any manner or in any form. The term includes the use of an e-cigarette which creates a vapor in any manner or in any form or the use of any oral smoking device for the purpose of circumventing the prohibition of smoking in this act.

Source: House Bill No. 682. Session of 2015. http://www.legis .state.pa.us/cfdocs/legis/PN/Public/btCheck.cfm?txtType= HTM&sessYr=2015&sessInd=0&billBody=H&billTyp=B& billNbr=0682&pn=2541. Accessed on November 28, 2015.

6   Annotated Bibliography

Introduction

Teenage substance abuse has been the subject of countless numbers of books, articles, Internet posts, reports, and other documents over the past half century. No collection of such documents can said to be complete. This chapter does provide, however, an introduction to some of the most recent and most important documents about this topic. Some resources appear in more than one format (such as print and electronic form) and are so indicated in the annotations.

Books

Abadinsky, Howard. 2014. *Drug Use and Abuse: A Comprehensive Introduction.* Belmont, OH: Wadsworth/Cengage Learning.
   This book begins with a general introduction to the biology of substance abuse and follows up with a discussion of the major types of psychoactive substances. It then continues with a review of drug legislation, drug policies, prevention and treatment programs, and decriminalization issues.

Bodden, Valerie. 2015. *Club and Prescription Drug Abuse.* Minneapolis: ABDO Publishing.

Students from Thomas Wootton High School in Rockville, Maryland, pledge not to drink alcohol until they are 21 years old. Questions remain as to the effectiveness of such programs in reducing substance abuse. (PRNewsFoto/Daimlerchrysler Corporate PR)

This book is intended for young adults. It provides a general introduction to the topic of club and prescription drug abuse with chapters on the history of drug abuse, drug abuse among young adults and children, why young people use drugs, club drugs and inhalants, prescription and OTC drugs, the cost of drug use, drugs and the law, and other prevention efforts.

Brady, Kathleen T., Jenna L. McCauley, and Sudie E. Back. 2014. "The Comorbidity of Post-Traumatic-Stress Disorder (PTSD) and Substance Use Disorders." In el-Guebaly, Nady, Giuseppe Carra, and Marc Galanter, eds. *Textbook of Addiction Treatment International Perspectives*. Milan: Springer Reference, 1985–2004.

The authors point out that evidence suggests that post-traumatic stress disorder and substance abuse, dependence, and addition is a growing problem worldwide. They discuss the nature of this comorbidity and some possible approaches to treatment.

Brown, Robert, and Sheryl Ryan, eds. 2014. *Substance Use and Abuse among Adolescents*. Elk Grove Village, IL: American Academy of Pediatrics.

This book provides basic information on all of the major psychoactive substances misused and abused by adolescents, with separate chapters on smoking, alcohol, marijuana, prescription stimulants, and performance-enhancing substances, along with chapters on the neurobiology of psychoactive substances, screening and intervention programs, and treatment programs.

Califano, Joseph A., Jr. 2014. *How to Raise a Drug-Free Kid: The Straight Dope for Parents*. New York: Touchstone Press.

This book is a conventional "how to" manual for parents who have to deal with substance-abusing children and adolescents. Theoretical principles and suggestions are translated in easily understood suggestions for parental behavior along with the assistance of other individuals and organizations.

Canfield, Jack, Mark Victor Hansen, and Kimberly Kirberger, eds. 2012. *Chicken Soup for the Teenage Soul on Tough Stuff: Stories of Tough Times and Lessons Learned.* Cos Cob, CT: Chicken Soup for the Soul Publishing.

> This book consists of a number of essays by young adults who have become involved at some point in their lives with destructive behaviors, such as substance abuse. The essays focus on how they recovered from such situations and the lessons they learned from their experiences.

Currie-McGhee. 2012. *Teenage Drug Abuse.* San Diego, CA: ReferencePoint Press.

> This book is intended for young adults of grade 8 and up. It provides a general introduction to the nature of substance abuse, its effects on kids, and methods of prevention and treatment.

Eldridge, Alison, and Stephen Eldridge. 2015. *Investigate Club Drugs.* Berkeley Heights, NJ: Enslow Publishers.

> This book is part of the publisher's Investigate Drugs series designed for young adults. It provides a good overview of the major club drugs, with special attention to their risks of dependence and addiction.

Fisher, Gary L., and Nancy A. Roget, eds. 2009. *Encyclopedia of Substance Abuse Prevention, Treatment, & Recovery.* Los Angeles: SAGE.

> This encyclopedia consists of entries on virtually every conceivable aspect of substance abuse prevention, treatment, and recovery.

Gogek, Ed. 2015. *Marijuana Debunked: A Handbook for Parents, Pundits and Politicians Who Want to Know the Case against Legalization.* Asheville, NC: Chiron Publications.

> The author is concerned about the growing use of marijuana by teenagers in the United States, and he points out a host of attitudes and beliefs about the drug that he claims are inaccurate or untrue.

Goode, Erich. 2015. *Drugs in American Society*, 9th ed. New York: McGraw-Hill.

This standard textbook provides one of the most comprehensive treatments of substance abuse issues in modern societies. It covers topics such as the history of drug use and drug control; a view of drug issues from the perspectives of the sociologist, the pharmacologist, and the media; the characteristics of major drugs; and drugs, crime, and drug control.

Hart, Carl L., and Charles Ksir. 2013. *Drugs, Society, & Human Behavior*, 15th ed. New York: McGraw-Hill.

This standard textbook provides general information on licit and illicit drugs, personal and social problems involved with their use, and treatment and prevention options.

Inciardi, James A., and Karen McElrath, eds. *The American Drug Scene: Readings in a Global Context*. New York: Oxford University Press.

This book contains a collection of 39 articles previously published in other places dealing with a variety of drug-related issues. The articles discuss topics such as the history of drug use in the United States, the history of marijuana use in Australia, why people take drugs, the use of crack cocaine on college campuses, and drug abuse among "nice" people.

Jaime, Everett, and Eliot R. Brown. 2012. *Baby Don't Smoke*. Prescott, AZ: Kalindi Press.

This graphic book is intended for young parents and pregnant teens in an effort to make the risks of smoking more realistic, with the hope that such at-risk individuals will be able to avoid the "lure" of smoking.

Julien, Robert M., Claire D. Advokat, and Joseph E. Comaty. 2011. *A Primer of Drug Action: A Comprehensive Guide to the*

Actions, Uses, and Side Effects of Psychoactive Drugs, 12th ed. New York: Worth Publishers.

This highly respected book contains detailed description of all classes of psychoactive drugs and their effects on the human body. Individual chapters also summarize current knowledge about the effects of drugs on the central nervous system.

Kaminer, Yifrah, ed. 2016. *Youth Substance Abuse and Co-occurring Disorders*. Washington, DC: American Psychiatric Association Publishing.

This technically oriented book includes essays on almost every essential issue related to adolescent substance abuse, such as screening, assessment, and treatment options; conduct disorder and delinquency; post-traumatic stress disorder; eating disorders; and youth gambling problems.

Kinney, Jean. 2015. *Loosening the Grip: A Handbook of Alcohol Information*. New York: McGraw-Hill Education.

This book provides a general overview on the topic of alcohol abuse and alcoholism, with chapters on the effects of alcohol on the body, how alcohol dependence develops, alcohol's effects on the body, populations at risk, and treatment and prevention programs.

Kuhn, Cynthia, et al. 2014. *Buzzed: The Straight Facts about the Most Used and Abused Drugs from Alcohol to Ecstasy*, 4th ed. New York; London: W.W. Norton & Company.

One of the standards in the field of substance abuse, this book provides a complete and well-written overview of psychoactive substances in general and the most commonly abused drugs in particular.

Levinthal, Charles F. 2016. *Drugs, Behavior, and Modern Society*, 8th ed. Boston: Pearson.

Now in its eighth edition, this textbook has long been a mainstay in classes about psychoactive substances and their place in society.

Lynam, Edward, and Ellen Bowers. 2014. *The Everything Parent's Guide to Teenage Addiction*. Avon, MA: Adams Media.

This book is intended to help parents understand and deal with teenager substance abuse issues. It includes chapters on What Causes Addiction?, Factors in Teenage Addiction, Why Does My Child Act that Way?, Prevention Methods, The Normal Teenage Brain versus the Addicted Teenage Brain, and Treatment Options for Teenagers.

Miller, Dennis K. 2016. *Taking Sides. Clashing Views in Drugs and Society*. New York: McGraw-Hill Education.

This book, like others in the "Taking Sides" series, presents contrasting views on a number of issues in the named field. In this case, those issues include drug laws, importation of drugs, the current drinking age, the over-prescription of opioids, naturopathic remedies for substance abuse, and drug addiction as a brain disease.

Miller, Richard J. 2015. *Drugged: The Science and Culture behind Psychotropic Drugs*. New York: Oxford University Press.

The author provides one of the most comprehensive overviews of the role of psychoactive drugs in human history, past and present, currently available. It approaches the topic in a format and language that is easily accessible to the layperson, making the issues involved in substance abuse easy to understand for almost all readers.

Rosner, Richard, ed. 2012. *Clinical Handbook of Adolescent Addiction*. Chichester, West Sussex, UK; Hoboken, NJ: John Wiley & Sons.

This book is a project of the American Society for Adolescent Psychiatry and is designed to provide users with easy access to the knowledge and tools needed for working with young adults who have become addicted to legal and illegal psychoactive substances.

Scheier, Lawrence M., ed. 2015. *Handbook of Adolescent Drug Use Prevention: Research, Intervention Strategies, and Practice*. Washington, DC: American Psychological Association.

The 30 articles in this anthology deal with a variety of substance-related topics, such as historical trends in drug abuse and treatment; epidemiology and etiology of substance abuse; school, family, and community-based prevention and treatment programs; evaluation of substance abuse programs; and media campaigns and their impact.

Steiker, Lori Holleran. 2016. *Youth and Substance Use: Prevention, Intervention, and Recovery*. Chicago, IL: Lyceum Books.

This book provides a comprehensive overview of many of the issues surrounding adolescent substance abuse. Chapters deal with topics such as overview of substance misuse, substance abuse for children and adolescents, substance misuse models and theories, substance misuse prevention, the role of parents and families in prevention and treatment, screening and assessment, support groups, and current issues in the field.

Stimmel, Barry. 2013. *Drug Abuse and Social Policy in America: The War That Must Be Won*. London; New York: Routledge.

The author looks at substance abuse from the policy standpoint. He begins by reviewing the fundamental facts about the nation's drug problem and then shows the role of tobacco, alcohol, and other large recreational and entertainment industries and of pharmaceutical companies. He then outlines policy issues and possible stances that should be taken to deal with a number of aspects of the nation's drug problems.

Swann, Maggie. 2013. *Get Real, Mum, Everybody Smokes Cannabis!: How Cannabis Claimed My Teenage Son and the Fight to Get Him Back*. Blackpool, England: Savage Mountain.

This book was written by a parent whose son became addicted to marijuana. It tells the story of what she had to go through to aid his recovery from that addiction.

White, Tony. 2013. *Working with Drug and Alcohol Users: A Guide to Providing Understanding, Assessment and Support.* London; Philadelphia: Jessica Kingsley Publishers.

This book is intended for counselors whose patients include teenagers who have become dependent upon or addicted to drugs or alcohol. The author describes the nature of addiction and dependence and describes counseling practices that may be useful in helping teenagers avoid or recover from misuse or abuse of drugs.

Young, Sian. 2012. *Teenage Kicks: A True Story of Dark Streets to Bright New Beginnings.* St. Albans, UK: Ecademy Press.

In this book, the author tells the story of how she overcame teenage substance addiction to become a successful business person who owns and operates her own company.

Articles

A number of peer-reviewed journals contain articles relating to youth substance abuse, some devoted exclusively to that topic. Among those journals are the following:

Addiction (ISSN: 1360-0443 [online])

Addiction Research and Theory (ISSN 1606-6359 [print] 1476-7392 [online])

Advances in Alcohol and Substance Abuse (ISSN: 0270-3106)

Journal of Addiction Research and Therapy. (ISSN: 2155-6105)

Journal of Child and Adolescent Substance Abuse (ISSN: 1067-828X [Print], 1547-0652 [Online])

Journal of Substance Abuse and Alcoholism (ISSN: 2373-9363)

Journal of Substance Abuse Treatment (ISSN: 0740–5472)

Research Journal of Drug Abuse (ISSN 2057-3111)

Substance Abuse (ISSN: 0889-7077 [Print], 1547-0164 [Online])

Substance Abuse Treatment Prevention and Policy (ISSN: 1747-597X)

Acri, Mary C., et al. 2012. "What Adolescents Need to Prevent Relapse after Treatment for Substance Abuse: A Comparison of Youth, Parent, and Staff Perspectives." *Journal of Child & Adolescent Substance Abuse*. 21(2): 117–129.
> For most adolescents who complete a treatment program for substance abuse, completion of the program itself is not the end of the recovery process. These researchers spoke with adolescents, parents, and staff members to determine the additional services that are required to ensure continued abstinence from psychoactive substance use.

Albers, Alison Burke, et al. 2015. "Flavored Alcoholic Beverage Use, Risky Drinking Behaviors, and Adverse Outcomes among Underage Drinkers: Results from the ABRAND Study." *American Journal of Public Health*. 105(4): 810–815.
> An emerging issue of concern in the field of substance abuse is the rapidly growing popularity of flavored alcoholic beverages, commonly known as alcopop. This study attempted to discover the extent to which adolescents have adopted a taste for such beverages and the patterns of use that have followed. They conclude that "FABs present an emerging public health problem among youths."

Amrock, S. M., et al. 2015. "Perception of E-Cigarette Harm and Its Correlation with Use among U.S. Adolescents." *Nicotine and Tobacco Research*. 17(3): 330–336.
> Research on adolescents' views about the safety of e-cigarettes is sparse. This study found that a large majority of both e-cigarette users and nonusers think that the

product is safer than conventional cigarettes, a belief that appears to contribute to increased vaping by both groups.

Anderson, Kristen G., Miranda Sitney, and Helene R. White. 2015. "Marijuana Motivations across Adolescence: Impacts on Use and Consequences." *Substance Use & Misuse.* 50(3): 292–301.
    Researchers followed a cohort of 434 individuals at four points in their lifetime, ages 12, 15, 18, and 25, to see how various motivations to use or not use marijuana predicted substance use in the early years of adulthood.

Antonio, M.C., and J.J. Chung-Do. 2015. "Systematic Review of Interventions Focusing on Indigenous Adolescent Mental Health and Substance Use." *American Indian and Alaska Native Mental Health Research.* 22(3): 36–46.
    The authors reviewed six substance abuse intervention programs designed specifically for American Indians and Native Alaskans and found that all programs reported "positive or expected outcomes."

Apa-Hall, Paula, Rochelle D. Schwartz-Bloom, and Elizabeth S. McConnell. 2008. "The Current State of Teenage Drug Abuse: Trend toward Prescription Drugs." *The Journal of School Nursing.* 24(3): S1–S16.
    This special supplement to volume 24, number 3, of the journal provides a good overview of the status of teenage drug use and abuse, with special attention to the issue of prescription drug abuse among adolescents.

Aston, Elizabeth V. 2015. "Are Risk Factors for Drug Use and Offending Similar during the Teenage Years?" *International Journal of Drug Policy.* 26(4): 396–403.
    The author asks whether substance abuse can be thought of as related to criminal behavior during adolescence and finds that the answer is "no" for younger adolescents, but "probably yes" for older adolescents. She suggests that these findings should affirm the need for thinking of and

treating substance use issues in early adolescence as a phenomenon different from criminal behaviors.

Baumann, Michael. 2014. "Awash in a Sea of 'Bath Salts': Implications for Biomedical Research and Public Health." *Addiction*. 109(10): 1577–1579.
  The author provides a good general introduction to the use and abuse of so-called bath salts (actually, synthetic analogues of the psychoactive compound cathinone). The article contains some very helpful additional references on the topic.

Bechtold, Jordan, et al. 2015. "Chronic Adolescent Marijuana Use as a Risk Factor for Physical and Mental Health Problems in Young Adult Men." *Psychology of Addictive Behaviors*. 29(3): 552–563.
  These researchers attempted to determine how four groups of males, ranging from nonusers to heavy users of marijuana in adolescence, differed in their adult health. They found no statistically significant differences among the four groups.

Bunnell, R. E., et al. 2015. "Intentions to Smoke Cigarettes among Never-Smoking US Middle and High School Electronic Cigarette Users: National Youth Tobacco Survey, 2011–2013." *Nicotine & Tobacco Research*. 17(2): 228–235.
  Researchers found that adolescence who took up vaping were twice as likely to switch to traditional cigarettes as were a group of control students who had never used any type of nicotine-delivery device.

Camenga, Deepa R., et al. 2014. "Trends in Use of Electronic Nicotine Delivery Systems by Adolescents." *Addictive Behaviors*. 39(1): 338–340.
  The authors attempt to estimate the prevalence of e-cigarettes, cigars, and other nicotine-delivery systems, along with an analysis of the characteristics of individuals who use such systems.

Choo, Esther K., et al. 2014. "The Impact of State Medical Marijuana Legislation on Adolescent Marijuana Use." *Journal of Adolescent Health*. 55(2): 160–166.

> The authors explored the question as to whether, and, if so, to what extent, the legalization of marijuana in some states affected marijuana use by adolescents in that state. They found no correlation between the two factors and concluded that legalization of marijuana has no effect on marijuana use by youth.

Cooper, Richard J. 2013. "Over-the-Counter Medicine Abuse—A Review of the Literature." *Journal of Substance Use*. 18(2): 82–107.

> This article is an excellent review of one of the topics of major concern in today's world, namely the misuse and abuse of over-the-counter medications by individuals, teenagers in particular.

Cornelius, Jack, et al. 2015. "Does Stress Mediate the Development of Substance Use Disorders among Youth Transitioning to Young Adulthood?" *The American Journal of Drug and Alcohol Abuse*. 40(3): 225–229.

> The authors attempted to find out if stress experienced during adolescence is a predictor of substance abuse in early adulthood. They found an association between stress in late adolescence (age 19) and early adulthood (age 22), but not between early adolescence (age 10–12) and early adulthood.

Crocq, Marc-Antoine. 2007. "Historical and Cultural Aspects of Man's Relationship with Addictive Drugs." *Dialogues of Clinical Neuroscience*. 9(4): 355–361.

> This article provides an excellent general introduction to the use and abuse of psychoactive substances in the early history of human societies.

D'Amico, Elizabeth J., Jeremy N. V. Miles, and Joan S. Tucker. 2015. "Gateway to Curiosity: Medical Marijuana Ads and

Intention and Use during Middle School." *Psychology of Addictive Behaviors.* 29(3): 613–619.

Adolescents who have been exposed to advertising for medical marijuana are more likely to have a favorable view toward the product and more willing to begin to use it.

Degenhardt, Louisa, et al. 2015. "Associations between Psychotic Symptoms and Substance Use in Young Offenders." *Drug and Alcohol Review.* 34(6): 673–682.

Researchers in this study found that one in eight adolescents who were substances abusers showed signs of psychotic personality.

Donaldson, Candice D., Brandon Nakawaki, and William D. Crano. 2015. "Variations in Parental Monitoring and Predictions of Adolescent Prescription Opioid and Stimulant Misuse." *Addictive Behaviors.* 45: 14–21.

This study was conducted to identify family factors that were relevant to an adolescent's decision to use or not use prescription medications for nonmedical purposes.

Emory, Kristen T., et al. "Receptivity to Cigarette and Tobacco Control Messages and Adolescent Smoking Initiation." *Tobacco Control.* 24(3): 281–284.

This study explored the effectiveness of anti-smoking advertisements as a mechanism for reducing the likelihood of adolescents' beginning to smoke. It found that such advertising was by far the most effective of anti-smoking programs and its use should be expanded.

Engle, Bretton, and Mark J. Macgowan. 2009. "A Critical Review of Adolescent Substance Abuse Group Treatments." *Journal of Evidence-Based Social Work.* 6(3): 217–243.

For this study, the authors found only 13 reports of treatment programs for which competent evaluations had been conducted, and of those, only two that met the more stringent requirement of "possible efficacy." They suggest that more, and more rigorous, evaluative studies are needed on group treatment programs.

Fischer, Benedikt, et al. 2015. "Effectiveness of Secondary Prevention and Treatment Interventions for Crack-Cocaine Abuse: A Comprehensive Narrative Overview of English-Language Studies." *International Journal of Drug Policy.* 26(4): 352–363.
Researchers reviewed articles on treatment programs for crack cocaine users published in English between 1990 and 2014 and found that none of the treatment methods used could be described as more than moderate and short term in their effectiveness.

Green, Kerry M., et al. 2016. "Outcomes Associated with Adolescent Marijuana and Alcohol Use among Urban Young Adults: A Prospective Study." *Addictive Behaviors.* 53: 155–160.
Researchers attempted to determine how moderate and high alcohol and alcohol/marijuana use in adolescence affected substance behavior during adulthood. They found that all three forms of adolescent behavior were correlated with substance abuse behavior in adulthood.

Griswold, Kim S., et al. 2008. "Adolescent Substance Use and Abuse: Recognition and Management." *American Family Physician.* 77(3): 331–336.
A significant fraction of adolescent substance abuse cases go undiagnosed and unrecognized. This article points out the critical role of family physicians in the frontline of this battle against addiction and recommends some actions that primary care physicians can take to correct this problem.

Hanson, Karen L., et al. 2011. "Changes in Neuropsychological Functioning over 10 Years Following Adolescent Substance Abuse Treatment." *Psychology of Addictive Behaviors.* 25(1): 127–142.
The authors report on a 10-year follow-up study of 213 subjects who experience substance abuse issues as

adolescents. They found that those individuals experienced a variety of mental issues at a greater rate than did a control group who were not substance users in adolescence. Thy conclude that the use of psychoactive substances at a time when the brain is still maturing has significant mental consequences.

Hassan, Areej, et al. 2009. "Adolescent Substance Abuse around the World: An International Perspective." *Adolescent Medicine: State of the Art Reviews*. 20(3): 915–929.

The authors note that data on adolescent substance abuse is not available from many countries in the world. But they do attempt to summarize that which is available.

Johnson, Joy, et al. 2009. "Relief-Oriented Use of Marijuana by Teens." *Substance Abuse Treatment, Prevention, and Policy*. 4(1): 1–10.

The authors found that teenagers who perceived that they had few or no viable options for the treatment of physical or emotional problems available to them turned to marijuana as a source of relief from their discomforts.

King, George, et al. 2010. "Neuropsychological Deficits in Adolescent Methamphetamine Abusers." *Psychopharmacology*. 212(2): 243–249. Also available online at http://www.ncbi.nlm.nih.gov/pmc/articles/PMC2939179/. Accessed on January 13, 2016.

The authors attempt to discover changes in brain structure and function resulting from amphetamine use. They find that amphetamine users have impaired executive functions compared to those in a control group. (Brain executive functions are brain functions that control activities such as memory, reasoning, and problem solving.)

Kloos, Angelica, et al. 2009. "Gender Differences in Adolescent Substance Abuse." *Current Psychiatry Reports*. 11(2): 120-126.

The authors note that gender differences among adult substance abusers have been well studied, although such is not the case for adolescents. Correcting that lacuna is an objective of this study.

Knight, John R., et al. 1999. "A New Brief Screen for Adolescent Substance Abuse." *Archives of Pediatrics & Adolescent Medicine.* 153(6): 591–596.
   This article describes the design and development of one of the most widely used screening tests used to determine substance abuse among adolescents. The test is known as the CRAFFT screening test for six key words in the protocol for the test: Car, Relax, Alone, Forget, Friends, Trouble.

Knudsen, Hannah K. 2009. "Smoking Cessation Services in Adolescent Substance Abuse Treatment: Opportunities Missed?" *Journal of Drug Issues.* 39(2): 257–276.
   The author notes that most adolescents who appear for treatment are also smokers, but that most treatment programs do not include smoking issues in their program. She reports on a survey of the inclusion of smoking cessation in substance abuse programs.

Knudsen, Hannah K., and C. B. Oser. 2009. "Availability of HIV-Related Health Services in Adolescent Substance Abuse Treatment Programs." *AIDS Care—Psychological and Socio-Medical Aspects of AIDS/HIV.* 21(10): 1238–1246.
   The authors point out that substance abuse has been found to increase an adolescent's risk for HIV/AIDS disease, suggesting that the inclusion of HIV services in substance abuse prevention programs would be a wise act. Their review of more than 100 substance prevention programs found that only half adopt this feature as part of their programs and only a quarter include HIV testing as part of the intake procedure.

Lorang, Melissa, et al. 2011. "Anabolic Androgenic Steroid Use in Teens: Prevalence, Demographics, and Perception of Effects." *Journal of Child & Adolescent Substance Abuse.* 20(4): 358–369.

The researchers explored patterns of use of anabolic ste-roids among a sample of 4,231 high school students, along with a study of the students' views about the use and possible effects of the drugs.

Lyoo, I. K., et al. 2015. "Predisposition to and Effects of Meth-amphetamine Use on the Adolescent Brain." *Molecular Psychiatry*. 20(12): 1516–1524.

Researchers report on their studies of brain composition in adolescents and adults who have and have not been methamphetamine users and come to the conclusion that "the adolescent brain, which undergoes active myelination and maturation, is more vulnerable to MA-related altera-tions than the adult brain. Furthermore, MA-use-related executive dysfunction was greater in adolescent MA users than in adult users." This observation, they say, "may pro-vide explanation for the severe behavioral complications and relapses that are common in adolescent-onset drug addiction."

Miech, Richard A., et al. 2015. "Trends in Use of Marijuana and Attitudes toward Marijuana among Youth before and after Decriminalization: The Case of California 2007–2013." *Interna-tional Journal of Drug Policy*. 26(4): 336–344.

Researchers asked whether the decriminalization of mari-juana use in California in 2012 added a new risk factor for adolescent use of the drug. The answer is yes.

Nakawaki, Brandon, and William D. Crano. 2012. "Predicting Adolescents' Persistence, Non-Persistence, and Recent Onset of Nonmedical Use of Opioids and Stimulants." *Addictive Behav-iors*. 37(6): 716–721.

This study was carried out to discover the factors involved in a young adult's decision to begin using opioids and stimulants for nonmedical purposes. A number of rele-vant and irrelevant factors are listed.

Nargiso, Jessica E., Erica L. Ballard, and Margie R. Skeer. 2015. "A Systematic Review of Risk and Protective Factors Associated with Nonmedical Use of Prescription Drugs among Youth in the United States: A Social Ecological Perspective." *Journal of Studies on Alcohol and Drugs.* 76(1): 5–20.

> This ambitious study attempted to identify those factors associated with the nonmedical use of prescription drugs. It found that some of those factors were accessibility of such drugs, parental attitudes and controls, educational attainment, and previous substance abuse.

Niño, Michael D., Tianji Cai, and Gabe Ignatow. 2016. "Social Isolation, Drunkenness, and Cigarette Use among Adolescents." *Addictive Behaviors.* 53(4): 94–100.

> The authors attempted to determine how social isolation is related to excessive use of alcohol and smoking and found that that relationship depended on the reason for one's isolation.

Nissen, Laura Burney, and Jessica Pearce. 2011. "Exploring the Implementation of Justice-Based Alcohol and Drug Intervention Strategies with Juvenile Offenders: Reclaiming Futures, Enhanced Adolescent Substance Abuse Treatment, and Juvenile Drug Courts." *Children and Youth Services Review.* 33: S60–S65.

> The authors describe efforts to combine substance abuse treatment and prevention programs with the juvenile justice system.

Paino, Maria. 2015. "Organizational Predictors and Use of Evidence-Based Practices in Adolescent Substance Abuse Treatment." 2015. *Substance Abuse.* 36(4): 462–469.

> The authors explore the likelihood of adolescent substance abusers' seeking treatment at conventional substance abuse treatment centers and report on the frequency and nature of the treatment that is available to teenagers.

Palamar, Joseph J., and Dimitra Kamboukos. 2014. "An Examination of Sociodemographic Correlates of Ecstasy Use among

High School Seniors in the United States." *Substance Use & Misuse*. 49(13): 1774–1783.

> Researchers found that a number of personal characteristics correlated with regular use of ecstasy, including living in a city, being gainfully employed, and being a regular user of other psychoactive substances.

Pomeranz, J. L., L. M. Taylor, and S. B. Austin. 2013. "Over-the-Counter and Out-of-Control: Legal Strategies to Protect Youths from Abusing Products for Weight Control." *American Journal of Public Health*. 103(2): 220–225.

> The authors reviewed information from state, national, and international law and precedent to come up with suggestions for reducing adolescents' access to potentially harmful over-the-counter drugs.

Scholes-Balog, Kirsty E., et al. 2016. "Developmental Trajectories of Adolescent Cannabis Use and Their Relationship to Young Adult Social and Behavioural Adjustment: A Longitudinal Study of Australian Youth." *Addictive Behaviors*. 53(4): 11–18.

> The research question for this study was how three levels of marijuana use (none, early onset, and later onset) affected a variety of outcomes in adulthood. They found a number of negative personal and social attributes by both early and late onset users and recommended that "[p]revention and intervention efforts to delay or prevent uptake of cannabis use should be particularly focussed on early adolescence prior to age 12."

Smyth, Bobby P., John Fagan, and Kathy Kernan. 2012. "Outcome of Heroin-Dependent Adolescents Presenting for Opiate Substitution Treatment." *Journal of Substance Abuse Treatment*. 42(1): 35–44.

> This study attempted to determine the success of methadone and buprenorphine substitution for the treatment of heroin addiction. It found that the procedure is generally successful and that about 20 percent of subjects were "clean" within a one- to two-year time frame.

Squeglia, L. M., J. Jacobus, and S. F. Tapert. 2009. "The Influence of Substance Use on Adolescent Brain Development." *Clinical EEG and Neuroscience*. 40(1): 31–38.

This article provides an excellent general introduction to the question of how psychoactive substances produced measurable changes in brain structure and activity.

Steinberg, Laurence. 2008. "A Social Neuroscience Perspective on Adolescent Risk-Taking." *Developmental Review*. 28(1): 78–106.

The author explores that question as to why substance use is an issue of particular concern during adolescence. He shows the connection between there being a period of high interest in risk-taking during brain development, and how that characteristic tends to dissipate toward the end of adolescence.

Unger, Jennifer B. 2015. "Preventing Substance Use and Misuse among Racial and Ethnic Minority Adolescents: Why Are We Not Addressing Discrimination in Prevention Programs?" *Substance Use & Misuse*. 50(8–9): 952–955.

The author notes that race and ethnicity are important factors in youth substance abuse so why is it, she asks, that such characteristics are not a more critical part of most prevention programs?

Usher, Kim, Debra Jackson, and Louise O'Brien. 2007. "Shattered Dreams: Parental Experiences of Adolescent Substance Abuse." *International Journal of Mental Health Nursing*. 16(6): 422–430.

The authors discuss the very personal questions as to how having an adolescent substance abuser affects that individual's parents, based on in-depth interviews with 18 parents with that experience.

Whiteside, Lauren K., et al. 2015. "Nonmedical Prescription Stimulant Use among Youth in the Emergency Department: Prevalence, Severity and Correlates." *Journal of Substance Abuse Treatment*. 48(1): 21–27.

This study explored a number of characteristics of 4,389 14- to 20-year olds who presented at an emergency department in Ann Arbor, Michigan, for nonmedical prescription substance abuse.

Workman, Judson W., et al. 2012. "PALS Prevention Program and Its Long-Term Impact on Student Intentions to Use Alcohol, Tobacco, and Marijuana." *Journal of Drug Education*. 42(4): 469–485.

The PALS (Prevention through Alternative Learning Styles) program has been developed to enhance students' knowledge about the harmful effects of alcohol, tobacco, and other drugs. This reports on the effectiveness of that program with middle school students, finding that it did in fact reduce students' stated interests in engaging in misuse of these substances.

Wu, Li-Tzy, et al. 2011. "Treatment Use and Barriers among Adolescents with Prescription Opioid Use Disorders." *Addictive Behaviors*. 36(12): 1233–1239.

The authors found in this study that adolescents who needed treatment for prescription drug abuse tended not to make use of available treatments for a variety of reasons, most important of which were stigma attached to treatment programs and perceived lack of need for such treatment.

Reports

"Adolescent Substance Abuse." 2011. National Center on Addiction and Substance Abuse. Columbia University. http://www .casacolumbia.org/addiction-research/reports/adolescent-sub stance-use. Accessed on November 27, 2015.

This report summarizes the result of an extensive study that involved interviews with 1,000 high school students, 1,000 parents of high school students, and 500 school personnel, as well as an exhaustive review of the literature on teenage substance abuse. The authors conclude that substance abuse by adolescents is the largest preventable and most costly health problem in the United States today. The report provides a wealth of data about the topic and is a "must reading" for anyone interested in the subject.

"The CBHSQ Report: A Day in the Life of American Adolescents: Substance Use Facts Update." 2013. Center for Behavioral Health Statistics and Quality. http://archive.samhsa.gov/ data/2k13/CBHSQ128/sr128-typical-day-adolescents-2013. htm. Accessed on January 12, 2016.

This collection of data comes from a variety of national surveys and provides statistics on tobacco and alcohol use, along with data on substance use and abuse by adolescents.

"A Century of International Drug Control." [2009]. United Nations Office on Drugs and Crime. http://www.unodc.org/doc uments/data-and-analysis/Studies/100_Years_of_Drug_Control. pdf. Accessed on January 14, 2016.

This report provides a detailed description of the state of drug use prior to the installation of international drug controls, a summary of the most important of those regulations, and the changes produced by their implementation beginning in the early twentieth century.

"Dextromethorphan. Pre-Review Report." 2012. World Health Organization. http://www.who.int/medicines/areas/quality_safety/ 5.1Dextromethorphan_pre-review.pdf. Accessed on November 27, 2015.

This document is one in a WHO series on specific substances of abuse. It includes detailed information about a range of aspects for the substance, such as its physical and chemical properties, pharmacology, toxicology, adverse reactions in humans, dependence potential, abuse potential, industrial uses, therapeutic applications, and marketing authorizations as a medicine.

"Drug Abuse Warning Network, 2013: National Estimates of Drug-Related Emergency Department Visits." 2013. Washington, DC: Center for Behavioral Health Statistics and Quality. Substance Abuse and Mental Health Services Administration. http://www.samhsa.gov/data/sites/default/files/DAWN2k11ED/ DAWN2k11ED/DAWN2k11ED.htm. Accessed on January 13, 2016.

> This report provides statistics about visits made to emergency departments (EDs) in the United States for reasons of substance use, misuse, and abuse. It is a treasure chest of information about virtually all psychoactive drugs used in the United States along with data on user characteristics.

"Drugs of Abuse." Drug Enforcement Administration. http:// www.dea.gov/pr/multimedia-library/publications/drug_of_ abuse.pdf. Accessed on November 27, 2015.

> This annual publication of the DEA is a superb introduction to the primary substances abused and misused by individuals in the United States, along with an explanation of the scheduling system used for such drugs and a complete list of the drugs included in each of the five schedules.

"E-Cigarette Reviews and News You Can Trust." 2015. e Cig One. http://ecigone.com/. Accessed on November 28, 2015.

> E Cig One was created in 2012 for the purpose of educating smokers about electronic cigarettes and to provide news and reviews about all aspects of the product. The e Cig One website provides information on virtually every aspect of the subject including the safety of e-cigarettes, the basics as to how they work, the best products for beginners, health effects of using e-cigarettes, and legal aspects of the products.

"Education under Arrest: The Case against Police in Schools." 2011. Justice Policy Institute. http://www.justicepolicy.org/ uploads/justicepolicy/documents/educationunderarrest_fullreport.pdf. Accessed on January 12, 2016.

This report considers the use of the so-called school to prison pipeline, in which schools tend to carry out "zero tolerance" drug policies that are likely to remove offending adolescents from schools and move them very quickly into the criminal justice system. The authors point out that this type of policy and program reduces the possibility of at-risk youths' receiving the benefit of substance education programs that are most commonly offered in a school setting.

Hedden, Sara L., et al. 2015. *Behavioral Health Trends in the United States: Results from the 2014 National Survey on Drug Use and Health.* Washington, DC: Center for Behavioral Health Statistics and Quality. Substance Abuse and Mental Health Services Administration.

This annual study collects basic information about the use of legal and illegal substances in the United States and analyzes those data on the basis of a number of demographic characteristics, such as age, gender, ethnicity and race, and previous experiences with substances. It is one of the most important sources of demographic data about substance use in the United States.

Hibell, Björn, et al. 2012. "The 2011 ESPAD Report: Substance Abuse among Students in 36 European Countries." http://www .espad.org/Uploads/ESPAD_reports/2011/The_2011_ESPAD_ Report_FULL_2012_10_29.pdf. Accessed on January 12, 2016.

This report provides a detailed overview of the state of substance abuse by adolescents in 36 European nations, with statistics for each nation, an overview for all 36 nations, a special trends from 1995 through 2011, and special sections on cannabis screening tests and polydrug use on the continent.

Kann, Laura, et al. 2013. "Youth Risk Behavior Surveillance—United States. 2013." *MMWR.* 63(4). Available online at http:// www.cdc.gov/mmwr/pdf/ss/ss6304.pdf. Accessed on November 27, 2015.

This publication is one of the most complete and detailed summaries of the statistics and data related to the abuse and misuse of substances by teenagers in the United States as of the publication date.

"Monitoring the Future: A Continuing Study of American Youth." Ann Arbor: Institute for Social Research. University of Michigan. http://www.monitoringthefuture.org/. Accessed on January 10, 2016.

The Monitoring the Future (MTF) research project is far and away the most important single resource on substance abuse patterns among American eighth, tenth, and twelfth graders, along with information about their attitudes about substance use and abuse. MTF researchers have produced a huge number of documents on specific aspects of American youth substance use and abuse over the 40 years of the project's existence.

"The Partnership Attitude Tracking Study." 2014. Partnership for Drug-Free Kids and MetLife Foundation. http://drugfree.scdn1.secure.raxcdn.com/wp-content/uploads/2014/07/PATS-2013-FULL-REPORT.pdf. Accessed on January 10, 2015.

This study is the 22nd version of research that has been conducted since 1987 to measure attitudes and behaviors associated with substance use and abuse among children and adolescents and their parents. Data for the most recent study was collected from existing literature as well as interviews with 1,000 young adults, 1,000 parents, and 500 school officials.

Stagman, Shannon, Susan Wile Schwarz, and Danielle Powers. 2011. "Adolescent Substance Use in the U.S.: Facts for Policymakers." National Center for Children in Poverty. http://www.nccp.org/publications/pdf/text_1008.pdf. Accessed on January 12, 2016.

This report presents some basic facts about substance abuse among adolescents from the special perspective of the sponsoring agency, the National Center for Children in Poverty.

It also provides some very specific recommendations for dealing with this problem for its target population.

"World Drug Report 2015." 2015. Vienna: United Nations Office on Drugs and Crime. https://www.unodc.org/documents/ mexicoandcentralamerica/eventos/2015/WDD2015/World_ Drug_Report_2015.pdf. Accessed on January 13, 2016.
This document is the most comprehensive and detailed report on world drug use currently available. It is produced annually.

Internet

"Addiction Science." 2015. National Institute on Drug Abuse. http://www.drugabuse.gov/related-topics/addiction-science. Accessed on January 13, 2016.
This excellent website provides a wide range of information on the effects of psychoactive substances on the human brain, particularly during adolescence. It has links to other publications on the same topic, including the Nature Outlook special edition on Addiction (http://www.nature.com/nature/outlook/addiction/), articles on the controversial nature of the brain disease model for addiction (http://www.sciencedirect.com/sci ence/article/pii/S2215036615002369), the NIDA publication "Drugs, Brains, and Behavior: The Science of Addiction" (http://www.drugabuse.gov/publications/drugs-brains-behavior-science-addiction/preface), and the NIDA publication "The Brain: Understanding Neurobiology through the Study of Addiction" (http://www.drugabuse .gov/publications/brain-understanding-neurobiology-through-study-addiction). (All references were accessed on January 13, 2016.)

"Adolescence and Substance Abuse." 2016. National Child Traumatic Stress Network. http://www.nctsn.org/resources/topics/ adolescence-and-substance-abuse. Accessed on January 12, 2016.

This website provides a general introduction to the issue of traumatic stress and its relationship to substance abuse, with a number of very useful links to related Internet and print resources.

"Adolescents." 2014. Get the Facts. DrugWarFacts.org. http:// www.drugwarfacts.org/cms/Adolescents#sthash.rQk2f8Wp .2nSLtmFW.dpbs. Accessed on January 12, 2016.
This excellent website provides links to a large number of references on specific aspects of youth substance abuse, such as basic data, young people and marijuana, sociopolitical research, adolescents and crime, families and youth, prevention and education, gateway theory, and data on adolescent substance use and abuse.

Aines, Ethan D. 2012. "The Archaeology of Alcohol." Carousing with the Ancients. http://www.eaines.com/archaeology/the-archaeology-of-ancient-alcohol/. Accessed on January 10, 2016.
This website provides one of the most complete and interesting histories of the role of alcohol consumption in ancient cultures. It also includes an excellent bibliography.

"Al-Anon Family Groups." 2016. http://www.al-anon.alateen.org/ for-alateen. Accessed on January 14, 2016.
Alateen is a specialty subgroup of Alcoholics Anonymous designed for children and adolescents whose lives have been affected by someone else's drinking. This website explains the resources that are available through Alateen and the ways in which one can become involved in the program.

"Alcohol Screening and Brief Intervention for Youth: A Practitioner's Guide." 2011. National Institute on Alcohol Abuse and Alcoholism. http://pubs.niaaa.nih.gov/publications/Practitioner/ YouthGuide/YouthGuide.pdf. Accessed on January 13, 2016.
This publication describes the use of a simple tool that can be used in the diagnosis and identification of underage individuals who are at risk for alcohol-related problems.

"Anabolic Steroids." 2013. Center for Substance Abuse Research. http://www.cesar.umd.edu/cesar/drugs/steroids.asp. Accessed on January 18, 2016.

> This website is an excellent general introduction to the topic of anabolic steroids, what they are, and the effects they have on humans, both good and bad.

Anderson, Brian T., et al. "Statement on Ayahuasca." 2012. International Journal of Drug Policy. http://canadianharmreduction.com/sites/default/files/Statement%20on%20Ayahuasca%20-%20IJDP%202012%20in%20press.pdf. Accessed on January 13, 2016.

> This editorial provides a broad general introduction to a psychoactive substance that has a long history of use in Brazil and whose use as a recreational drug has spread throughout South and North America in the last few years.

"Assessment of Khat (Catha Edulis Forsk)." 2006. World Health Organization. http://www.who.int/medicines/areas/quality_safety/4.4KhatCritReview.pdf. Accessed on January 13, 2016.

> This WHO document provides a very detailed description of the chemistry, pharmacology, toxicology, dependence potential, epidemiology, and other characteristics of this psychoactive substance.

Barker, Joanne. 2016. "When Teens Lie about Drugs: A Guide for Parents." WebMD. http://www.webmd.com/parenting/teen-abuse-cough-medicine-9/when-teenagers-lie-about-drugs?page=1. Accessed on January 14, 2016.

> This article recommends six things parents can do when they suspect that their children may be abusing drugs, but will not admit to doing so.

Bellum, Sara. 2012. "Helping Children of Addicted Parents to Find Help." NIDSA for Teens. https://teens.drugabuse.gov/blog/

post/helping-children-addicted-parents-find-help. Accessed on January 14, 2016.

This website discusses the problems facing children of substance abusers and refers specifically to Children of Alcoholics Week for additional information on the problem. Responses and replies in the blog portion of the website are of particular interest.

Bellum, Sara. 2014. "Let's Talk about Khat." NIDA for Teens. https://teens.drugabuse.gov/blog/post/lets-talk-about-khat. Accessed on January 12, 2016.

This website provides a good general introduction to the use of khat by teenagers with an useful link to additional information.

"The Best Electronic Cigarette Guide for 2015." http://info-elec tronic-cigarette.com/. Accessed on November 28, 2015.

This blog contains a number of articles by a variety of writers on all aspects of the discussion over the use and legalization of e-cigarettes.

Buck, Jordan M., and Jessica A. Siegel. 2015. "Frontiers in Neuroscience." http://journal.frontiersin.org/article/10.3389/fnins.2015 .00151/full. Accessed on January 13, 2016.

The authors provide a summary of current research information on the effects of methamphetamine use in both clinical settings and animal models. They conclude that methamphetamine use during adolescence "results in increased risky sexual behaviors and psychiatric problems in humans."

"Children, Adolescents, Substance Abuse, and the Media." 2010. The Council on Communications and the Media. American Academy of Pediatrics. http://pediatrics.aappublications.org/con tent/126/4/791. Accessed on January 12, 2016.

This policy statement by the American Academy of Pediatrics reviews the role that the media have in reporting and commenting on adolescent substance abuse and makes some recommendations about the future role of media in dealing with this issue.

"Circle of Healing." 2014. Office for Victims of Crime. http:// ovc.ncjrs.gov/topic.aspx?topicid=28; https://www.youtube.com/ watch?v=VhL4ZlceMS4&feature=youtu.be. Accessed on January 13, 2016.
   This program was developed by the U.S. Office for Victims of Crime as a teaching tool for Native American youth who are at risk for substance abuse. It consists of seven videos with accompanying print materials.

Davies, Leah. 2016. "Educator's Guide to Children Affected by Parental Drug Abuse." http://www.kellybear.com/TeacherArti cles/TeacherTip66.html. Accessed on January 14, 2016.
   Problems encountered by children of parents who are substance abusers are largely ignored. This article describes how to identify such individuals and the types of support that may be available for them.

Dryden-Edwards, Roxanne. "Club Drugs." 2015. eMedicine Health. http://www.emedicinehealth.com/club_drugs/article_em .htm. Accessed on January 14, 2016.
   This article provides a general overview of club drugs and then discusses in detail the properties and effects of those drugs, which include amphetamines, ecstasy, inhalants, PCP, ketamine, and so-called date rape drugs.

"Comorbidity: Addiction and Other Mental Illnesses." 2010. National Institute on Drug Abuse. https://www.drugabuse.gov/ sites/default/files/rrcomorbidity.pdf. Accessed on January 13, 2016.
   Comorbidity is the condition in which two or more illnesses or disorders occur in the same individual at the same time. The abuse of alcohol and marijuana is an example of comorbidity. This publication discusses some common types of comorbidity, its frequency in the population, means

of diagnosing comorbidity, and some treatment programs that are available for the condition.

"The Cool Spot." 2016. National Institute on Alcohol Abuse and Alcoholism. http://www.thecoolspot.gov/. Accessed on January 13, 2016.
This website is intended for boys and girls between the ages of 11 and 13. It is designed to help such individuals resist peer pressure to begin drinking and provides information and skills that can be used in avoiding the risks of alcohol abuse and dependence.

"The CRAFFT Screening Tool." 2016. The Center for Adolescent Substance Abuse Research. http://www.ceasar-boston.org/CRAFFT/. Accessed on January 12, 2016.
This web page provides an introduction to the CRAFFT screening tool used for the diagnosis of possible substance abuse problems with adolescents. Links to the tool itself and other relevant resources are available on the website.

Cunha John P. 2016. "Date Rape Drugs." MedicineNet.com. http://www.medicinenet.com/date_rape_drugs/article.htm. Accessed on January 14, 2016.
This article explains the basics of date rape drugs, suggests ways of avoiding becoming involved in a date rape, how to know if one has, indeed, been date raped, and if a date rape has occurred.

Cuzen, Natalie L., et al. 2015. "Methamphetamine and Cannabis Abuse in Adolescence: A Quasi-Experimental Study on Specific and Long-term Neurocognitive Effects." BMJ Open 5(1): 5:e005833 doi:10.1136/bmjopen-2014-005833.
This article describes a study designed to identify the changes in an individual's brain resulting from either methamphetamine or cannabis. It also summarizes previous research on the use of the two drugs together on brain structure and function.

"Drug Facts: Spice." 2015. NIDA for Teens. https://teens.druga-buse.gov/drug-facts/spice. Accessed on January 12, 2016.

> This website provides an excellent introduction to the drug commonly known as *spice* or *synthetic marijuana*, with sections on "What Is Spice?," "How Is Spice Used?," "How Does Spice Affect the Brain?," and "Can You Get Addicted to Spice?"

"Drug Schedules." 2016. U.S. Drug Enforcement Administration. http://www.dea.gov/druginfo/ds.shtml. Accessed on January 12, 2016.

> This website provides legal definitions for the five drug schedules created by the Controlled Substances Act of 1970. It also has a number of links to other related topics, such as a text of the act itself and an alphabetical list of all controlled substances and the schedule to which they belong.

DuPont, Robert L., et al. 2013. "America's Dropout Crisis: The Unrecognized Connection to Adolescent Substance Abuse." Institute for Behavior and Health. http://www.preventteendruguse.org/pdfs/AmerDropoutCrisis.pdf. Accessed on January 14, 2016.

> This report discusses the connection between school drop-out rates among adolescents and substance misuse and abuse. The authors note that researchers are not sure of the direction in which this relationship goes—whether dropping out leads to substance abuse or vice versa—but that, in any case, the connection has largely been ignored in the past, a situation that should be changed.

"Entheogens Including Salvia, LSD, Peyote, and Mushrooms." 2014. Get the Facts. DrugWar Facts.org. http://drugwarfacts.org/cms/Entheogens#Ayahuasca. Accessed on January 13, 2016.

> This website provides general information and a number of very useful links on the topics mentioned in its name, with an additional section on the meaning and use of the term *entheogen*.

"The Films." 2016. Home Box Office (HBO). https://www.hbo
.com/addiction/thefilm/index.html?current=5. Accessed on January 12, 2016.

This website provides access to a number of extraordinary documentary films dealing with many aspects of adolescent substance abuse. Among the titles are "The Adolescent Addict," "A Mother's Desperation," "The Science of Relapse," "Brain Imaging," "Opiate Addiction: A New Medication," and "Insurance Woes."

"Get Smart about Drugs." 2016. U.S. Drug Enforcement Administration. http://www.getsmartaboutdrugs.com/. Accessed on January 14, 2016.

This website provides a host of materials primarily aimed at parents, educators, and caregivers about ways of preventing adolescents from becoming involved with psychoactive substances. The two main sections deal with news articles about substance abuse and "trending topics," with special features on subjects such as opiod abuse, prescription drug abuse, synthetic drugs, heroin, new addictive substances, and the role of social media in substance abuse.

Grigoriadis, Vanessa. 2013. "Travels in the New Psychedelic Bazaar." *New York Magazine.* http://nymag.com/news/features/synthetic-drugs-2013-4/. Accessed on January 12, 2016.

This article discusses the history of designer drugs and analyzes recent trends in the development and use of such drugs.

"Helping Children from Dysfunctional Families." 2016. Alcoholics Victorious. http://alcoholicsvictorious.org/acoa. Accessed on January 14, 2016.

This article discusses the issues confronting children in families with one or adult substance abusers and the ways in which they can be helped in dealing with these issues.

"Is Your Teen Using? Signs and Symptoms of Substance Abuse." Partnership for Drug-Free Kids. http://www.drugfree .org/resources/is-your-teen-using-signs-and-symptoms-of-sub-stance-abuse/. Accessed on January 12, 2016.

   This web page provides guidance for parents, friends, and other acquaintances of the signs and symptoms that they can look for in adolescents who may be abusing psychoac-tive substances.

"Just Think Twice." 2016. U.S. Drug Enforcement Administra-tion. http://www.justthinktwice.com/. Accessed on January 14, 2016.

   This website uses a variety of media formats to provide information and give advice on the risks of adolescents' using psychoactive substances. Especially interesting is a set of biographical videos of individuals who have died from substance abuse.

Knight, John, et al. 2016. "Adolescent Alcohol and Substance Use and Abuse." American Academy of Pediatrics. Bright Future Handbook. https://brightfutures.aap.org/Bright%20Futures%20 Documents/Screening.pdf. Accessed on January 12, 2016.

   Bright Futures is a national health promotion and pre-vention initiative program sponsored by the American Academy of Pediatrics. This handbook is one in a series of similar resources written for the program that provides background about alcohol and substance use and abuse among adolescents, along with an extensive discussion of methods for preventing, diagnosing, and treating the condition.

Levy, Sharon. 2016. "Drug and Substance Use in Adoles-cents." Merck Manual. Professional Version. https://www.merck manuals.com/professional/pediatrics/problems-in-adolescents/ drug-and-substance-use-in-adolescents. Accessed on January 12, 2016.

This review of adolescent substance abuse issues is provided by one of the most highly respected sources of information about medical topics, the Merck Manual, for practitioners in the field. A comparable essay designed for the general public can be found at https://www.merckmanuals.com/home/children's-health-issues/problems-in-adolescents/substance-use-and-abuse-in-adolescents.

"Making the Connection: Trauma and Substance Abuse." 2008. National Child Traumatic Stress Network. http://www.nctsn.org/sites/default/files/assets/pdfs/SAToolkit_1.pdf. Accessed on January 13, 2016.
Increasing evidence suggests that trauma may be an important risk factor for the development of substance abuse, dependence, and addiction. This publication outlines the character of that problem and suggests possible systems of prevention and treatment.

McFadden, Cynthia, Aliza Nadi, and Tracy Connor. 2015. "'Devil's Drug': Flakka Is Driving Florida Insane." NBC News. http://www.nbcnews.com/news/us-news/devils-drug-flakka-driving-florida-insane-n471531. Accessed on January 14, 2016.
Flakka is a new designer drug that has been called "more dangerous than crack cocaine." Its use is spreading throughout the United States and to other developed countries in the world. This article discusses this trend and the potential harm associated with the substance.

"Media and Adolescent Substance Abuse." 2011. Johns Hopkins Children's Center. http://www.hopkinschildrens.org/media-and-adolescent-substance-abuse.aspx. Accessed on January 12, 2016.
This article raises the question as to how advertising and other media presentations about alcohol and other psychoactive substances affect adolescents' attitudes about the use of such substances.

"Mescaline." 2010. Science in Context. http://ic.galegroup.com/
ic/scic/ReferenceDetailsPage/DocumentToolsPortletWindow?di
splayGroupName=Reference&jsid=6136ddee7859183bb7f359
4c8cdef566&action=2&catId=&documentId=GALE%7CCV2
645000032&u=gotitans&zid=af1c2c1b5c6309cb697cd501a79
7bd69. Accessed on January 13, 2016.

This web page provides a good general introduction to the
psychoactive substance mescaline, along with its potential
effects on the human body and current use among adolescents and adults.

"Methamphetamine (Meth)." 2016. NIDA for Teens. https://
teens.drugabuse.gov/drug-facts/methamphetamine. Accessed on
January 13, 2016.

This article in the very useful NIDA for Teens series provides basic information on almost every aspect of methamphetamine use by adolescents, along with suggestions
for additional reading.

"Parents 360: Synthetic Drugs: Bath Salts, K2/Spice: A Guide for
Parents and Other Influencers." 2012. The Partnership at Drug-
Free.org. http://www.preventteendruguse.org/pdfs/Parents360-
SyntheticsBathSaltsK2SpiceParentsGuideFINAL21312.pdf.
Accessed on January 14, 2016.

This PowerPoint format presentation provides a general
introduction to "bath salts" and "synthetic marijuana"
(K2/Spice), with suggestions for ways that parents and
other adults can help children and adolescents to avoid
involvement with such products.

"Performance-Enhancing Drugs and Teen Athletes." 2016. Mayo
Clinic. http://www.mayoclinic.org/healthy-lifestyle/tween-and-
teen-health/in-depth/performance-enhancing-drugs/
art-20046620. Accessed on January 13, 2016.

This article provides a good general introduction to the
nature of anabolic steroids, their use by adolescents, and
their possible effects on the human body and emotions.

"Prevent Teen Drug Use." 2016. http://www.preventteendru guse.org/index.html. Accessed on January 14, 2016.

This excellent website provides a number of very useful links to articles, activities, and organizations aimed at reducing substance abuse among children and adolescents.

"Principles of Adolescent Substance Use Disorder Treatment: A Research-Based Guide." 2014. National Institute on Drug Abuse. https://teens.drugabuse.gov/sites/default/files/podata_1_17_14_0. pdf. Accessed on January 12, 2016.

This publication provides a superb introduction to and overview of treatment services for adolescent substance abusers. It begins with some major principles on which such programs should be based, provides answers to a number of frequently asked questions, and supplies suggestions for specific programs and resources in the field.

"Psilocybin." 2016. Hallucinogens. http://hallucinogens.com/ psilocybin/. Accessed on January 12, 2016.

This article provides a general introduction to psilocybin and "magic mushrooms," one of the natural sources of that compound. It provides links to a number of other online articles that also discuss this psychoactive compound.

"Recent Declines in Adolescent Inhalant Use." 2014. Substance Abuse and Mental Health Services Administration. http://www .samhsa.gov/data/sites/default/files/sr174-inhalants-2014/sr 174-inhalants-2014/sr174-inhalants-2014.htm. Accessed on January 13, 2016.

This report provides data from the most recent version of the National Study on Drug Use and Health showing that inhalant abuse by adolescents appears to be dropping by significant levels over the past few years.

"Reducing Adolescent Substance Abuse Initiative." 2016. National Council for Behavioral Health. http://www.thenationalcouncil .org/practice-improvement/reducing-adolescent-substance- abuse-initiative/. Accessed on January 12, 2016.

This web page describes a two-year program designed to train providers in the use of the Screening Brief Intervention and Referral to Treatment Process (SBIRT) for identifying and dealing with substance abuse among adolescents. The program was scheduled to run from October 2014 to September 2016, with a six-month follow-up phase to follow its completion date.

Robertson, Elizabeth B., Susan L. David, and Suman A. Rao. "Preventing Drug Abuse among Children and Adolescents," 2nd ed. 2003. Washington, DC: National Institute on Drug Abuse. https://d14rmgtrwzf5a.cloudfront.net/sites/default/files/pre ventingdruguse_2_1.pdf. Accessed on November 28, 2015.

This somewhat dated publication contains, nonetheless, some very valuable basic information about risk and protective factors for substance abuse, the community's role in drug abuse prevention, some general principles that can be used in developing substance abuse prevention programs, and examples of successful programs of this kind.

Roland, Takeesha. 2016. "Rohypnol Addiction and Recovery Facts." Recovery.org. http://www.recovery.org/topics/rohypnol-facts/. Accessed on January 14, 2016.

This article provides a good general overview of Rohypnol, with special emphasis on its use as a "date rape" drug.

"The Salvia Divinorum Research and Information Center." 2015. http://www.sagewisdom.org/. Accessed on January 13, 2016.

This website provides detailed information on virtually every aspect that can be imagined of this psychoactive substance, including its legal status worldwide, instructions for growing the plant, a user's guide in many languages, its use in religious and ceremonial events, and reports from those who have used the drug for a variety of purposes.

"The Science behind Drug Abuse." 2015. National Institute on Drug Abuse. https://teens.drugabuse.gov/. Accessed on November 27, 2015.

This website provides an array of resources designed to help teenagers understand the factual basis behind the campaign to reduce youth substance abuse. It has separate sections on drug facts, interactives and videos on substance abuse, teen prescription abuse, and related topics.

"6 Parenting Practices Help Reduce the Chances Your Child Will Develop a Drug or Alcohol Problem." 2012. Partnership for Drug Free Kids. http://www.preventteendruguse.org/pdfs/HelpReducetheChancesYourChildWillDevelopaDrugorAlcoholProblem.pdf. Accessed on January 14, 2016.
This pamphlet reviews six "research-supported" suggestions for actions that parents can take to reduce their children's risk for developing substance abuse problems.

"Substance Abuse." 2015. Healthy Children.org. https://www.healthychildren.org/English/ages-stages/teen/substance-abuse/Pages/default.aspx. Accessed on November 28, 2015.
This web page is available on a website operated by the American Academy of Pediatrics. It contains a number of excellent articles on various aspects of substance abuse by children and adolescents, such as the dangers of cocaine, parent's role in preventing substance abuse, the risks posed by e-cigarettes, and home drug testing information for parents.

"Teen Drug Abuse." 2015. MedicineNet.com. http://www.medicinenet.com/teen_drug_abuse/article.htm. Accessed on November 27, 2015.
One of the most reliable and dependable websites for information about health and medical issues, MedicineNet.com provides an excellent general introduction to the topic of teenage substance abuse.

"Teen Drug Abuse: 14 Mistakes Parents Make." 2016. CBS News. http://www.cbsnews.com/pictures/teen-drug-abuse-14-mistakes-parents-make/. Accessed on January 14, 2016.

This news report is based on a series of recommendations made by Dr. Joseph Lee, spokesman for the American Academy of Child and Adolescent Psychiatry.

"Teen Drug Abuse: Help Your Teen Avoid Drugs." 2015. Mayo Clinic. http://www.mayoclinic.org/healthy-lifestyle/tween-and-teen-health/in-depth/teen-drug-abuse/art-20045921. Accessed on November 27, 2015.

This website focuses especially on ways in which parents and other adults can help prevent teenagers from becoming involved in substance abuse to begin with.

"Topic Overview." 2015. WebMD. http://www.webmd.com/parenting/guide/teen-alcohol-and-drug-abuse-topic-overview. Accessed on November 27, 2015.

This website provides a broad, general introduction to the subject of adolescent substance abuse, with recommendations for a number of other resources on the topic.

"Welcome to the Center for Adolescent Substance Abuse Research (CeASAR)." 2016. http://www.ceasar.org/. Accessed on January 12, 2016.

CeASAR is a facility for research, training, and clinical services in the field of adolescent substance abuse at Children's Hospital, Boston. It is a very important source for the most up-to-date information on the causes, characteristics, prevention, and treatment of adolescent substance use disorder.

"What Is Date Rape?" 2016. Teens Health. http://kidshealth.org/teen/your_mind/problems/date_rape.html. Accessed on January 14, 2016.

This web page explains what date rape means and provides a number of very specific and practical actions one can take to reduce the risk of being involved in a date rape.

"World Alcohol and Drinking History Timeline." 2016. Alcohol: Problems and Solutions. http://www.alcoholproblemsand

solutions.org/timeline/Alcoholic-Beverages-from-Antiq
uity-through-the-Ancient-Greeks.html. Accessed on January 10,
2016.

This website provides a detailed timeline of important
events in the history of alcohol and drinking. It includes a
bibliography of more than 70 additional resources.

CVS/pharmacy

KATHLEEN A GAGE

NALOXONE 2 MG/2 ML
SYRINGE

ADMINISTER 1ML IN EACH NOSTRIL
NOSTRIL ADAPTOR. IF NOT RESPONSE
AFTER 3 TO 5 MINUTES, REPEAT

Refills require authorization

Qty-4

Store Phone: (401) 467-7796
Rx # 987994
Prescriber: JOSIAH DANIEL RICH

▲ open

Luer-Lock Prefilled Syringe

Rx Only   NDC 76329-3369-1 | STOCK NO. 3369

NALOXONE
HYDROCHLORIDE
INJ, USP
(1 mg/mL)

INTRAVENOUS, INTRAMUSCULAR
...CANEOUS USE
...TAGONIST

2 mg
per
2 mL

LUER-JET™ LUER-LOCK PREFILLED SYRINGE
2 mL single dose disposable prefilled syringe
Single use, do not reuse or resterilize.

2 mL
NALOXONE HYDROCHLORIDE
INJECTION, USP
1 mg/mL

The use of natural plant products to produce altered states of consciousness dates to the earliest years of human history. There has hardly been a period since then when substances such as cocaine, opiates, marijuana and other cannabis products, and a host of other natural and synthetic materials have not been used for such effects. This chapter lists a number of important events in the history of the use of psychoactive substances in human cultures, along with a number of efforts to control the use of such products.

ca. 10,000 BCE   Among products discovered at the earliest agricultural sites, dating to about 10,000 years ago, are cannabis, tobacco, and mandrake, which contains hallucinogenic alkaloids.

ca. 7000–9000 BCE   Prehistoric rock art suggests the use of psychedelic mushrooms by early humans.

ca. 7000 BCE   Seeds of the betel nut, still chewed today for their stimulant effects in many parts of the world, are found at sites dating to 7,000 years ago.

ca. 7000 BCE   Clay vessels containing remnants of wine dating to about 7000 BCE are found at the site of a Neolithic village in Iran.

This photo shows Narcan, a drug that can reverse the effects of an overdose of a substance such as heroin or other opiate. (AP Photo/Stephan Savoia)

ca. 6000 BCE   The first cultivation of tobacco in the New World dates to about 6,000 BCE.

ca. 4300 BCE   The first recipes for making beer, recorded on clay tablets from Babylonia, date to about 4300 BCE.

ca. 3400 BCE   Possible first mention of the *hul gil* plant in Sumerian texts, a plant (*gil*) that brings joy (*hul*) to anyone who ingests it.

3300 BCE   The earliest written records of the use of opium date to about 3300 BCE.

3000 BCE   Charred seeds of the cannabis plant found in a ritual brazier at a burial site in modern-day Romania, suggesting that they were used in a religious ceremony.

ca. 2000 BCE   The Chinese emperor Shen Nung is said to have written the first (or one of the first) books on the use of drugs in medical treatment, *Pen Ts'ao*.

ca. 1300 BCE   Approximate date of the "poppy goddess," or the "Minoan goddess of narcotics," whose characteristic features have suggested to some scholars a woman in a state of ecstasy supposedly induced by the ingestion of an opium-like substance.

ca. 1300 BCE   The first evidence for the cultivation of the opium poppy in Egypt, near the city of Thebes. Opium produced in these fields is later exported to Mesopotamia, North Africa, Greece, and other parts of Europe.

ca. 600 BCE   The text called *Sushruta Samhita* is generally regarded as the first medical/herbal text produced in ancient India.

50–75 CE   The Roman physician Pedanius Dioscorides compiles one of the first materia medicas ever written, and certainly one of the most influential books of this type. In five volumes, the book describes more than 600 plants and minerals that can be used to produce more than a thousand medicinal substances.

Fifth century CE   In his book, *Persian Wars*, Greek historian Herodotus records the use of cannabis as a recreational drug by the Scythians.

620 CE   In one of the earliest attempts at regulating drinking, the Prophet Muhammad prohibits the consumption of alcohol by Muslims (Qur'an 2:219 and 5:91).

1484   Pope Innocent VIII bans the use of cannabis. His action was part of the church's program against heretics because common belief at the time was that witches used cannabis as an "antisacrament" in place of wine at their "black masses."

1493   Christopher Columbus and his crew, returning from America, introduce the use of tobacco products to Europe.

ca. 1500   Portuguese traders discover the benefits of smoking opium for recreational purposes because it produces nearly instantaneous psychoactive effects.

ca. 1525   The Swiss-Austrian physician and alchemist Phillip von Hohenheim (better known as Paracelsus) introduces the use of a tincture of opium called *laudanum* to medical practice in Europe. He is said to have learned about the beneficial effects of the substance during his visits to the Middle East. Both the inventor and the date are subject to considerable historical dispute.

1590   A Japanese law makes possession of tobacco illegal. Anyone found with the substance is subject to imprisonment and/or loss of property.

1613–1614   John Rolfe, husband of the Native American princess Pocahontas, sends the first shipment of tobacco from the New World to Europe.

1633   The Sultan Murad IV of Turkey declares the use of tobacco a capital offense, punished by hanging, beheading, or starvation.

1638   A Chinese law declares the use of tobacco a capital offense, to be punished by beheading.

1690   The British Parliament passes an Act for the Encouraging of the Distillation of Brandy and Spirits from Corn, which results in the production of about a million gallons of alcoholic beverages, primarily gin, only four years later.

1729   Chinese emperor Yung Ching issues an edict prohibiting the smoking or other use of opium except for medical purposes.

The edict reflects the growing objections to the use of opium as a recreational drug, in contrast to its medical applications.

1736   Concerned about the widespread popularity of gin among all classes, the British Parliament passes the Gin Act, which raises taxes on the drink to 20 shillings per gallon, a point at which only members of the upper classes can afford the substance.

1785   In his book *An Inquiry into the Effects of Ardent Spirits upon the Human Body and Mind*, American physician Benjamin Rush calls the intemperate use of alcohol a disease and lists a number of symptoms, such as unusual garrulity, unusual silence, profane swearing and cursing, a clipping of words, fighting, and certain extravagant acts which indicate a temporary fit of madness, such as singing, roaring, and imitating the noises of brute animals. He estimates the annual death rate from alcoholism at about 4,000 in a population of about six million.

1789   An estimated 200 farmers living in the vicinity of Litchfield, Connecticut, meet to form the nation's first temperance society.

1791   The U.S. Congress enacts the nation's first tax on whiskey, the so-called "whiskey tax."

1793–1797   Opposition to the whiskey tax of 1791 leads to outbreaks of violence in various parts of Pennsylvania, all of which are eventually put down by federal forces.

1799   Chinese emperor Jiaqing bans growing, production, and use of all forms of opium.

ca. 1800   Members of Napoleon's army, returning from the war in Egypt, bring with them information about the use of cannabis (in the form of hashish and marijuana) to France. Medical personnel are impressed by the pain-killing properties of the drug, and some members of the general public are more interested in its use as a recreational drug.

1805   German chemist Friedrich Sertürner extracts morphine from opium. He names the substance after Morpheus, the Greek god of dreams.

1819   German chemist Friedrich Ferdinand Runge isolates caffeine from coffee.

1821   English essayist Thomas De Quincey publishes his *Confessions of an English Opium-Eater*," an autobiographical account of his experiences in the use of opium as a recreational drug.

1827   The Merck company chooses morphine and aspirin as the two drugs it first begins producing in bulk quantities. Its success with these two drugs largely establishes Merck as one of the world's largest and most successful drug companies for well over a century.

1839–1842   The First Opium War is fought between Great Britain and China over the importation of the drug into China by British traders, although other issues are also involved in the conflict.

1848   German chemist Georg Merck discovers papaverine.

1856–1860   The Second Opium War is fought between Great Britain and China over ongoing issues about the trade in opium and related political questions.

1859   German chemist Albert Niemann obtains pure cocaine from coca leaves.

1870   In New York City, a group of "scientific and medical gentlemen" found the American Association for the Cure of Inebriates, with the goals of studying the condition of "inebriety," discussing its proper treatment, and bringing about a "co-operative public sentiment and jurisprudence." The action was significant because it was one of the first times that the medical profession acknowledged that alcoholism might be a hereditary disease that could be treated like other medical conditions.

1875   The city of San Francisco adopts an ordinance prohibiting the smoking of opium, apparently the first law in the United States to deal with the practice.

1879   An act is introduced into the U.S. Congress to create a system of controls over the production and sale of foods and drugs in the United States. The act fails in the Congress, and is re-introduced nearly 200 times over the next 27 years, before it is finally adopted in 1906.

1884   Largely through the influence of the Women's Christian Temperance Union, the New York state legislature passes a bill requiring the inclusion of an anti-alcohol curriculum in all schools in the state. Pennsylvania follows suit the next year, as do many other states in succeeding years.

1887   Romanian chemist Lazar Edeleanu first synthesizes amphetamine in an effort to make ephedrine synthetically. With no known use, the compound is essentially forgotten for about 40 years.

1893   Japanese chemist Nagayoshi Nagai synthesizes methamphetamine.

1897   German chemical researcher Felix Hoffmann rediscovers a method for making heroin, but also understands the potential of the drug for medical use. Heroin eventually becomes one of the best-selling drugs for Hoffman's employer, Aktiengesellschaft Farbenfabriken pharmaceutical company, later the Bayer company.

1902   Physician C. B. Burr writes in *The Journal of the American Medical Association* about the problems of morphine addiction and its treatment. This article is one of the earliest commentaries on the addictive properties of morphine and heroin and their potential medical implications.

1906   The U.S. Congress passes the Pure Food and Drug Law, among whose provision is a requirement that all products containing alcohol be labeled to indicate that fact.

1909   The U.S. Congress passes the Smoking Opium Exclusion Act, the first federal regulation of the nonmedical use of a substance. The law bans the importation, possession, and smoking of opium.

1909   The first international conference on the topic of the control of narcotic drugs is held in Shanghai, China. The conference laid the groundwork for the International Opium Convention, signed at The Hague, Netherlands, in 1912.

1910 New York becomes the first state to adopt a drunk driving law.

1912 The International Opium Convention is signed at The Hague, Netherlands, by delegates from China, France, Germany, Italy, Japan, the Netherlands, Persia (Iran), Portugal, Russia, Siam (Thailand), the United Kingdom, and the United States.

1914 Partly as a condition of the provisions of the International Opium Convention, the U.S. Congress adopts the Harrison Narcotic Act, which provided primarily for the licensing of individuals involved in the opium trade, along with taxes on the sale of the drug.

1915 The U.S. Bureau of Narcotics opens the first narcotics clinic in the United States. The goal of the clinics is to help addicts maintain their drug habits in a healthful atmosphere. Eventually, 44 such clinics were opened. When they proved to be a failure, they were closed. The last one ceased operation in 1923.

1919 Secretary of State Francis Polk certifies the ratification of the Eighteenth Amendment to the U.S. Constitution, placing severe restrictions on the manufacture, sale, and transportation of "intoxicating liquors" within the United States. The amendment was eventually ratified by every state in the union except for Connecticut and Rhode Island.

1919 The International Opium Convention is incorporated into the conditions of the Versailles Peace Treaty signed at the end of World War I. This action obligated all signatories to the peace treaty to become signatories to the opium treaty also.

1922 The Narcotic Import and Export Act restricts the importation of crude opium except for medical use.

1924 The Heroin Act of 1924 bans the manufacture, importation, possession, and use of heroin for any reason whatsoever in the United States, including all medical applications.

1928 American physician Charles E. Terry and his wife, Mildred Pellens, publish one of the most comprehensive studies on opium in U.S. history, "The Opium Problem."

1931   At a meeting held in Geneva, a group of nations adopt the Convention for Limiting the Manufacture and Regulating the Distribution of Narcotic Drugs in an effort to bring under control the manufacture, distribution, and use of a number of narcotic drugs. The convention establishes two groups of drugs, one consisting of morphine, cocaine, heroin, and di-hydrohydrooxycodeinone and related compounds, and one consisting of codeine, ethylmorphine, and related compounds. The convention enters into force in 1933.

1932   German chemist Otto Eisleb synthesizes the first synthetic opioid, pethidine, which is eventually made commercially available under the trade names of Dolantin and Demerol.

1932   The U.S. Congress passes the Uniform State Narcotic Act, designed to make state drug laws consistent with each other. All 50 states eventually adopted their own versions of the act, which has been amended and updated a number of times since 1932.

1932   The pharmaceutical firm of Smith, Kline, and French markets amphetamine as Benzedrine, an over-the-counter inhalant for respiratory congestion.

1933   Secretary of State Cordell Hull certifies the ratification of the Twenty-First Amendment to the United States, nullifying the Eighteenth Amendment and ending national laws against the manufacture, sale, and transportation of alcohol beverages in the United States.

1935   Two American alcoholics William Griffith ("Bill") Wilson and Robert Holbrook ("Bob") Smith found Alcoholics Anonymous.

1941–1945   The U.S. government distributes both amphetamine and methamphetamine to military personnel to improve their performance in battle.

1942   The Opium Poppy Control Act prohibits the growing of opium poppies in the United States.

1951   Lois W., wife of Bill W., co-founder of AA, and Anne B. found Al-Anon, a support group for families and friends of problem drinkers.

1956   The Narcotics Control Act further increases federal penalties for violations of federal drug laws.

1957   The teenage son of alcoholic parents and members of Alcoholics Anonymous in California form Alateen, an organization designed to provide support for the children of one or more alcoholic parents. A year later, the organization is adopted by Al-Anon as a special committee of the organization.

1964   In the largest and most definitive study of its kind, the so-called Grand Rapids Study finds that the risk of a driver's being involved in an accident rises sharply with his or her blood alcohol concentration. These findings are replicated a number of times in the future with a variety of modifications in variables studied.

1965   An advisory committee to the Surgeon General issues a report, *Smoking and Health*, that represents the first significant review of the health effects of smoking. The report is instrumental in the passage in the same year of the Federal Cigarette Labeling and Advertising Act, which, among other provisions, requires that all cigarette packages carry the warning label: "Caution: Cigarette Smoking May Be Hazardous to Your Health."

1970   The U.S. Congress adopts the Controlled Substances Act of 1970, an act designed to update and consolidate the dozens of federal laws dealing with all aspects of a number of types of illicit drugs. A key provision of the law was the creation of five *Schedules*, categories of drugs, based on their potential for medical use and their potential harm to users.

1971   President Richard M. Nixon declares a "war on drugs," calling for an aggressive antidrug policy at both federal and state levels. He calls drug abuse "Public Enemy #1" in the United States.

1972   The National Commission on Marijuana and Drug Abuse (also known as the Shafer Commission, named after its chairman) issues its report, recommending, among other things, that simple possession of marijuana be decriminalized and that all distinctions between legal and illegal drugs be dropped. The commission had been created by the U.S. Congress by Public Law 91–513 to study the problem of substance abuse in the United States. President Richard M. Nixon declined to implement any of the commission's recommendations.

1973   As part of the Reorganization Plan No. 2 of 1973, President Richard M. Nixon establishes the Drug Enforcement Agency to replace the Bureau of Narcotics and Dangerous Drugs, the Office of Drug Abuse Law Enforcement, and a handful of other federal agencies with drug control responsibilities.

1973   The Methadone Control Act provides funding for the establishment of clinics through which recovering heroin addicts can receive methadone therapy. Doctors at this point are no longer allowed to write prescriptions for methadone for the same purpose.

1974   The National Institute on Drug Abuse is created to conduct research on drug abuse and drug addiction.

1978   The U.S. Congress passes the American Indian Religious Freedom Act that acknowledges the elements of traditional Native American religious ceremonies and the conflicts that may arise between those ceremonies and some U.S. laws. It declares that Native Americans do have the right to practice their traditional religious customs. The use of peyote is implicitly, but not explicitly, guaranteed by this act.

1984   The U.S. Congress passes the National Minimum Drinking Age Act (also known as the Uniform Drinking Age Act) requiring all states to raise the minimum age for drinking to 21. Any state that refuses to adopt this standard is subject to loss of 10 percent of the funds due it annually under the Federal Aid Highway Act.

1984   First Lady Nancy Reagan launches her "Just Say No" campaign against drug use.

1986   The U.S. Congress passes the Anti-Drug Abuse Act of 1986. The act consists of two major titles, one dealing with Anti-Drug Enforcement, and the other with International Narcotics Control. The first title is divided into 21 subtitles dealing with a host of issues, perhaps the most important of which is Subtitle E: Controlled Substances Analogue Enforcement Act of 1986, which states that substances that are chemically and pharmacologically similar to substances listed in Schedule I or Schedule II of the Controlled Substances Act of 1970 (known as analogues of the listed drugs) are also classified as Schedule I drugs. Perhaps the most controversial section is Subtitle B: Drug Possession Penalty Act of 1986, which establishes the so-called 100-to-1 rule, in which possession of 100 grams of powder cocaine (the drug of choice among wealthy white Americans) is considered to be legally equivalent to 1 gram of crack cocaine (used most commonly by blacks).

1988   The Anti-Drug Abuse Act of 1988 for the first time imposes penalties on the users of illegal drugs. Prior to this time, penalties for illegal drug use were limited to the producers and distributors of such substances.

1994   The Omnibus Crime Bill, introduced by then-senator Joseph Biden (D–DE) introduces the death penalty for anyone convicted to operating large-scale drug distribution programs, one of the first times the death penalty is permitted for crimes in which a death is not involved.

1996   The U.S. Congress passes the Drug-Induced Rape Prevention and Punishment Act, which provides for penalties of up to 20 years in prison for supplying a drug to another person with the intent of committing a crime, such as rape, against that person. The primary motivation for the act is the spread of so-called date rape, in which one person provides a second person with a psychoactive drug—most commonly ketamine, gamma hydroxybutyrate (GHB), gamma butyrolactone (GBL), or Rohypnol—without that second person's knowledge or approval.

1996   California voters pass Proposition 215, the Compassionate Use Act of 1996, which allows individuals with a doctor's prescription to grow small amounts of marijuana for their own personal medical use.

1996   The U.S. Congress passes the Comprehensive Methamphetamine Control Act, which further restricts the sale of precursors used in the production of methamphetamine, such as pseudoephedrine, iodine, red phosphorus, and hydrochloric acid.

1997   The tobacco industry reaches a settlement with 46 state attorneys general to pay $360 billion over a period of 25 years to fund anti-smoking campaigns, to add health warnings to cigarette packages, and to pay substantial fines if the number of teenage smokers is not reduced.

2000   The Drug Addiction Treatment Act of 2000 allows certain qualifying physicians to treat patients with opioid addictions using substances on Schedules III, IV, and V of the Controlled Substances Act. The only drug that meets this specification is buprenorphine.

2001   In the case of *United States v. Oakland Cannabis Buyers' Cooperative* 532 U.S. 483 (2001), the U.S. Supreme Court unanimously rules that marijuana has no medical value and that its sale by the Oakland Cannabis Buyers' Cooperative (and similar organizations) is illegal.

2005   The U.S. Congress passes and President George W. Bush signs the USA PATRIOT Improvement and Reauthorization Act which includes, as an unrelated amendment, a version of the Combat Meth Act, originally proposed by Senator James Talent (R-MO). One of the primary features of the act is the imposition of severe restrictions on the sale of cough and cold products whose ingredients can be used in the manufacture of methamphetamine.

2005 In the case of *Gonzalez v. Raich* 545 U.S. 1 (2005), the U.S. Supreme Court rules, by a vote of 6 to 3, that it is illegal for medical doctors to write prescriptions for their patients to use marijuana for medical purposes.

2009 The administration of President Barack Obama announces that it will cease using the term "drug wars" as the concept is counterproductive to the current approach to substance abuse as a medical problem.

2010 The U.S. Food and Drug Administration approves a new formulation of OxyContin designed to deter abuse of the opioid narcotic.

2013 The Pew Research Center reports that, for the first time in history, a majority of Americans favor the legalization of cannabis for recreational purposes.

2014 The U.S. House of Representatives passes a bill prohibiting the Drug Enforcement Agency from using funds to arrest medical cannabis patients in states with medical cannabis laws.

2016 As of January 1, 2016, 22 states and the District of Columbia have legalized the use of medical marijuana. In addition, four states have legalized the use of controlled amounts of cannabis products for recreational use.

Glossary

Many discussions of substance abuse involve terminology that is unfamiliar to the average person. In some cases, the terms used are scientific or medical expressions used most commonly by professionals in the field. In other cases, the terms may be part of the so-called street slang that users themselves employ in talking about the drugs they consume, the paraphernalia associated with drugs, or the kind of experiences that accompany drug use. This chapter lists and defines some terms that may be unfamiliar to some readers.

addiction   A long-lasting and typically recurring psychological and/or physiological need for one or more substances, such as alcohol or tobacco, that generally results in permanent or long-lasting changes in the neurochemistry of the brain.

alkaloid   A naturally occurring organic compound containing one or more basic nitrogen atoms found in plants often displaying medicinal properties.

analgesic   A drug capable of relieving pain.

analog (also analogue)   A chemical compound similar in structure to some other chemical compound.

anorectic   A substance that reduces the appetite.

antidepressant   A drug that reduces or moderates depression, resulting in an elevation in one's mood.

antitussive   A cough suppressant.

ataxia   Loss of control of muscular movement, manifested in an unsteady gait, unsteady movements, and clumsiness; a common symptom of mild drug overdose.

BAC   Acronym for *blood alcohol content* or *blood alcohol concentration*, a measure of the amount of alcohol present in a person's body, usually represented as percentage content or percentage concentration, as 0.08 (i.e., 0.08 percent).

barbiturate   A substance derived from the chemical barbituric acid ($C_4H_4N_2O_3$).

bhang   A concoction or infusion made with leaves and flowers from the hemp plant, widely used on the Indian subcontinent as a recreational drug and as a drug for religious and ceremonial purposes.

binge drinking   Excessive consumption of alcohol over a relatively brief period of time, which typically results in nausea, vomiting, loss of control over one's bodily functions and, in extreme cases, more serious symptoms, such as coma and death.

blackout   Loss of memory about a particular event, such as the taking of a drug or overconsumption of alcohol.

cannabinoid   Any one of the substances found in the cannabis plant, *Cannibis sativa*, or, more generally, that has a chemical structure similar to that of tetrahydrocannabinol (THC) or that binds to cannabinoid receptors in the body.

chemical dependence   A condition that develops when one's body undergoes changes that result in a continual physiological need for a particular drug or other substance.

club drug   *See* **designer drug**.

controlled substance analog   *See* **designer drug**, definition 2.

cross-addiction   Addiction to two substances belonging to different classes, such as alcohol and cocaine.

delirium   A medical condition characterized by severe confusion; rapid changes in brain function; rambling or incoherent speech; sensory misperceptions; sleep disruption; drowsiness; memory loss; and disorientation with respect to time, place, or persons.

delirium tremens   A medical condition associated with the withdrawal of alcohol among chronic alcoholics, characterized by uncontrollable trembling, hallucinations, severe anxiety, excessive sweating, and feelings of terror.

dependence   A condition in which an individual develops a fixation on or craving for a drug that is not necessarily so severe as to be classified as an addiction but that may, nonetheless, require professional help to overcome.

designer drug   (1) A synthetic chemical compound developed for the treatment of a specific disease or group of diseases; (2) A psychoactive chemical that mimics the effects of a banned drug deliberately synthesized to avoid antidrug laws. Also known as a controlled substance analog, club drug, or rave drug.

dissociative drug   A substance that produces feelings of analgesia, disconnection, and alienation.

dysphoria   A condition of unusually severe depression and/or anxiety, mental and/or physical discomfort, and general malaise.

empathogen   A drug capable of producing strong emotional features, such as emotional closeness, love, and affection. The term *entactogen* has been suggested as a synonym for the word.

enabling   The act of supporting or contributing to the destructive behavior of a substance abuser, sometimes based on the enabler's best intentions of helping that person.

endogenous   Produced naturally within the body.

entactogen   *See* **emphathogen**.

flashback   Recurring emotional or sensory experiences that take place independently, and often at much later times, than an initial experience which, in the case of drugs, was the occasion of having consumed those drugs.

hallucinogen A drug that causes profound distortions in a person's perceptions of reality, causing an individual to see images, hear sounds, and feel sensations that seem real but do not exist.

inhalant A substance of low volatility, such that it can be easily absorbed through the respiratory system.

intervention An event in which a group of individuals confront an alcoholic or a substance abuser with the demand for specific action by that person to begin dealing with his or her addiction.

mainlining Taking a drug by injection into a vein.

narcotic Any drug that, in small doses, produces insensitivity to pain, dulls the senses, and induces deep sleep, but in larger doses may result in numbness, convulsions, and coma.

neuron A nerve cell.

neurotransmitter A chemical that carries a nerve impulse between two neurons.

oneirogen A substance that produces a dream-like state of consciousness.

opiate Any drug or other substance derived from or chemically related to opium.

opiate receptor Specialized receptor cells in neurons that bind to natural analgesic molecules present in the body.

OTC drug *See* **over-the-counter drug**.

overdose (verb) To take an excessive, risky, and potentially fatal quantity of a harmful substance.

over-the-counter drug A drug that can be purchased without a prescription.

paranoia A psychological disorder characterized by delusions of persecution or grandeur.

pharmacopoeia A catalog of drugs, chemicals, and medicinal preparations.

phenylethylamines   A class of drugs whose members contain three functional groups—the phenyl group ($-C_6H_5$), ethyl group ($-C_2H_5$), and amine group ($-NH_2$)—that form the basis of a very large number of natural and synthetic compounds with a variety of psychotropic effects. Drugs in this class may act as anorectics, antidepressants, bronchodilators, entactogens, hallucinogens, or stimulants.

precursor chemical   A chemical used to make some other substance, as, for example, the raw materials used to make illicit drugs.

prescription drug   A drug that can be purchased only with a medical prescription provided by a registered medical provider, such as a physician or a physician's assistant.

psychedelic   A substance capable of producing perceptual changes, such as vivid colors and weird shapes, as well as altered awareness of one's mind and body.

psychoactive   *See* **psychotropic**

psychoanaleptic   *See* **psychostimulant**.

psychostimulant   A type of stimulant that acts to increase brain activity specifically; also known as a psychoanaleptic.

psychotomimetic   A drug that produces psychotic-like effects that may include delusions and hallucinations.

psychotropic   Having an effect on the mind.

rave drug   *See* **designer drug**.

relapse   The return of a condition, such as addiction to or dependency on a drug, which had formerly been successfully overcome.

Schedule (drug)   A category into which the federal government classifies certain drugs based on their potential medical use and their possibility of illicit recreational applications.

serotonin   A neurotransmitter associated with a number of mental and emotional functions, including appetite, learning, memory, mood, muscular contraction, and sleep. A number of drugs reduce or increase the amount of serotonin available in the brain, thereby moderating one or more of these actions.

smokeless tobacco   Tobacco that is consumed by some method other than smoking, as, for example, chewing tobacco or snuff.

snuff   Finely ground tobacco which is inhaled rather than smoked.

stimulant   When used in connection with drugs, a substance that temporarily increases physiological activity in the body, with a number of associated effects, such as increased awareness, interest, physical activity, wakefulness, endurance, and productivity. Physiological changes include increased heart rate and blood pressure.

synaptic gap   The space between two neurons.

tolerance   Developing immunity to the effects caused by a substance such that one requires a larger amount of the substance over time to achieve the same results obtained from smaller amounts earlier on in its use.

twelve-step program   A program for recovery from alcoholism, drug addiction, and other behavioral problems originally proposed by Alcoholics Anonymous in its 1939 book *Alcoholics Anonymous: The Story of How More Than One Hundred Men Have Recovered from Alcoholism.*

withdrawal symptoms   The physical, mental, and emotional effects that an individual experiences when he or she discontinues use of a substance to which he or she has become addicted or dependent.

Index

Note: Page numbers followed by t indicate a table on the designated page.

About the Author

David E. Newton holds an associate's degree in science from Grand Rapids (Michigan) Junior College, a BA in chemistry (with high distinction), an MA in education from the University of Michigan, and an EdD in science education from Harvard University. He is the author of more than 400 textbooks, encyclopedias, resource books, research manuals, laboratory manuals, trade books, and other educational materials. He taught mathematics, chemistry, and physical science in Grand Rapids, Michigan, for 13 years; was professor of chemistry and physics at Salem State College in Massachusetts for 15 years; and was adjunct professor in the College of Professional Studies at the University of San Francisco for 10 years.

The author's previous books for ABC CLIO include *Global Warming* (1993), *Gay and Lesbian Rights—A Resource Handbook* (1994, 2009), *The Ozone Dilemma* (1995), *Violence and the Mass Media* (1996), *Environmental Justice* (1996, 2009), *Encyclopedia of Cryptology* (1997), *Social Issues in Science and Technology: An Encyclopedia* (1999), *DNA Technology* (2009), *Sexual Health* (2010), *The Animal Experimentation Debate* (2013), *Marijuana* (2013), *World Energy Crisis* (2013), *Steroids and Doping in Sports* (2014), *GMO Food* (2014), *Science and Political Controversy* (2014), *Wind Energy* (2015), and *Fracking* (2015). His other recent books include *Physics: Oryx Frontiers of Science Series* (2000), *Sick!* (4 volumes) (2000), *Science, Technology, and Society: The Impact of Science in the 19th Century* (2 volumes; 2001), *Encyclopedia of Fire* (2002), *Molecular Nanotechnology: Oryx Frontiers of Science Series* (2002), *Encyclopedia of Water* (2003), *Encyclopedia of Air* (2004), *The New Chemistry* (6 volumes; 2007), *Nuclear Power* (2005), *Stem Cell Research* (2006), *Latinos in the Sciences, Math, and Professions* (2007), and *DNA Evidence and Forensic Science* (2008). He has also been an updating and consulting editor on a number of books and reference works, including *Chemical Compounds* (2005), *Chemical Elements* (2006), *Encyclopedia of Endangered Species* (2006), *World of Mathematics* (2006), *World of Chemistry* (2006), *World of Health* (2006), *UXL Encyclopedia of Science* (2007), *Alternative Medicine* (2008), *Grzimek's Animal Life Encyclopedia* (2009), *Community Health* (2009), *Genetic Medicine* (2009), *The Gale Encyclopedia of Medicine* (2010–2011), *The Gale Encyclopedia of Alternative Medicine* (2013), *Discoveries in Modern Science: Exploration, Invention, and Technology* (2013–2014), and *Science in Context* (2013–2014).